Sailing is a Breeze:
Learning to Sail a Laser, Sunfish, or Other Small Boat

THOMAS P. MARTIN, PHD., FACSM
Wittenberg University
Springfield, OH 45501

ILLUSTRATED BY JOSH KOENIG

american press
BOSTON, MASSACHUSETTS

WARNING

This is an instruction book to a potentially dangerous activity. It is not intended to be the only source of information for those wishing to learn to sail. It is recommended that this book be used in conjunction with instruction from a certified sailing instructor. You should read, understand and appreciate the sailing hazards and risks presented in Chapter 1 before starting your sailing experience. At the same time, it is virtually impossible to cover every hazard you might encounter while sailing. Sailing is a RISK activity. You should strive to eliminate or minimize potential risks through knowledge, preparation and safe sailing practices. Neither the author, publisher, nor booksellers assume liability for any injury or death which might result from any interpretation of sailing techniques and/or practices described in this book. By the use of this book, the reader hereby releases the author, publisher, and booksellers of ***Sailing is a Breeze: Learning to Sail a Laser, Sunfish or Other Small Boat*** from liability for any injury, including death, that might result.

Copyright © 2006 by American Press
ISBN 0-89641-433-7

All rights reserved. No part of this publication may be reproduced, stored in a retrieval system, or transmitted, in any form or by any means, electronic, mechanical, photocopying, recording, or otherwise, without the prior written permission of the copyright owner.

Printed in the United States of America.

Dedication

This book is dedicated to my mother, Cecile Knistoft Martin—the person who taught me to sail through life's glorious days and storms with joy, humility, sensitivity, perseverance, and hope.

Acknowledgements

I learned to sail from Ohio Division of Watercraft (ODW) officers who were Red Cross certified sailing instructors. They used a small ODW book that was titled "Sailing is a Breeze." When I started teaching sailing at Wittenberg University, I used the same book and continued to use it until it went out of print in the nineties. At that time, I decided to use information from the book and put together one of my own. Each year I would get feedback from my students and ODW officers as to how the book could be improved. This book has evolved from that process.

I would like to thank the ODW officers who so freely gave of their time and talents: John Peters, Gary Hale, Marilyn Hinderer, Scott Jones, Jim Mayhugh, and Emily King. A special thanks to Doug Golding (ODW) for the information he provided on sailing risks. Also, I want to acknowledge that some figures in this book (i.e. H.E.L.P. position, Huddle position, PFDs, and buoys) were taken from the public domain Ohio Boat Operator's Guide 2005/06 printed by the Ohio Department of Natural Resources, Sam Speck Director.

I believe you will be impressed by the detailed figures in this book—they are the work of Josh Koenig. I want to thank Josh for his cooperation as well as compliment him on his fine work. Thanks as well to M.J. Fox and Marci Taylor, American Press editors, for their help and support during this project.

Last but not least, thanks to my wife Helen for her help and encouragement on and off the water.

Tom Martin
Springfield, Ohio

Preface

Sailing is a wonderful and rewarding leisure time activity as well as an exciting sport. Man has always been attracted to water. Perhaps it's because we can't live without it. Our bodies are 60% water! We can survive weeks without food but only a few days without water. It seems logical that we would be attracted to this essential compound of life.

At the same time, most sailors would agree that they sail for enjoyment, relaxation, and personal satisfaction. Feeling, moving, interacting with the elements of our natural world (environment) can be a positive, rewarding, and uplifting experience. Stimuli from all senses are constantly relayed to the brain providing an incredible instantaneous database for feelings and cognitive processes. Water, waves, currents, temperature (water and air), humidity, wind, sky, sun, clouds, fog, stars, and wildlife are seen, heard, felt, and sometimes even smelled and tasted. The beauty and power of nature are awesome and provide an aesthetic and spiritual dimension to the sailing experience.

There are also psychological and social benefits inherent in sailing. Understanding and using the forces in nature to sail across the water under varying conditions develops/reinforces a feeling of confidence and control. Being prepared and knowing how to handle changes in conditions and potential problems builds self-confidence, reinforces self-sufficiency, and positively impacts self-image. Sailing with family and friends (or future friends!) can result in a great deal of positive social interaction and pleasure. Working, playing, and communicating with others while sailing can be a meaningful and valuable way to develop/improve relationships off the water.

The sailor can also choose the solitude of sailing solo, as well as the excitement and challenge of competition. The diversity of potential experiences is amazing. At the same time, there is one common element that should be a part of all leisure sailing experiences—FUN! The greater your knowledge, and the more extensive your sailing experiences, the more enjoyment you are likely to have.

This book is written for the individual who wants to learn to sail a Laser, Sunfish, or other small boat. It is appropriate for use in a summer camp setting, class setting (e.g. school or marina), or for personal instruction in conjunction with a certified sailing instructor. The Laser and Sunfish are both one-design boats, meaning that all boats of the class are identical. The Laser is the most popular racing class sailboat in the world. The Sunfish, which was the first off-the-beach sailboat, is the most popular sailboat ever produced. Therefore, these boats are readily available at sailing sites. It has been said that if one can sail a Laser or Sunfish, he/she "KNOWS HOW" to sail, and can transfer that knowledge to any sailboat afloat.

This book details the basic knowledge, skills, and progression of learning to sail a Laser, Sunfish, or other small catboat. A catboat has one mast stepped well forward, a boom, and one sail. This is the place to start for someone who wants to learn to sail. This book follows a progressive format leading the reader step by step through the information and knowledge necessary to prepare for, practice, and learn basic sailing skills. It begins with an emphasis on sailing safety. Hazards and risks are reviewed with special emphasis on preventing hypothermia and the importance of wearing a personal flotation device (PFD). Information on line (rope) and tying basic knots follows in preparation for the next chapter which describes hull designs, rigs, and rigging of small boats. This is followed by a detailed description and rigging instructions for the Laser and Sunfish. The next chapter is titled "How a Sailboat Sails." It provides the information and terminology the sailor needs to know and understand in order to learn basic sailing skills and techniques. The prospective sailor should now have a basic understanding of sailing risks, sailboat design, rigging, and how a sailboat sails.

The next chapter, "Sailing Techniques," presents a progressive sequence of skills and techniques from launching to landing the sailboat. The order of presentation and practice is important from both safety and learning perspectives. On water practice begins with sailing on the "easiest" point of sail—a beam reach. While sailing on a beam reach, the beginner learns basic boat controls, how to put the boat in the safety position, how to get the boat out of "irons," how to turn around ("come about"), and how to right a capsized boat. When the sailor is able to perform these skills as captain and linesman, he/she is ready to move on to other points of sail.

The next practice sequence involves sailing alternately on a close reach and broad reach. "Fine tuning" the sail, that is, adjusting it in relation to the wind and the direction of the boat (point of sail) is emphasized. When this is accomplished the sailor is ready to practice sailing on a run (the most unstable point of sail). The last basic skill to be learned is jibing. Once the basic skills are learned, the sailor is ready to repeat the progression solo. Sailing a triangle course clockwise and counter clockwise (solo) is the test to determine if basic sailing skills have been learned.

Upon successful completion of the triangle course, the individual can proudly proclaim "I can sail!" Now he/she can advance to learning the intermediate sailing skills covered in the next chapter. This chapter contains information on equipment adjustments and intermediate sailing techniques that can make sailing more efficient and enjoyable. The following chapter, "Right of Way and Racing," reviews basic boating "rules of the road" and introduces the sailor to racing. The final chapter contains information on aids to navigation, as well as the transport, care, storage, and purchase of sailboats. It ends with information on sailing certification.

There are five Appendices: (A) Resources and References—an up-to-date listing of Internet sites related to sailing as well as video and book references; (B) Sailing Class Information—for formal sailing classes; (C) Exercises and Review Questions—to test knowledge and understanding; (D) Answers to Exercises and Review Questions—to provide immediate feedback and self-evaluation of learning; and (E) Nautical Dictionary—for definition of sailing terms.

Maximize learning by completing the Exercises and Review Questions in Appendix C after reading each chapter, that is, *before* moving on to the next chapter.

Once the basic knowledge and skills are obtained, the sailor will be able to enjoy sailing as a recreational activity. Further, "knowing how to sail" will open the door to other opportunities for enjoyment, challenge, and excitement. The sailor will be in a position to move on to a larger more sophisticated boat. Perhaps a boat with onboard accommodations and the world of cruising will beckon, or the competitive individual might be drawn to the excitement and challenge of racing. One thing is certain; the individual will have expanded his/her horizons and developed skills that can be used for a lifetime.

x

Contents

PREFACE VII

Chapter

1. Sailing Safety 1

    A. HAZARDS AND RISKS 1
        1. Immersion or Drowning 1
        2. Cold Water Immersion 2
        3. Hypothermia 2
        4. Heat Cramps, Heat Exhaustion, and Heat Stroke 2
        5. Severe Weather: Storms, Lightning, and High Winds 3
        6. Offshore Winds 3
        7. Poor Visibility: Darkness, Heavy Rain, Fog 3
        8. Underwater Obstructions: Rocks, Logs, Glass, and Shallow Water 4
        9. Inexperience and/or Unfamiliarity with Equipment 4
      10. Overhead Power Lines 4
      11. Equipment Failure or Misuse 5
      12. Back Injury 5
      13. Collision: Fixed Obstructions, Other Boats, and Swimmers 5
      14. Sailing in an Area where there is No Means of Communication with other Boats or People 5
      15. Fisherman 6
      16. Interaction with a Power Boat or Rescue Boat 6
      17. Medical Considerations 6
      18. Alcohol, Legal and Illegal Substances 6
      19. Loss of Property 6
      20. Tripping, Falling, Etc. 7
      21. Currents, Tides, and Channels 7
      22. Natural Hazards 7
      23. Summary 7

B. Hypothermia 8
  1. Symptoms 8
  2. Prevention and Survival 9
  3. Treating Mild to Moderate Hypothermia 10
  4. Severe Hypothermia 11
  5. Mammalian Diving Reflex 11
C. Personal Flotation Devices (PFDs) 11
  1. Types of PFDs 11
  2. US Coast Guard PFD Requirements 13
D. Additional Safety Guidelines
   and Emergency Procedures 14
  1. Weather 14
  2. Float Plan 15
  2. Self-Rescue Procedure 15
  4. Hand/Arm Signals 16
  5. Towing 17
  6. State Laws 17
E. Summary 17
F. Exercises and Review Questions 17

2. Line and Knots 19

A. Types of Line 19
B. Selected Knots 20
C. Line Hardware 24
  1 Cleats 24
  2 Other Line Hardware 25
D. Coiling and Throwing Line 26
E. Exercises and Review Questions 27

3. Small Boats 29

A. Hull Designs 29
B. Sailing Terminology 29
  1. Basic Boat Terms 30
  2. Hull Terms 31
  3. Spar, Steering Assembly, and Depth Terms 32
  4. Sail and Running Rigging Terms 33

    C. SAILS 34
    D. RIGS AND RIGGING 35
    E. OTHER DINGHY SAILBOATS 36
    F. EXERCISES AND REVIEW QUESTIONS 38

4. Laser and Sunfish 39

    A. LASER 39
        1. Description 39
        2. Rigging 41
        3. Derigging 44
        4. Exercises and Review Questions 44
    B. SUNFISH 45
        1. Description 45
        2. Rigging 45
        3. Derigging 47
        4. Exercises and Review Questions 47

5. How a Sailboat Sails 49

    A. CENTER OF GRAVITY AND CENTER OF BUOYANCY 49
    B. BOAT AXES 50
    C. HEELING 51
    D. RUNNING 53
    E. REACHING 53
    F. POINTS OF SAIL 54
    G. TACKING 56
    H. TERMS RELATED TO BOAT MOVEMENT AND DIRECTION 57
    I. THEORY OF SAILING 60
        1. Sail Aerodynamics 60
        2. Boat Lateral Resistance 63
        3. Sail Center of Effort 65
        4. Center of Lateral Resistance 66
    J. EXERCISES AND REVIEW QUESTIONS 67

6. Sailing Techniques 69

- A. INTRODUCTION 69
- B. PROGRESSION 70
- C. WIND SPEED AND DIRECTION 70
  1. Wind Speed 70
  2. Wind Direction 71
- D. LAUNCHING 74
  1. From Beach 74
  2. From Dock 77
- E. BEAM REACH 78
- F. BASIC BOAT CONTROLS 79
- G. ADJUSTING TO FORCE OF WIND 80
- H. SAFETY POSITION AND STOPPING THE BOAT 81
- I. GETTING OUT OF "IRONS" 83
- J. COMING ABOUT 83
- K. CAPSIZE RECOVERY 88
  1. Standard Capsize Recovery Technique 88
  2. Scoop Capsize Recovery Technique 89
- L. LANDING 90
  1. At Beach 90
  2. At Dock 93
- M. CLOSE REACH AND BROAD REACH 94
- N. RUN 96
- O. JIBING 98
  1. Jibing While on a Run 98
  2. Jibing From a Broad Reach 100
- P. PRACTICE 103
- Q. EXERCISES AND REVIEW QUESTIONS 105

7. Intermediate Sailing Skills 107

- A. INTRODUCTION 107
- B. SAILING EFFICIENTLY 107
  1. Telltales 107

		2. Sailing Upwind 108
		3. Pinching 109

    C. USING BODY WEIGHT 110
        1. Boat Balance 110
        2. Steering Boat 111
        3. Roll Tack 111
        4. Capsize Step Over Technique 112

    D. SAIL AND DAGGERBOARD ADJUSTMENTS 113
        1. Sail Shape 113
        2. Daggerboard Adjustments 115

    E. STOPPING ALONGSIDE ANOTHER BOAT 116
    F. "MAN OVERBOARD" RECOVERY 117
    G. PICKING UP A MOORING 117
    H. EXERCISES AND REVIEW QUESTIONS 117

8. Right of Way and Racing 119

    A. RIGHT OF WAY 119
        1. Starboard Tack Rule 119
        2. Same Tack Rule 120
        3. Overtaking Rule 121
        4. Turning Rule 121
        5. Prudential Rule 121

    B. RACING 122
    C. EXERCISES AND REVIEW QUESTIONS 124

9. Useful Information 125

    A. AIDS TO NAVIGATION 125
        1. Buoys 125
        2. Lights 127
        3. Flags 127

    B. TRANSPORTING EQUIPMENT 127
        1. Car-Topping 127
        2. Trailering 128

- C. CARE AND STORAGE 129
    1. Regular Care and Maintenance 129
    2. Short and Long Term Storage 130
- D. HULL IDENTIFICATION NUMBER (HIN) 131
- E. PURCHASING A BOAT 131
- F. CERTIFICATION 132
    1. American Sailing Association 132
    2. United States Sailing Association 133
- G. EXERCISES AND REVIEW QUESTIONS 133

Appendices

A. Resources and References 135
- A. BOATING ORGANIZATIONS 135
- B. SAILING ORGANIZATIONS AND SELECTED WEB SITES 135
- C. ONE-DESIGN SAILING ASSOCIATIONS 136
- D. SAILING VIDEOS 136
- E. BOOK REFERENCES 137
- F. BOOKLET 138

B. Sailing Class Information 139
- A. INTRODUCTION 139
- B. SAILING CLASS RULES 139
- C. SAILING CLASS EVALUATION 141
- D. CLOTHING/GEAR CHECKLIST 141
- E. FIRST ASSIGNMENT 142
    1. Student Information 143
    2. Affirmation and Liability Release 144

C. Exercises and Review Questions **145**
D. Answers **165**
    A. Answers for Labeled Figures in Chapter 3 165
    B. Answers to Exercises and Review Questions in Appendix C 168
E. Nautical Dictionary **173**

Chapter 1
Sailing Safety

A. HAZARDS AND RISKS

Welcome to the exhilarating sport of sailing. The sport offers a great deal of fun for sailors of all ages. However, just like many other outdoor activities (e.g. climbing, canoeing, backpacking, sky diving, SCUBA diving, etc.), it is considered a RISK activity. As in all risk activities, the general idea is to gain maximum enjoyment while taking minimum risks. This is accomplished by risk management, which is done by knowledge and awareness of the risks, properly using sufficient safety equipment, and following proper safety guidelines. Unlike many other risk activities, sailing risks can be reduced enough to consider the sport quite safe, provided known precautions are taken. The following information is intended to alert the beginning sailor to the hazards and risks he/she could encounter. It includes simple safety guidelines to follow in order to avoid or minimize each hazard or risk. Also included are some basic emergency procedures in case the sailor comes face to face with certain hazards.

Although this list of known hazards is quite extensive, it should not be considered a complete listing. The sailor needs to be constantly on the alert for unforeseen hazards. No person should take up the sport of sailing without fully understanding and appreciating the following information. If the beginning sailor has any doubts or questions concerning this information, a certified sailing instructor should be consulted before participating in the sport. Once the beginning sailor understands this information, he/she should be ready to attempt the activity with an acceptable level of safety and minimal risk.

1. Immersion or Drowning

Like any activity involving water, the possibility of immersion or drowning exists. The beginning sailor should expect to spend some time in the water. Wearing a properly fitted, U.S. Coast Guard approved, Personal Flotation Device (PFD) can minimize the risk of drowning. Sailors should be familiar with their state laws concerning the possession and wearing of PFDs. Personal Flotation Devices (PFDs) are covered in more detail in Section C.

2. Cold Water Immersion

A sailor runs the risk of unexpectedly falling into cold water. The body reacts to this shock with an involuntary gasp for breath called the "Gasp Reflex." If the face is in the water during this first involuntary gasp, water rather than air may be taken into the lungs. Therefore, the head should always be kept above water when falling from a boat. Avoiding very cold water conditions can eliminate this risk.

3. Hypothermia

Prolonged exposure to cold water and air temperatures combined with the effects of wind chill, could cause a drop of internal body temperature (**hypothermia**). Hypothermia is a serious health problem and prevention is a necessity. Preventing hypothermia is easily accomplished by wearing protective clothing appropriate to water and air temperatures. Extremely cold conditions should be avoided. The topic of hypothermia is covered in more detail in Section B.

4. Heat Cramps, Heat Exhaustion, and Heat Stroke

Under most conditions, body temperature (98.6 F) is higher than the environmental temperature and the body can easily dissipate the heat of metabolism and physical activity to the environment. Blood vessels under the skin dilate (increase in size) to bring blood close to the surface where heat can escape and cool the body (convection). The body is also cooled by evaporation of sweat. As external temperature and/or physical activity increase, sweating increases to cool the body. The evaporation of sweat has a major cooling effect on the body. However, when humidity is high, sweat cannot evaporate as quickly. It stays on the skin and has little or no cooling effect. Further, sweating can result in loss of fluids (dehydration) and heat stress.

Hot and/or humid weather can lead to heat-related problems. Elevated body temperature and loss of fluids can result in heat cramps, heat exhaustion, and heat stroke. **Heat cramps** are painful muscle contractions that are believed to be due to a combination of fluid and salt loss as a result of heavy sweating. **Heat exhaustion** is the first stage of heat-related illness. Dehydration and elevated body temperature result in symptoms such as cool/moist/pale skin, nausea, headache, dizziness, and exhaustion. **Heat stroke** is a heat emergency; symptoms include vomiting, changes in consciousness, rapid/weak pulse, rapid/shallow breathing, and red/hot skin, which may be dry or moist.

Heat cramps, heat exhaustion, and heat stroke can be prevented by:
- Avoiding the hottest part of the day
- Avoiding direct sun light
- Wearing light weight and light colored clothing and a hat with a wide brim
- Decreasing level of activity

Sailing Safety

- Maintaining hydration. Drink large amounts of fluids. Avoid beverages with caffeine and alcohol. They are diuretics and will result in loss of fluid.

Skin exposure to the sun is another often overlooked danger. Everyone is familiar with the discomfort and pain of sunburn. But long term exposure to the sun is even a more serious concern, it can cause skin cancer. It is recommended that a sun block of at least 30 SPF, with protection against both IVA and UVB rays, be applied about 30 minutes before sun exposure. Polarizing sunglasses (with strap) are also recommended.

5. *Severe Weather: Storms, Lightning, and High Winds*

Severe weather has been a contributing factor in many serious boating accidents. It can result in breakage of equipment, loss of property, personal injury, and even death. A sailboat (consider the high metal mast) runs the risk of being struck by lightning, particularly if caught in a thunderstorm. High winds could prevent the safe operation of a sailboat or make it uable to return to the safety of shore. Sailing in heavy weather requires a high skill level.

The logical safety precaution is to avoid severe weather conditions. Check local weather forecasts before and during a boating trip. If foul weather is predicted and you choose to risk it, remain close to shore. Always be alert to weather changes and keep a lookout for approaching dark clouds. Return to the nearest shore immediately if threatening weather approaches. A thunderstorm with lightning is a high-risk situation. Stay away from your mast and metal fittings. If possible, make sure the boat is grounded. Consider taking down the mast. Sailors on small boats may purposely capsize and turtle their boat (i.e. turn it upside down—mast pointed to bottom of water) and then sit on the bottom of the boat. Stay with your boat, never swim for shore. Be prepared to signal for assistance with hand signals, distress flag, whistle, horn, light, and/or radio. See Section D, "Additional Safety Guidelines and Emergency Procedures."

6. *Offshore Winds*

During the process of learning to sail you will drift down wind. Sailing back upwind may require skills you don't yet have. Stay within an area where you know you will be able to return to shore. Do not allow yourself to drift further down wind than you can paddle back. See Section D 3, "Self-Rescue Procedure."

7. *Poor Visibility: Darkness, Heavy Rain, and Fog*

Never sail in darkness or poor visibility, including heavy rain and fog. A greater risk of collision with an obstruction exists in low visibility and the possibility of being struck by another vessel is a hazard. If visibility becomes reduced while you are out sailing, return to shore immediately. Coast Guard regulations specify lighting and sound signals to be used during limited visibility.

8. *Underwater Obstructions: Rocks, Logs, Glass, and Shallow Water*

Water is not crystal clear and hazards below the water's surface may not be visible. Generally, this is more of a hazard when in shallow water near shore. There could be rocks, broken glass, or other hazardous debris on or protruding from the bottom. Use footwear and walk slowly and carefully when in the water. If you are stepping or falling from your craft, make ever effort to enter the water feet first or rear end first and distribute the force so you do not go very far underwater. Never dive or fall headfirst when entering the water.

9. *Inexperience and/or Unfamiliarity with Equipment*

Sailing is a sport. Like any sport, sailing requires knowledge and skill in order to perform efficiently and safely. Knowledge is obtained through formal (e.g. classes) and self-instruction (e.g. reading, videos, study, etc.). Skills are learned and fine-tuned by actual sailing. Know your boat, its parts, its operation, as well as basic sailing techniques before attempting to sail. When learning, sail with another individual, preferably a certified sailing instructor. Discussing technique, while performing, aids the learning process. Also, it is helpful to have another individual on board in the event of a problem. Lines may become loose. Equipment might come apart. The boat could capsize. The skilled sailor should be able to handle these conditions alone; however, assistance when learning is advisable.

> *Caution:* Beginning or novice sailors should not take children sailing. The adult sailing with children should be a skilled and experienced sailor, one who exudes confidence and performs with skill. A novice sailor with a child on board raises the level of risk to an unacceptable level.

10. *Overhead Power Lines*

The mast of a sailing vessel is very tall and some power lines are quite low. If the mast comes in contact with a power line it could cause electrocution or severe injury. Do not allow any part of your equipment to contact a power line. Be sure to check maps and inspect the area where you will be rigging your boat and sailing. Be aware of power lines when unloading and rigging your boat on shore and when sailing on the water. Also, be aware that rain, tides, and flood conditions can raise water level and bring a boat closer to overhead power lines.

Sailing Safety

11. Equipment Failure or Misuse

Equipment failure, breakage, or misuse could lead to an accident resulting in injury or even death. Equipment can fail or break during severe weather or even with normal use; therefore, the sailor must always be aware of this possibility and have a pre-planned procedure for handling the situation. At the same time, most equipment problems can be prevented with proper care and inspection of equipment. Equipment should be inspected regularly for excessive wear and to be sure that it is operating properly. Before each sail, the parts and rigging of the sailboat should be examined to be sure that they are working properly; this is especially true if someone else has rigged the boat.

12. Back Injury

Sailboats are heavy and stepping a mast can be very strenuous. Do not exceed your physical limitations when unloading or loading a boat from a trailer or stepping or unstepping a mast. Use proper lifting techniques and always request assistance if you do not feel comfortable handling the equipment.

13. Collision: Fixed Obstructions, Other Boats, and Swimmers

When sailing, keep a lookout for obstructions; a collision could cause injury or even death. Obstructions include, but are not limited to, fixed obstructions both above and below the water surface, other boats, other sailors, swimmers, buoys, etc. Your vision will be partially obstructed by your sail, so you must constantly be aware of your surroundings and maintain a proper lookout. Stay several boat lengths from any obstacle. Stop if you must to avoid a collision. If you must stop immediately, luff your sails by releasing the main sheet and/or turn the boat into the wind. You cannot control the actions of other boaters; so you must plan ahead and stay well away from other boating traffic. Know and obey the "Rules of the Road (i.e. Right of Way—Chapter 8)," they are the law. Stay away from designated swim areas. Stay in control of your craft and always be courteous to other individuals.

14. Sailing in an Area where there is No Means of Communication with other Boats or People

In the event of a problem or emergency, it may be necessary to request and obtain assistance. Therefore, there should always be a way of communicating with other boats and people. This can be accomplished by sailing in an area where there are other boats and/or people and by being prepared to use a variety of distress signals and equipment, for example, hand signals, a distress flag, whistle, horn, light, radio, and/or cellular phone (keep in waterproof bag). Be sure equipment is secure so it will not be lost if the boat capsizes. Also, always file a "Float Plan" with a responsible person. That plan should include the area you are sailing, your destination, your route, and your time of return. If you are not back at the designated time, the individual can mount a search operation.

15. Fishermen

Avoid fishermen. Do not cross closely behind a boat as it may be towing a fishing line. Stay well away from anchored boats for safety and courtesy. Do not approach the shoreline in an area where there are fishermen. Remember that recreation areas are for multiple uses and must be shared.

16. Interaction with a Power Boat or Rescue Boat

If approached by a power boat or rescue boat follow the directions of the operator very closely. The operator should shut off the engine before making contact. Do not approach a powerboat until the engine is shut off and you are instructed to do so. A whirling propeller(s) is a serious hazard. In an emergency situation, it may be necessary to tow you and your equipment back to shore. Follow directions closely when being towed.

17. Medical Considerations

Sailing occurs in an outdoor environment; therefore, emergency medical attention may not be immediately available. It could take time to reach a phone or radio to call for help and it does take time for medical assistance to reach your location. Always carry or have easy access to a well-stocked first aid kit for minor injuries. It is recommenced that sailors be trained in Cardio-Pulmonary Resuscitation (CPR). It is also recommended that you carry a cellular phone in a secured waterproof bag. However, be aware that cellular phones do not work in all locations; so, have alternate plans in case of an emergency.

18. Alcohol, Legal and Illegal Substances

Operating a watercraft under the influence of alcohol and/or drugs is dangerous and illegal. Violators will be subject to state law. Be aware that other boaters may be SUI (Sailing Under the Influence) and could potentially put you at risk. Avoid contacts with these individuals and report all suspicious activity. You will be providing a service to your fellow boaters. Further, even legal drugs may impair your ability to safely operate a sailboat. Therefore, consult your physician concerning safety precautions related to your medication(s).

19. Loss of Property

Do not take anything on the water that you would be upset about losing. This includes jewelry (especially rings because fingers will shrink in cold water), watches, unsecured

Sailing Safety

glasses, a favorite hat, etc. Leave keys on shore and lock any valuables you forgot to leave at home in the trunk of your vehicle.

20. Tripping, Falling, Etc.

One must always be alert while in an outdoor setting. Trips or falls could result in injuries ranging from minor cuts and bruises to a more severe injury. Rough terrain along access routes and shorelines must be negotiated carefully. Watch for obstructions, loose rocks, wet and slippery areas, brush, logs, hazardous litter such as broken glass, etc.

21. Currents, Tides, and Channels

Sailors need to be aware of currents when sailing on a river or in a tidal zone. This is particularly true if the current is moving in the same direction as the wind. This condition will make it more difficult for the sailor to make headway when wanting to sail upwind. For example, it will be easy (and fast) to leave a harbor with an off-shore breeze and an ebb tide (going out). However, it may be impossible to return to the harbor until the tide changes. There are normally two high and two low tides a day on the east and west coasts of the U.S. Know the sailing area and use charts and tidal (current) information to plan your sail.

In areas where there are channels, be aware that larger boats must follow the channel route. This will limit their ability to maneuver. Also, large boats have a great deal of momentum and take a long time to stop. Therefore, stay out of their way!

22. Natural Hazards

The hazards related to adventuring into the great out-of-doors are too numerous to list. Some examples are insects, animals, thorn bushes, poison ivy, and weather. In a water environment, the ultra violet rays are more intense than on land due to reflection from the water. Therefore, sunburn is a common problem. Use sunscreen or sun block, sunglasses, a hat, etc. to prevent this very real sailing hazard.

23. Summary

There are many risks and hazards related to sailing. A prime objective of the sailor should be to eliminate or minimize these risks through knowledge, preparation, and appropriate action. At the same time, the sailor must realize that unforeseen problems can occur—equipment failure, unseen underwater obstructions, unexpected change in weather, etc. Therefore, the sailor should consider any potential problems before sailing and have a course of action planned should a problem materialize. Also, be prepared to help others. There is a U.S. Coast Guard *Law* that states you must render assistance to "any individual in danger at sea," provided you can do so safely. The first source of assistance during an emergency is usually from other boats that are in the vicinity.

B. Hypothermia

Hypothermia—below normal body temperature, can be a life threatening medical condition. Any temperature below 98.6 degrees F (normal body temperature) will result in heat loss. Heat loss to the environment through radiation, conduction, convection, and evaporation is a normal occurrence and serves to help maintain the body in a homeostatic or balanced thermal condition. It is when heat loss is greater than heat production that problems arise. In general, body temperature is controlled by putting on or taking off clothing and/or increasing or decreasing physical activity.

Environmental conditions that lead to or accelerate heat loss are potential problems for the sailor. Cold temperatures, wetness (rain, sweat, or immersion in water), and wind can lead to excessive heat loss. These environmental conditions combined with inadequate/improper clothing, fatigue, and/or dehydration can put the sailor at great risk. Approximately 90% of boating fatalities are due to drowning and nearly half of those can be attributed to the effects of immersion in cold water. Cold water cools the body 25-30 times faster than cold air of the same temperature; the colder the water, the greater the risk of hypothermia.

The major heat loss areas of the body are the head, neck, armpits, sides of the chest, and groin. This is because there is limited musculature in these areas and blood vessels run near the surface of the body. The head accounts for approximately 50% of heat loss. Therefore, all these areas need to be protected with appropriate clothing (wearing a PFD provides additional insulation) to maintain body temperature. Body position and movement in the water can also greatly affect heat loss. This topic is covered under Prevention and Survival.

Hypothermia may develop gradually or when sudden immersion in the water causes rapid cooling of the body. Watch for what can be described as the "umbles"—stumbles, mumbles, fumbles, and grumbles. If hypothermia is not stopped and reversed, a predictable progression of symptoms will follow:

1. Symptoms

- Shivering is the first sign and becomes vigorous with continued exposure
- Skin color becomes flushed initially, but later may turn blue
- Slurred speech
- Clumsiness and poor coordination (particularly in hands, e.g. can't tie knot, zip zipper, etc.)
- Withdrawn and apathetic
- Heart rate and blood flow slows down
- Limbs become stiff as muscles get rigid
- Mental confusion
- Shivering ceases as body is no longer able to warm itself
- Unconsciousness eventually occurs
- Heart failure may occur but drowning usually occurs first

Sailing Safety

2. *Prevention and Survival*

- Always dress for the water temperature and be prepared for cold water immersion
- Layer clothing and use fabrics that insulate even when wet, e.g. polypro, fleece and wool (*not cotton*)
- Protect the head, neck, sides, and groin which are high heat loss areas
- A windbreaker or raincoat will help reduce heat loss from wind chill
- Wear a PFD at all times. It provides both flotation *and* insulation.
- Get out of the water as quickly as possible
  Right, re-enter, and bail out your overturned boat
  Climb onto the bottom of your overturned boat if unable to right it
- In general, do not attempt to swim to shore unless you are *certain* you can make it. Swimming will reduce your survival time as much as 50%. Most individuals *overestimate* their ability to swim in cold water, especially when clothed! Furthermore, staying with your boat makes you an easier rescue target.
- Minimize movement, do not attempt to remove clothing which traps water that will be warmed by the body's heat
- Assume the Heat Escape Lessening Position (H.E.L.P.). While floating in a life jacket, draw your knees together toward your chest, cross your ankles and hold your upper arms tightly to your sides. Keep your head, neck, and face out of the water. If there is more than one person, assume the HUDDLE position. In comparison to treading water, either of these positions will increase your survival time by 50 %.
- Remain as still as possible, however painful. Intense shivering and severe pain in cold water are natural body reflexes, which will not kill you, but heat loss will! Thrashing flushes the warmer water away from the body.

Heat Escape Lessening Position

Fig. 1-1a H.E.L.P.

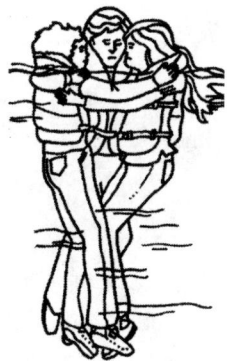

Fig. 1-1b HUDDLE

Water does not have to be icy cold; it just has to be colder than you are, to cause hypothermia. Factors such as body size, percent body fat, protective clothing, and most importantly, the way you behave in the water, will determine the rate of body heat loss. Contrary to popular belief, alcohol decreases rather than increases survival time. This is because alcohol causes vasodilatation (i.e. opening) of peripheral blood vessels.

> **When Air Temperature + Water Temperature < 140° F**
> **Dress to Prevent Hypothermia**
>
> **When Air Temperature is 55 degrees or Below**
> **Or when Air Temperature + Water Temperature < 110° F**
> **Wear a Wet or Dry Suit**

The more energy (heat) that is expended while in the water, the faster body temperature will drop and the sooner the individual will become hypothermic. Survival time can be increased or decreased depending on body position and activity while in the water. Predicted survival time for an average adult in three water temperature conditions are as follows:

Predicted Survival Time

Water Temperature degrees	Swimming hours	Treading Water hours	HELP/HUDDLE Wearing PFD
70	10	13	18
55	2	3	4.5
35	0.75	1.25	1.75

Note, wearing a life jacket and using the H.E.L.P. or HUDDLE position significantly increases survival time.

3. Treating Mild to Moderate Hypothermia

- To reduce heat loss: use dry clothing, add layers of clothing, cover entire body with blanket, find shelter, increase physical activity
- Give hot liquids: hot "sweet" drinks will add heat, energy, and help maintain hydration
- Give food as tolerated
- Avoid alcohol (vasodilator), caffeine (diuretic), and tobacco/nicotine (vasoconstrictor)
- Provide external source of heat (e.g. fire) heated shelter (e.g. car), etc.

4. Severe Hypothermia

- Should be handled by a professional as soon as possible
- Professionals are trained in proper methods for reducing heat loss, administering fluids and food, and utilizing various techniques for elevating temperature

5. Mammalian Diving Reflex

Some apparent drowning victims may not be dead! The Mammalian Diving Reflex, which is triggered by cold water, shuts down blood circulation to most parts of the body except the heart, lungs, and brain. Do not assume that a person who is cyanotic (blue skin) and who has no detectable pulse or breathing is dead. Administer CPR and get medical help as quickly as possible.

C. PERSONAL FLOTATION DEVICES (PFDs)

Body weight, volume, percent fat, lung volume, clothing, and water conditions are just some of the variables that determine if a person will float. Most people can float; however, adults need 7-12 pounds of additional buoyancy to float with their heads above water. That is why the *minimum* amount of floatation in a U.S. Coast Guard (USCG) approved adult Personal Floatation Device (PFD) is 15.5 pounds, more than enough to serve the purpose.

For a PFD to function properly, it must fit correctly. A PFD that is too tight will be restrictive. One that is too loose will tend to "ride up" negating its ability to keep the head above water. Always select a PFD for your weight and body size and make sure it fits correctly and comfortably. Try it on and be sure you know how to adjust and secure it properly.

1. Types of PFDs

There are four types of PFDs or life jackets approved by the USCG for use on recreational boats. Throwable devices (Type IV) may be helpful but are not approved as "official" PFDs because they are not made to be worn.

Type I Off-Shore Life Preserver

This is a vest or yoke type device generally found on commercial craft. It is designed to turn most unconscious persons from a face down to a face up position in the water. It must provide a minimum buoyancy of 22 pounds for an adult.

Type II Near-Shore Life Vest

This vest usually looks like a horse collar and is worn like a bib around the neck. It has the ability to turn the face upward like the Type I, but because it has less buoyancy (15.5 pound minimum), it will not perform as well as the Type I under the same conditions.

Type III Special Purpose Flotation Aid

There are many styles and colors of approved special purpose flotation aids. Examples of special purpose flotation aids would be those designed specifically for water skiing, hunting, kayaking, etc. They have the same amount of buoyancy as the Type II but *are not* designed to turn an unconscious person face up. Type III designs do, however, allow for greater comfort and often have features which are useful in specific settings (e.g. pockets, straps, etc.).

Type IV Throwable Devices

Devices such as buoyant cushions, ring buoys, and horseshoe buoys are designed to be thrown to a person and ***not worn***. To use these devices, simply throw them overboard to a person in the water. The person then clutches the device to their chest while awaiting rescue. Throwable devices ***do not*** meet USCG carriage requirements. An appropriate sized USCG approved PFD must be available for each person on board.

Type V Special Use Devices

An inflatable life vest is an example of a special use device. Regulations for "Special Use Devices" specify they ***must be worn*** whenever the boat is underway and the wearer is on deck in order to meet Coast Guard carriage requirements.

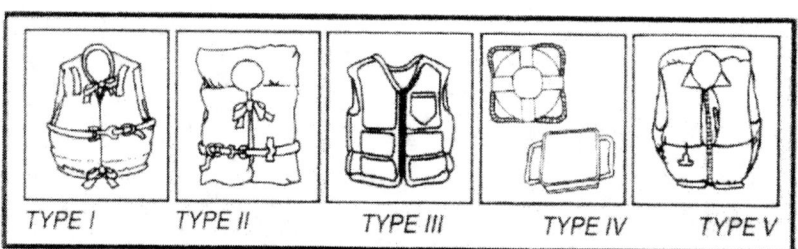

Fig. 1-2 Types of Personal Flotation Devices (PDFs)

Increase the Life of Your PFD

1. Clean/rinse your PFD with fresh water before storing.
2. Drip-dry your PFD and put it away in a ventilated location. Do not dry it on a radiator or other direct heat source.
3. Store your PFD indoors out of direct sunlight.
4. Do not put heavy objects on your PFD. Also, do not use it as a kneeling pad or boat fender. Crushed PFDs lose buoyancy.
5. Do not leave your PFD on board for long periods when the boat is not in use.

Sailing Safety

According to the U.S. Coast Guard's Office of Boating Safety, 703 people died in boating accidents in 2003, 201 of these deaths occurred when someone fell overboard and 284 involved alcohol. Of the 481 people that drowned, 86% *were not* wearing a PFD! The Coast Guard estimates that the lives of approximately 390 of these individuals could have been saved, **if they had been wearing a PFD!**

2. U.S. Coast Guard PFD Requirements

The following are United States Coast Guard (USCG) Carriage Requirements. See Federal Regulations and Safety Tips for Recreational Boats, United States Coast Guard, 2004 www.uscgboating.org/safety/fedreqs/equ_pfd.htm for additional information. Every person on board a watercraft must wear or have ready access to a USCG approved Personal Flotation Device (PFD) which meets the following five conditions:

- **U.S. Coast Guard Approved**—An approval label or stamp will appear on the PFD. Ski belts *are not* Coast Guard approved.

- **Appropriate Size for the Intended Wearer**—A wearable type device must fit the passenger for which it was intended. Sizes are indicated on the PFD label. For children, they are marked: less than 30, 30-50, less than 50 and 50-90 pounds according to the child's weight. Infants under 30 pounds require an infant sized device.

- **Readily Accessible**—PFDs should be in clear view to all passengers and easy to access in an emergency. PFDs in locked lockers, under anchors and line, or enclosed in plastic bags are **NOT** readily accessible.

- **In Good and Serviceable Condition**—All stitching, straps, buckles, and zippers must be intact and in working order. The PFD must be free of tears, rot, punctures, and water logging (especially kapok filled devices).

- **Correct Type and Number of PFDs on Board**—All recreational boats must carry one wearable PFD (Type I, II, or III) for each person on board. On boats 16 feet long or more, except canoes and kayaks, there must be a Type I, II, or III wearable PFD for each person on board **PLUS** a Type IV throwable. A Type V hybrid device may be used to meet carriage requirements if it is worn above deck.

State and local park authorities may have additional PFD regulations. For example, according to Ohio law, children under 10 years of age on boats less than 18 feet in length must wear a properly sized Type I, II or III PFD at all times while the vessel is being operated. Check the regulations in your state and at your sailing location.

> **The Four Major Causes of Drowning**
> 1. Not wearing a life jacket
> 2. Abuse of alcohol
> 3. Lack of sufficient swimming skills
> 4. Hypothermia

When choosing a PFD, consider that reds and oranges are very visible at sea, whereas whites and blues are not (making it difficult to see a person who has fallen overboard).

D. ADDITIONAL SAFETY GUIDELINES AND EMERGENCY PROCEDURES

1. Weather

Various aspects of weather have already been covered. This section presents a general overview of practical information that can be used in determining and/or evaluating weather conditions. The sailor should know the current air temperature, water temperature, wind speed, wave height, and tide status as well as the local weather forecast before setting sail.

Forecast: The sailor should know the weather forecast for the time planned on the water. There are many sources of weather information. Some are more up-to-date and accurate than others.

- **News media:** newspapers, radio stations, and television stations all have some form of weather information. Some weather reports will give a marine forecast for the local area.

- **Internet:** there is a great deal of weather information on the internet. A good place to start is at the National Weather Service's web page for local forecasts www.srh.noaa.gov and/or marine forecasts www.nws.noaa.gov/om/marine/marine_map.htm The Weather Channel also has a web site where you can check local conditions including water temperature, wave height and the marine forecast www.weather.com/activities/recreation/boatandbeach/ On-line services such as AOL also provide local forecasts.

- **Telephone:** local forecasts are often available by telephone. Check the local telephone directory or call information.

- **VHF radio:** The National Weather Service provides marine weather forecasts on special VHF radio channels. Weather radios, which carry these specific channels, are available for purchase.

- **Sailing Site:** Some sailing sites (e.g. marinas) have current barometric pressure and wind speed measures as well as the local forecast.

Knowledge and Experience: The best weather forecast is no substitute for weather knowledge and experience. Start with the most accurate weather forecast available. However, be

Sailing Safety

alert to the immediate conditions and how they may be changing. Look for signs/signals of change. The knowledgeable sailor will use both general and specific indicators of change in deciding when to sail and also in deciding when to come off the water:

- "Red sky at night—sailors delight; red sky in the morning—sailors take warning."
- A halo around the moon indicates precipitation. The larger the halo, the nearer the rain.
- "When smoke descends, good weather ends."
- The higher the clouds the better the weather.
- If the sky changes, so will the weather.
- High pressure (barometric) is associated with clear, dry weather. Low pressure is associated with cloudy, rainy weather. Increasing pressure indicates that weather will soon be good. Decreasing pressure indicates that a storm is on the way.
- A rapid change in temperature indicates changing weather conditions.
- Large dark clouds on the horizon signal an approaching storm.
- If there is thunder and/or lightning, the small boat sailor should get off the water. The speed of sound is around 760 mph or about one-fifth of a mile per second. Therefore, count the number of seconds following a flash of lightning until you hear thunder and then divide by five. This calculation will give a good estimate of your distance (in miles) from the lightning/thunder.

2. Float Plan

Small boats are not normally sailed very far from their put-in and take-out points. However, if this is going to be the case, the sailor should be prepared and stow some basic equipment on board. Examples of items to consider would be foul-weather clothing, water, food, paddle, distress flag, duct tape, knife, first-aid kit, light, whistle, spare parts, and something to bail with. The sailor should also write down and file a float plan with a responsible person. The **float plan** should describe where you are going, when you will return, the names of the people on board, and a description of your boat. Leave the float plan with a responsible person who will call the local authorities and/or Coast Guard if you are seriously overdue.

3. Self-Rescue Procedure

In the event of equipment failure, insufficient wind, or other problem that prevents you from sailing back to shore, you may have to Self-Rescue. Depending on conditions, you may choose to enter the water and pull or push your boat, lie on the deck at the bow and paddle with your arms, or sit on the deck and use a paddle you have brought for this purpose. In very heavy wind, it may be necessary to dismantle your sailing rig and lash it to the boat before paddling to shore. The best procedure is to prevent the need for Self-Rescue by inspecting your

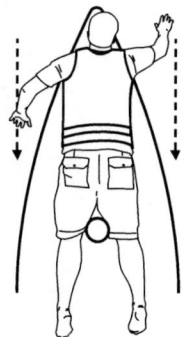

Fig. 1-3 Self-Rescue

equipment carefully, remaining near shore, and gaining knowledge and experience in operating a sailboat.

4. *Hand/Arm Signals*

If you need assistance and cannot Self-Rescue, use a distress flag or the international distress signal. The international distress signal involves waving both arms back and forth over your head. When using the distress signal continue waving until the rescuer responds with the same signal. *This distress signal is for emergency use only.* To signal you are OK, raise your arm to the side and, with your elbow held high, place your finger tips on top of your head.

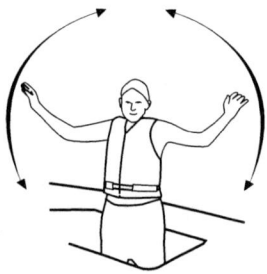 

Fig. 1-4a Distress Signal   **Fig. 1-4b I'm OK**

Hand/Arm signals are also helpful for communication between instructor and student. Noise from wind, waves, and luffing sails can make voice communication difficult to impossible. When the arms are swung back and forth across the chest with the palms down, the instructor is directing the student to go into the Safety Position. When the arm begins in an extended position with the palm up and is then flexed with the fingers closing, the instruction is to "Sheet-In." When the arm begins in a flexed position with the fingers closed and is then extended with the fingers opening, the instruction is to "Sheet-Out." **Sheeting** refers to pulling in (trimming) or letting out (easing) the line that controls the sail, the mainsheet.

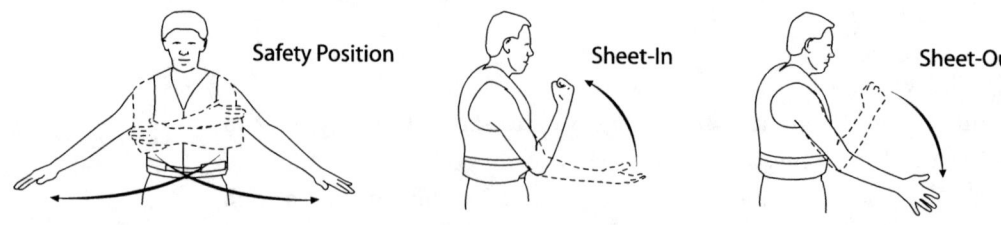

Fig. 1-5 Instructor Signals

Sailing Safety

5. Towing

If there is an equipment problem or conditions become calm and you are too far out to self-rescue, you may need a tow. Some boats will have a line attached to the bow called a **painter**. This line is used to control the boat in launching and landing. It can also be used for towing. If there is no painter, a line will need to be attached from the rescue craft to your boat. If a line is not readily available, the mainsheet can be detached and used for this purpose. A good place to attach this line on a small sailboat is around the bottom of the mast. Lower the sail or make sure the mainsheet is slack and the sail is free to move when being towed. Also, raise the daggerboard half-way and use body weight to keep the boat balanced.

6. State Laws

Each state has laws pertaining to the safe operation of watercraft. Contact the appropriate agency in the state where you live/sail to obtain this free information. These laws include specifications related to reckless operation, operating under the influence, Right of Way, meaning of various buoys, Lake Zones, etc.

E. SUMMARY

There are many hazards and risks related to the sport of sailing. The intent of the information in this chapter is to make the prospective sailor aware of potential hazards and risks. Awareness of these hazards and risks, along with knowledge of appropriate precautions and safety procedures, will not only prevent accidents but also result in a more enjoyable sailing experience.

F. EXERCISES AND REVIEW QUESTIONS

Appendix C, Exercises and Review Questions, is presented to assist you in the learning process. It is organized by chapter. It is recommended that you do the exercises and answer the questions related to each chapter as soon as you finish reading it. **Therefore, go to the Chapter 1 Exercises and Review Questions in Appendix C and complete them before proceeding to Chapter 2.**

Chapter 2
Line and Knots

A. TYPES OF LINE

Rope being used on a boat is referred to as "**Line**." Lines are used to rig, secure, and control a sailboat. Sailing commands are transmitted to the boat through lines, movement of the rudder, and shifting of body weight.

There are four standard types of line; laid rope, solid braid, dynamic kernmantle and static kernmantle. Laid rope is made from natural or synthetic fiber strands that are wound together. Solid braid line is made from strands that are woven together. Dynamic kernmantle line has a braided sheath woven over a twisted core which acts as a shock absorber. Static kernmantle line has a protective sheath woven tightly over the load-bearing parallel fibers in the core. Modern sailing lines are made from synthetic fibers (e.g. dacron, nylon and polypropylene) and are practically carefree, unlike the mildew and rot-prone natural fiber lines of the past.

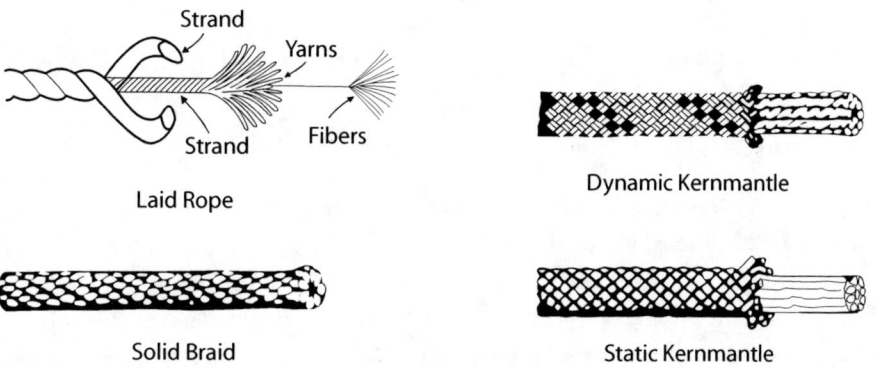

Fig. 2-1 Types of Line

Dacron line is used for halyards and sheets (lines used to raise and control sails) because it has very little stretch. Nylon is used for anchors and dock lines because it does stretch. Polypropylene is used for mooring lines because it floats. Sailing lines are expensive due to the method of construction and the cost of man-made fibers. Proper care of lines will minimize the need (and cost) of replacement.

Follow these simple DO's and DON'Ts:

DO

1. Take care to keep lines out of dirt, mud, and sand.
2. Remove dirt/sand from lines before storage, rinse in nearby fresh water or use a gentle hose stream. Dirt/sand clinging to a line will work itself between the fibers and cause damage.
3. Rinse lines that have been used in saltwater in fresh water to remove salt.
4. Store lines clean, dry, out of direct sunlight, and away from extreme heat. Nylon, polyester, and polypropylene lines are severely weakened by prolonged exposure to ultra violet light.
5. Treat the ends of freshly cut lines so they will not unravel. An electric cutter or "hot knife" works well. If not available, tape the line, cut in the center of the tape, and then hold the end of the freshly cut line to a match until the core and mantle melt and run together. Let it cool slightly, and then twirl the end between your thumb and forefinger to produce a hard tight taper.

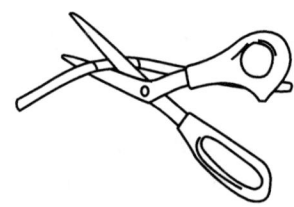

Fig. 2-2 Cutting a Taped Line

DON'T

1. Don't put wet lines into closed sailbags. Be sure the line is clean and dry before storing. A line that remains wet will be ruined.
2. Don't use a cut or frayed line. If the core is exposed, the line should be replaced.

B. SELECTED KNOTS*

*Go to www.ussailing.org Getting Started—Online Education—Small Boat Course—Knots & Lines to see videos on how to tie knots.

A knot will transform a simple line into a useful tool. Sailors need to develop skill in tying several simple knots. These knots are best learned through practice. Using sailing knots for everyday tasks such as tying packages, securing roof rack items, hanging clothesline, etc., will help make tying knots second nature.

The following are basic terms used in knot tying. **Bight** is that section of line used in the knot and beyond. **Running end** is the part of line used in making the knot. **Standing part** is the part of line *not* used in forming the knot. To form an **overhand loop**, cross the running end *over* the standing part. To form an **underhand loop**, cross the running end *under* the standing part.

Line and Knots

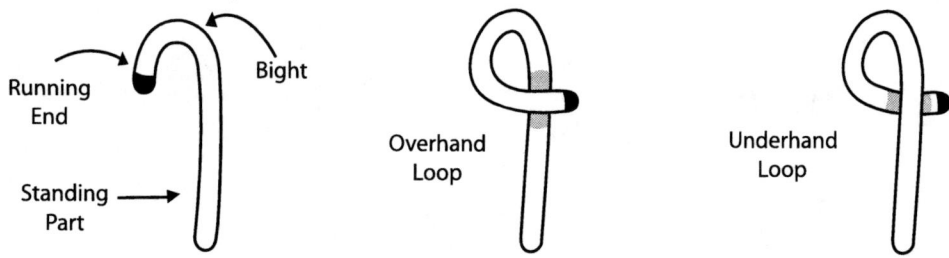

Fig. 2-3 Knot Tying Terms

A **turn** is taken when an overhand or underhand loop is made around an object or a section of the standing part. A **round turn** is taken when a second loop is added.

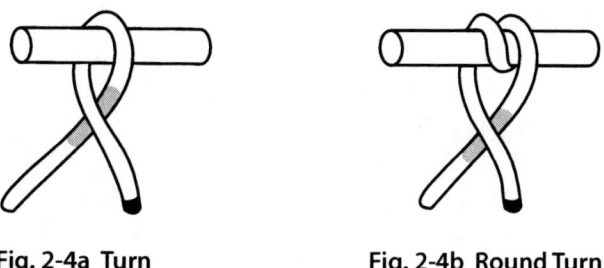

Fig. 2-4a Turn **Fig. 2-4b Round Turn**

The **overhand knot** is the simplest of all knots. It is sometimes used as a "stopper knot" in the end of a line, however, it *is not* recommended because it jams easily and is difficult to untie.

Fig. 2-5 Overhand Knot

Do Not Use

The recommended "stopper knot" is the **Figure 8** (shaped like an 8) because it holds well and is easy to untie by pushing the running end and standing part toward the middle of the knot. The figure 8 is used to prevent lines from running through blocks, eyes, and jam cleats. Take a bight at the end of the line and make an overhand loop, pass the running end under the standing part and back through the loop as indicated. Pull on both ends and "firm" the knot in place. See Fig. 2-6.

Fig. 2-6 Tying a Figure 8 Knot

The **square** (or reef) **knot** can be used to tie off two ends of a line that is under tension or to join together two lines of equal size. Hold one end of line in each hand. First, take the end in your left hand and put it over and around the line in your right hand, switch hands, and pull both ends to tighten (like tying your shoe) and provide enough free line at each end to repeat the process. Now, take the end that is in your right hand and put it over and around the line in your left hand, switch hands, and pull both ends tight.

The square knot is probably the most useful and popular of all knots. It will hold firmly when under tension and is easy to untie by pushing the lines coming out of each end toward the center of the knot. Caution, crossing your lines incorrectly (e.g. going left over right and then left over right again), will result in a "granny knot" that is not secure and will easily come apart.

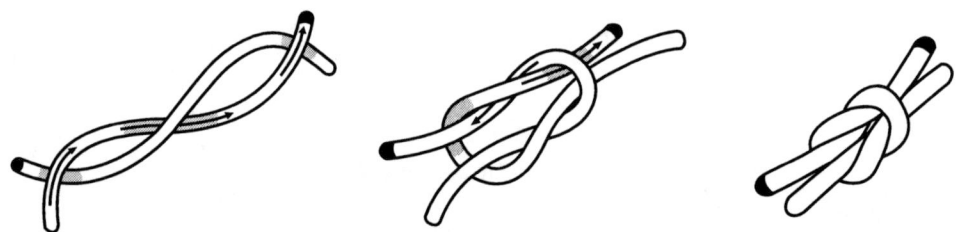

Fig. 2-7 Tying a Square Knot

A **clove hitch** is not a very secure knot, but can be used to temporarily moor to a piling or tie a line around a spar. Make a loop around the piling or spar and then a second loop crossing over the first loop. Bring the running end under the second loop and pull both ends tight.

Line and Knots

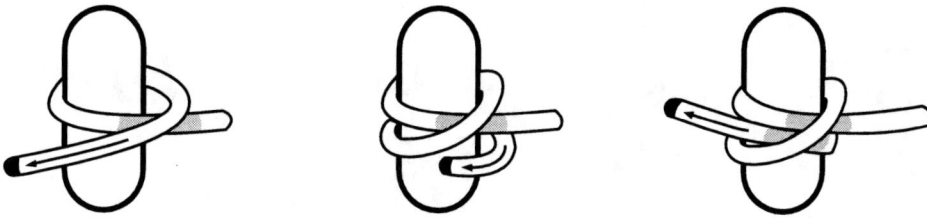

Fig. 2-8 Tying a Clove Hitch

A **round turn** secured **with two half hitches** is a good way to attach a line for extended mooring. After completing the round turn, the running end goes around and through twice to form the two half hitches. Pull the running end tight while pushing the two half hitches together against the round turn. This can also be used as a utility knot to secure one end of a line.

Fig. 2-9 Use a Round Turn and Two Half Hitches to Secure the End of a Line

The **bowline** (pronounced "bolin") is used whenever a loop is required that will not slip, jam, or fail. It is a favorite knot of sailors and is often used to tie off the mainsheet to the block at the end of the boom and to attach lines to the sail. It can be easily untied when not under tension.

First make an overhand loop in the standing part with enough lead to form the loop of the bowline. Bring the running end up through the bottom of the overhand loop, around the standing part, and then back down through the overhand loop. When done, hold the running end against the loop of the bowline that has just been formed and then pull on the standing part to tighten the knot. The Boy Scout story still works in learning to tie this not. First make the overhand loop and then think of the tip of the running end being a rabbit! The rabbit comes out of his hole and goes around the tree (the standing end). He sees the fox; so he goes back in his hole. Hold the running end against the loop and pull the standing end, and there you have it—a bowline! See Fig. 2-10.

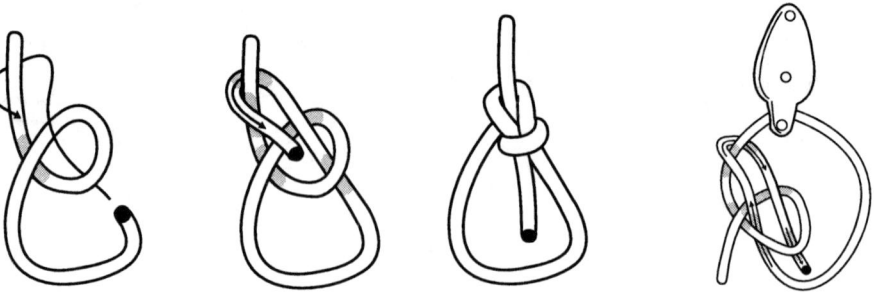

Fig. 2-10a Tying the Bowline   Fig. 2-10b Bowline on a Block

C. Line Hardware

Various hardware devices are used to hold and direct line.

1. Cleats

Cleats are objects on boats and docks that are there for the purpose of securing line without having to tie a knot. Attaching a line to a **horn shaped cleat** is easily accomplished by first taking the line around the base of the cleat, then forming a figure 8 around the cleat and finally securing the running end under the last loop with a half hitch lying parallel to the figure 8 turn.

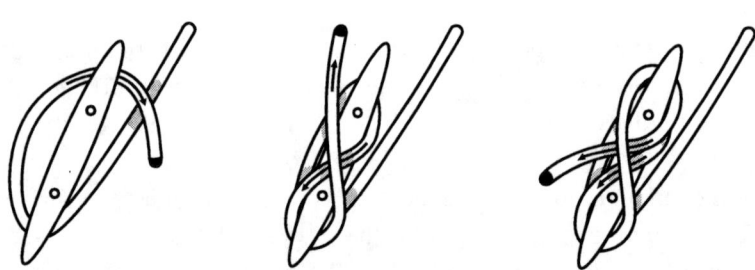

Fig. 2-11 Tying Off to a Horn Cleat

There are three kinds of "jamming" cleats. The **clam, cam, and jam cleats** are used to secure a line, while still providing for easy adjustment. The **clam cleat** is made of hardened plastic or aluminum and has notches that will hold a line that is run through it. To make the line fast to a clam cleat, pull it through the cleat and hold it down, then, while continuing to

Line and Knots

apply tension, pull the standing part backward somewhat to secure the line in the grooves of the cleat. To release the line, pull and lift.

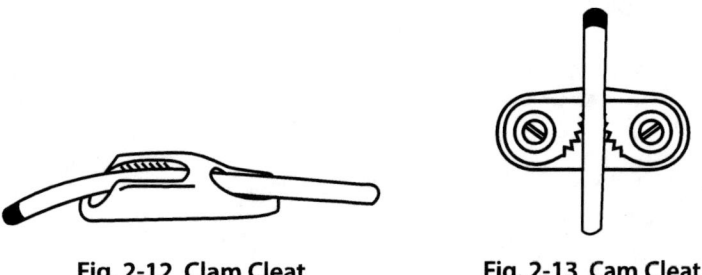

Fig. 2-12 Clam Cleat   Fig. 2-13 Cam Cleat

The **cam cleat** holds a line between two rotating sets of cam teeth. It operates by rotating in one direction as a line (e.g. mainsheet) is pulled down and through it. When the tension is released, the grooved cam clamps down on the line holding it in place. To release the line from the cam cleat, pull it up with a quick snap—maintain hold of the line for control.

The **jam cleat** looks like a horn cleat except that there is a notch in the front horn that can grab a line with only one wrap. There is a jam cleat located on the tiller of a Laser. It is used for tying off the rudder line.

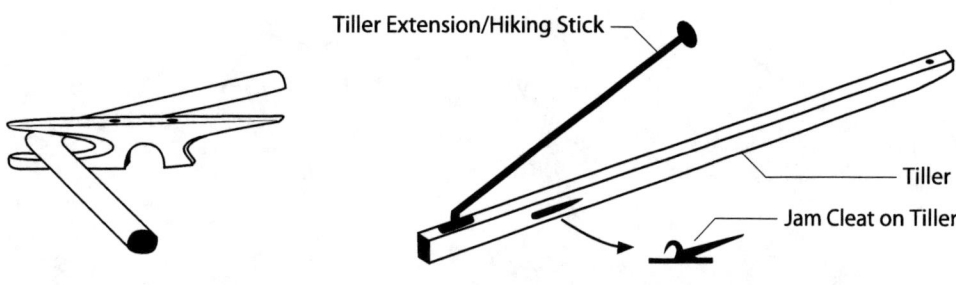

Fig. 2-14a Jam Cleat   Fig. 2-14b Jam Cleat on a Tiller

2. Other Line Hardware

Sailboats have hardware that is used to support and change the direction of line. An **eye strap** is a metal strap that keeps a line in place while providing free passage. A **fairlead** ("fairleed") is an eye through which a line is led to change its direction. A **block** is a nautical pulley; it is used to change the direction of a moving line while reducing friction and also, depending on pulley arrangement, to increase force on a line. See Fig. 2-15.

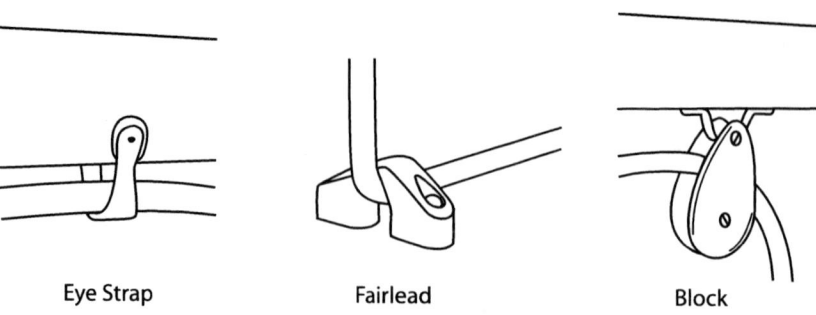

Fig. 2-15 Line Hardware

D. Coiling and Throwing a Line

Coiling and securing a line (e.g. mainsheet) is a good way to store it and prevent tangles. First coil the line keeping each coil the same length by using an arm's length for each coil. Then, take the remaining end and wrap it three or four times around the middle of the entire coil. Next, pull the end of the line through the coil to form a loop, drop the loop back over the coil, and then pull on the end to tighten.

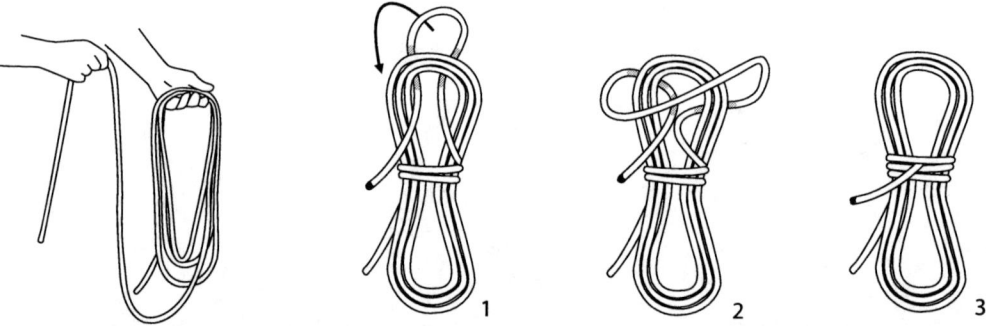

Fig. 2-16a Coiling Line

Fig. 2-16b Securing a Coiled Line

Throwing a line is sometimes necessary when docking or preparing to tow a boat. It may seem like a simple task but it should be practiced so it can be done quickly and accurately. Start with a coiled line and separate it into a small section and a larger section. Place the small section in the throwing hand and throw it while allowing the line to uncoil from the other hand.

Line and Knots 27

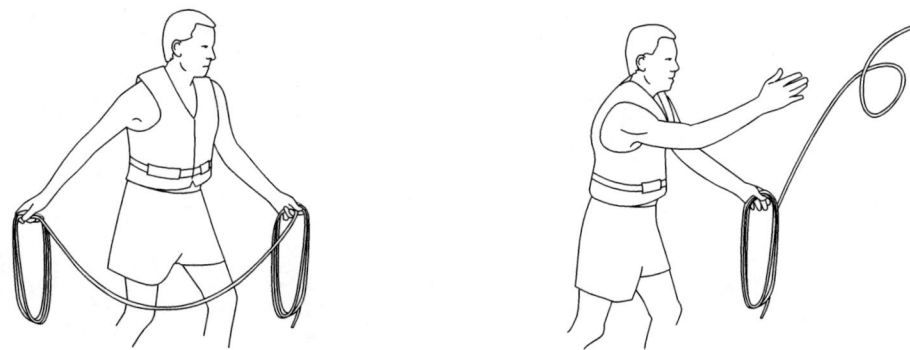

Fig. 2-17 Throwing a Coiled Line

E. EXERCISES AND REVIEW QUESTIONS

Complete Exercises and Review Questions for Chapter 2 in Appendix C *before* **proceeding to Chapter 3.**

Chapter 3
Small Boats

Sailboats that are less than 20 feet long are called "small boats."

A. HULL DESIGNS

There are many designs (kinds) of small sailboats. Major differences between boats are related to both hull design and sail rigging. The **hull** is the body of the boat. There are two main types of hull designs, centerboard and keel. Small boats that have retractable centerboards are called dinghies. Boats that have keels are called keelboats. Centerboard boats have large flat boards that are lowered vertically (daggerboards) or pivot as they are raised/lowered. Centerboards provide lateral stability (i.e. lateral resistance), that is, they prevent the boat from sliding sideways in the water. In addition to providing lateral stability, keels have ballast (i.e. are weighted) to help prevent the wind in the sails from capsizing the boat. The fixed keel is typically more stable, stronger, and safer than the swing keel. However, the swing keel has the advantage of allowing the boat to enter shallow water and is more easily loaded on a trailer.

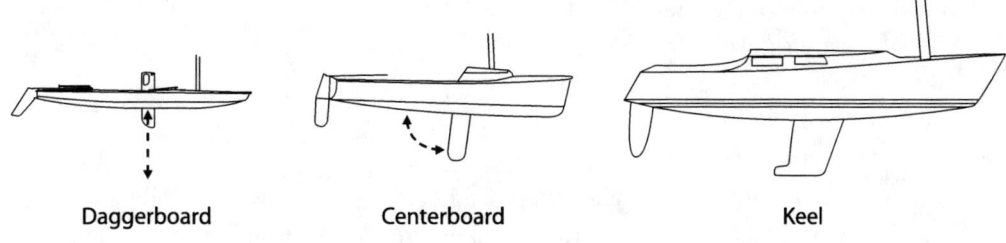

Daggerboard   Centerboard   Keel

Fig. 3-1 Hull Designs

B. SAILING TERMINOLOGY

Knowing sailing terminology is important for a clear understanding of sailboat design, function, and control. As with a foreign language, you must first learn the vocabulary and then how the terms are used before you can become proficient. The following sections present basic sailing terms: (1) Basic Boat Terms; (2) Hull Terms; (3) Spar, Steering Assembly, and Depth Terms; and (4) Sail and Running Rigging Terms. The terms are first defined, and then you are asked to *write* each term next to the appropriate number on the diagram. The act of physically writing the name while noting the location on the diagram will help you learn the name and function of the generic sailboat parts that are covered in this chapter. These labeling exercises *(and the ones in Appendix C—Exercises and Review Questions)* will help you learn the name and function of the different parts of your boat.

In addition to these labeling exercises, it is recommended that you verbally name the parts of your boat as you **"rig it"** (put it together). It is best if you have a knowledgeable person present who can correct you, if necessary, and provide you with immediate feedback. However, even if you don't, still name the parts and describe what you are doing "out loud." For example, "I am putting the tiller under the traveler so it doesn't get caught on the traveler when I am sailing."

Further, while learning, verbally describe (using correct terminology) what you are going to do before you do it (and while you are doing it), e.g. launching, steering, tacking, landing, etc. Verbally describing your plans and actions will assist you in the learning process.

A "Nautical Dictionary" can be found in Appendix E. It provides a quick reference for learning sailing terms.

Using the diagram that follows each set of definitions, write each term next to the correct number on the diagram. As you use each term cross it out and continue until all terms have been used. Answers can be found in Appendix D.

1. Basic Boat Terms

Though there are many designs of sailboats, basic boating terms apply to all of them.

Fore —forward ("for-rad"), toward the front
Ahead—in front of the boat
Aft—at, near, or toward the stern
Astern—behind the boat
Amidships—between fore and aft; the middle of the boat
Beam—widest point of the boat
Abeam—the bearing 90° from ahead; perpendicular to the boat
Starboard—right side of the boat when looking toward the front
Port—left side of the boat when looking toward the front; note, left and port each have four letters
Length Over All (LOA)—the distance measured along the centerline of the boat from the tip of the bow to the stern

Small Boats 31

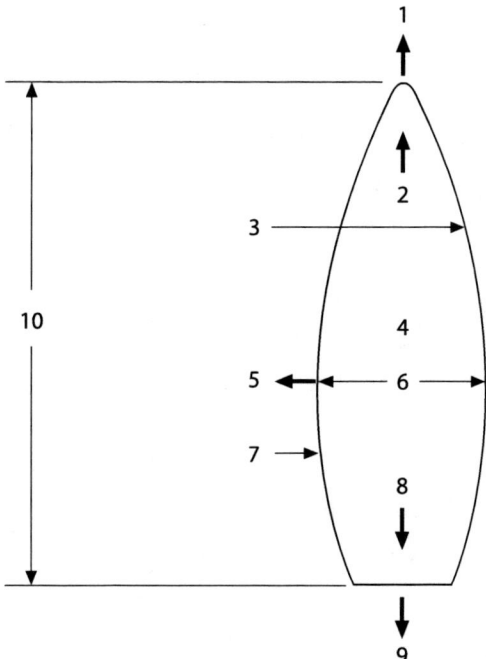

Fig. 3-2 Basic Boat Terms

2. Hull Terms—Label on Next Page

Stern—the back of the boat

Transom—the stern surface of the boat

Gudgeon (Gudgeon bracket)—fitting (bracket) on the transom into which a pintle pin from the rudder head is inserted to hold the rudder onto the boat

Traveler line—line at the stern of the boat to which the mainsheet is attached

Traveler block—pulley on traveler to which mainsheet is attached

Cockpit—open area behind the mast where you sit or place your feet

Gunwale ("gunnel")—edge of the boat at deck level; term from the past when ships carried guns along a wall

Hiking strap—line or webbing across cockpit; feet are placed under it in order to hike (lean) out to balance the boat

Mainsheet swivel block—pulley through which mainsheet runs

Daggerboard trunk—slot or housing for daggerboard

Mast step hole (Tabernacle)—place to mount the mast in the deck of the boat

Deck—the horizontal flat surface enclosing the hull

Bow—the front of the boat

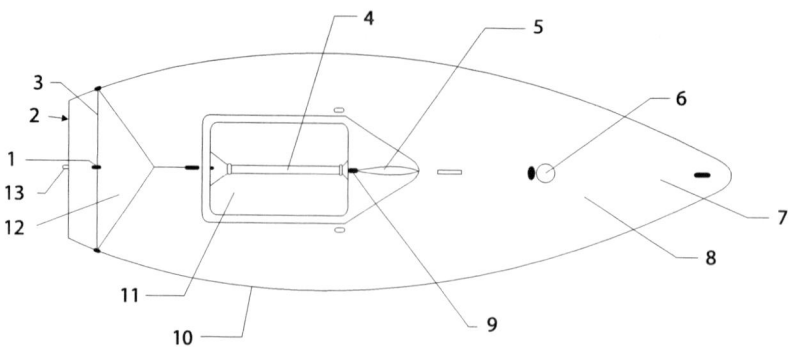

Fig. 3-3 Hull Terms

3. Spar, Steering Assembly and Depth Terms

Spar is a term for a mast, boom, sprit, gaff, or other pole that is used to support the sail. The **steering assembly** consists of the rudder and its controlling elements as well as the daggerboard (centerboard). It is what enables the sailor to control the direction of the boat. **Depth** terms relate to how the boat floats in the water and the minimum depth of water in which the boat can sail.

> **Mast**—the vertical pole that supports sail
> **Boom**—horizontal spar that attaches to the mast and supports the foot of the sail. Be careful, it got its name by hitting people in the head!
> **Boom vang**—line system secured to the boom; it controls tension on the boom, holds it in place, and prevents it from lifting
> **Gooseneck**—hinged or swivel fitting that attaches the boom to the mast
> **Forward boom block**—forward pulley on boom through which mainsheet runs
> **Aft boom block**—aft pulley on boom through which mainsheet runs
> **Waterline**—the level at which the boats floats
> **Freeboard**—distance from the waterline to the deck or gunwale
> **Draft**—distance from waterline to the deepest part of the boat
> **Daggerboard**—centerboard that is inserted vertically by hand; it provides lateral resistance
> **Daggerboard stop**—projection that prevents the daggerboard from sliding all the way through the daggerboard slot
> **Rudder blade**—flat blade attached to stern; used to steer the boat
> **Pintle pin**—pin that attaches rudder to gudgeon on the transom of the hull
> **Tiller**—bar or handle used to turn the rudder and steer the boat
> **Tiller extension/Hiking stick**—extension of the tiller, used to steer the boat when leaning out (hiking)

Small Boats

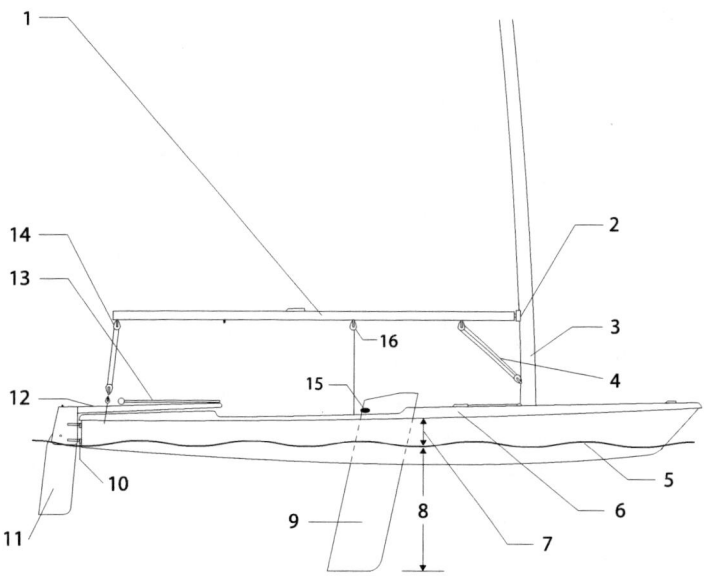

Fig. 3-4 Spar, Steering Assembly and Depth Terms

4. Sail and Running Rigging Terms—Label on Next Page

Most small boats have a triangular sail. Each side and corner of the sail has a name. The sail is put on (e.g. sailsock placed over mast on Laser) or hoisted into place by a **halyard** (e.g. Sunfish). A line used to trim a sail is called a **sheet**. **Running rigging** consists of the halyard, sheets and other lines used to hoist, trim, and control the sail.

> **Mainsail** ("mainsul")—the principal sail attached to the main mast
> **Luff**—the front side or leading edge of a sail. When the sail flutters along the luff edge (e.g. when the boat heads into the wind) it is said to be "luffing."
> **Foot**—the bottom side or edge of a sail
> **Leech**—the back side or edge of a sail
> **Clew**—lower back corner of a sail
> **Tack**—lower front corner of a sail
> **Head**—top corner of a sail
> **Batten**—thin wooden or plastic strip inserted in a pocket along the leech of a sail to help hold the sails' form
> **Batten pocket**—pocket for holding batten
> **Outhaul line**—line used to adjust the foot edge tension of the sail; it pulls out on the clew of the sail
> **Downhaul line**—line used to adjust the luff edge tension of the sail; it pulls down on the tack of the sail
> **Mainsheet**—line which controls the boom and therefore the position of the mainsail

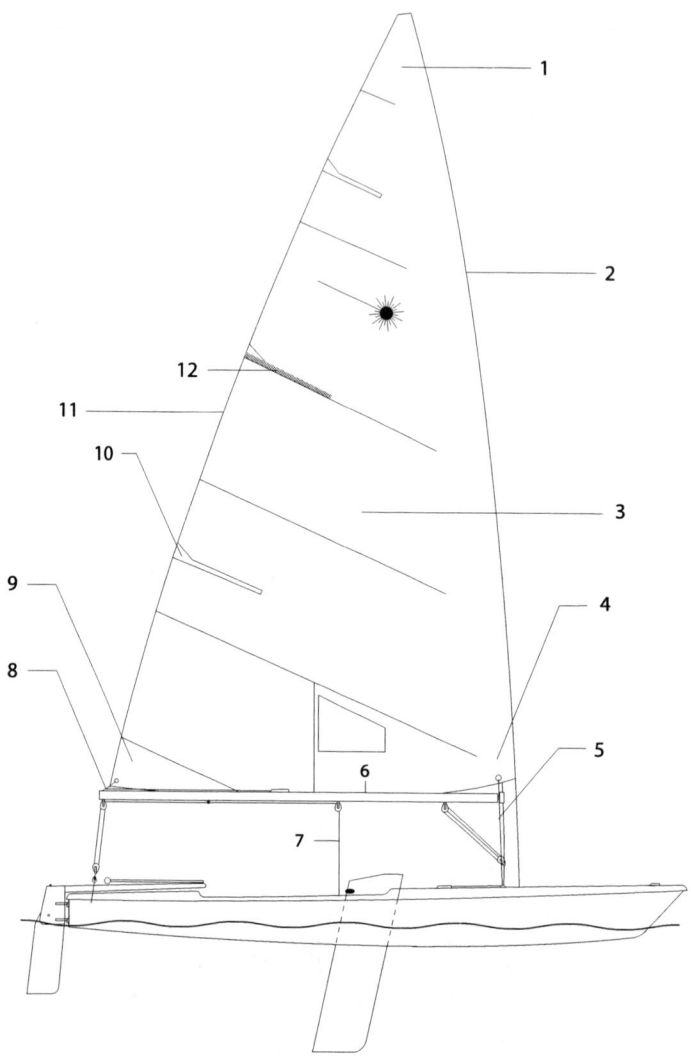

Fig. 3-5 Sail and Running Rigging Terms

C. Sails

Sails come in many shapes and sizes. Unlike bed sheets, which are flat or two-dimensional, sails are made to have "shape." So, **shape of** a sail refers to the number of sides of a sail; **shape in** a sail refers to its curved three-dimensional airfoil design. The sailmaker builds "shape" into the sail. The sailor can adjust shape in a sail by lines that are attached to its corners. Sails are adjusted according to wind conditions. This topic is covered in more depth in Chapter 7.

Small Boats

Many sails use thin wooden or plastic strips (battens) inserted in pockets (batten pockets) along the leech of the sail in order to increase stiffness and help the sail hold its form. It is important that battens be inserted properly so they do not "pop out" while sailing.

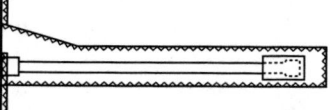

Fig. 3-6 Batten in Batten Pocket

Sails on small boats are typically taken off, cleaned, dried, and then stored after each outing. The recommended way to fold a sail is as follows. Use a clean/clear area (e.g. grass) and layout the sail on the ground with the foot facing the wind. The sail can be folded by one person but it is recommended that two be used. One person takes a position at the tack and the other at the clew of the sail. Both individuals "pull" as the sail is accordion folded (12-15 inch folds) in order to minimize wrinkles. When done, the sail is folded toward the luff edge, then rolled and placed in a sail bag.

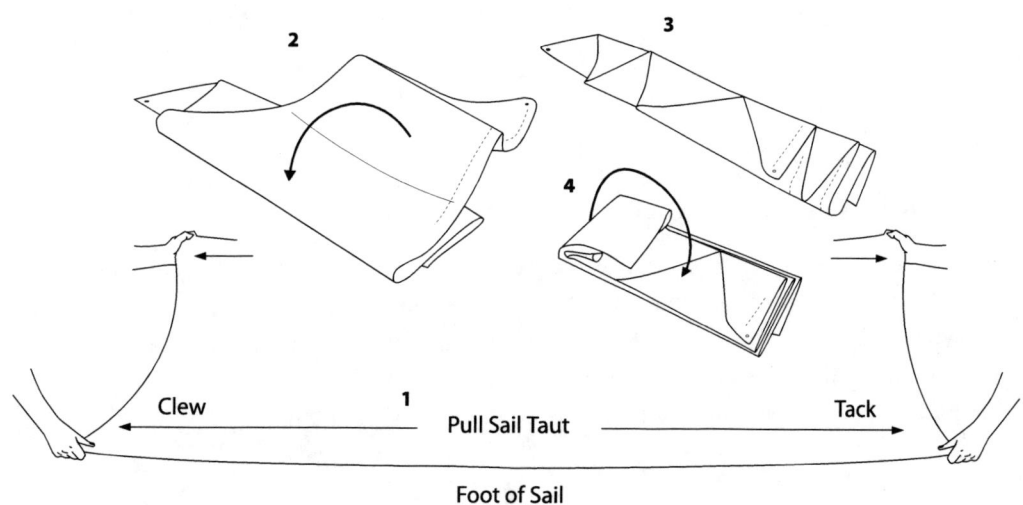

Fig. 3-7 How to Fold a Sail

D. Rigs and Rigging

There are numerous kinds of sailboats and sailboat "rigs." **Rig** refers to the number and arrangement of spars (e.g. masts, booms, sprits, etc.) and sails on a boat. **Rigging** refers to the wires and lines that are used to support and control the rig. **Standing rigging** is the rigging used to attach and hold the mast to the boat. Lines used to control the sail are called the **running rigging**.

The simplest sailboat is the **catboat**; it has one mast stepped well forward and a single sail. The **Laser**, which has one mast, one boom, and a mainsail, is called a Marconi rigged catboat. The **Sunfish**, which has a mast, boom, lateen (upper boom), and an equilateral triangular sail is called a lateen rigged catboat. The **Optimist**, which has a mast, boom, mainsail, and sprit, is called a sprit rigged pram (catboat with square flat bow).

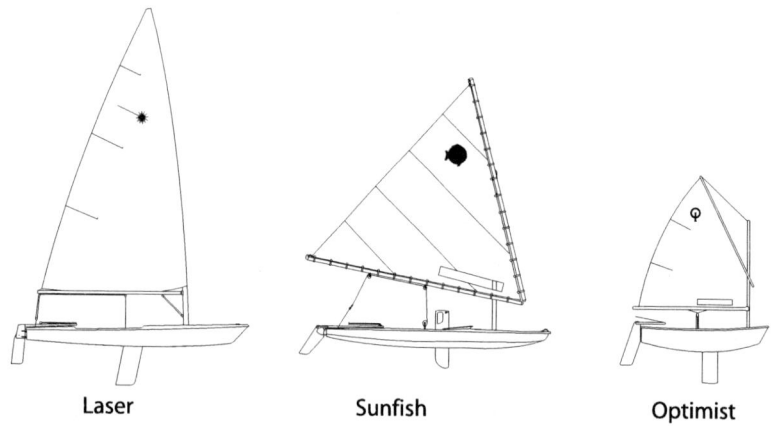

Fig. 3-8 Catboats

E. Other Dinghy Sailboats

The term **dinghy** refers to a small centerboard boat that is less than 17 feet long. Dinghies come in different sizes and shapes and also with various riggings. Dinghies are the boats of choice when learning to sail. The following are examples of additional one-design dinghy catboats. Each of these boats has a sailing association(s) as well as a competition schedule. Selected addresses and web sites related to each of these boats are listed in Appendix A.

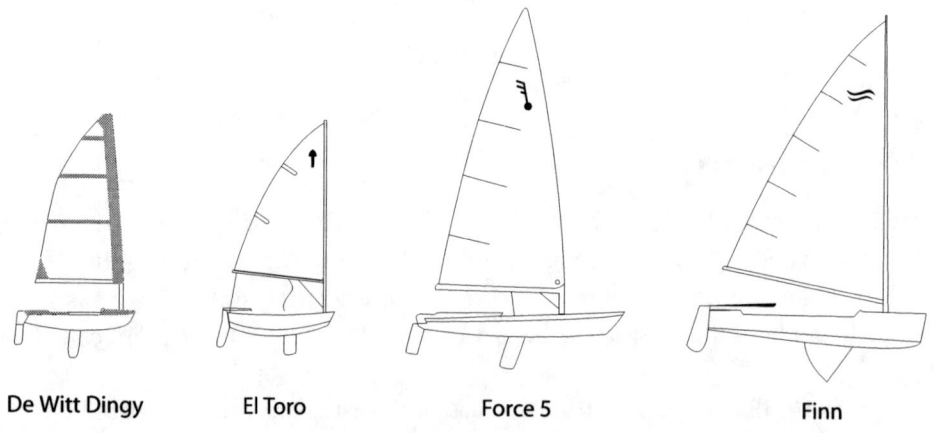

Fig. 3-9 Other Catboats

Small Boats

When a jib sail is added to the sail plan, the rig becomes a sloop-rigged dinghy. The jib sail not only increases the total sail area; it also directs more air over the leeward side of the mainsail producing greater force for propulsion of the boat through the water. The Day Sailer is an example of a sloop rig sailboat.

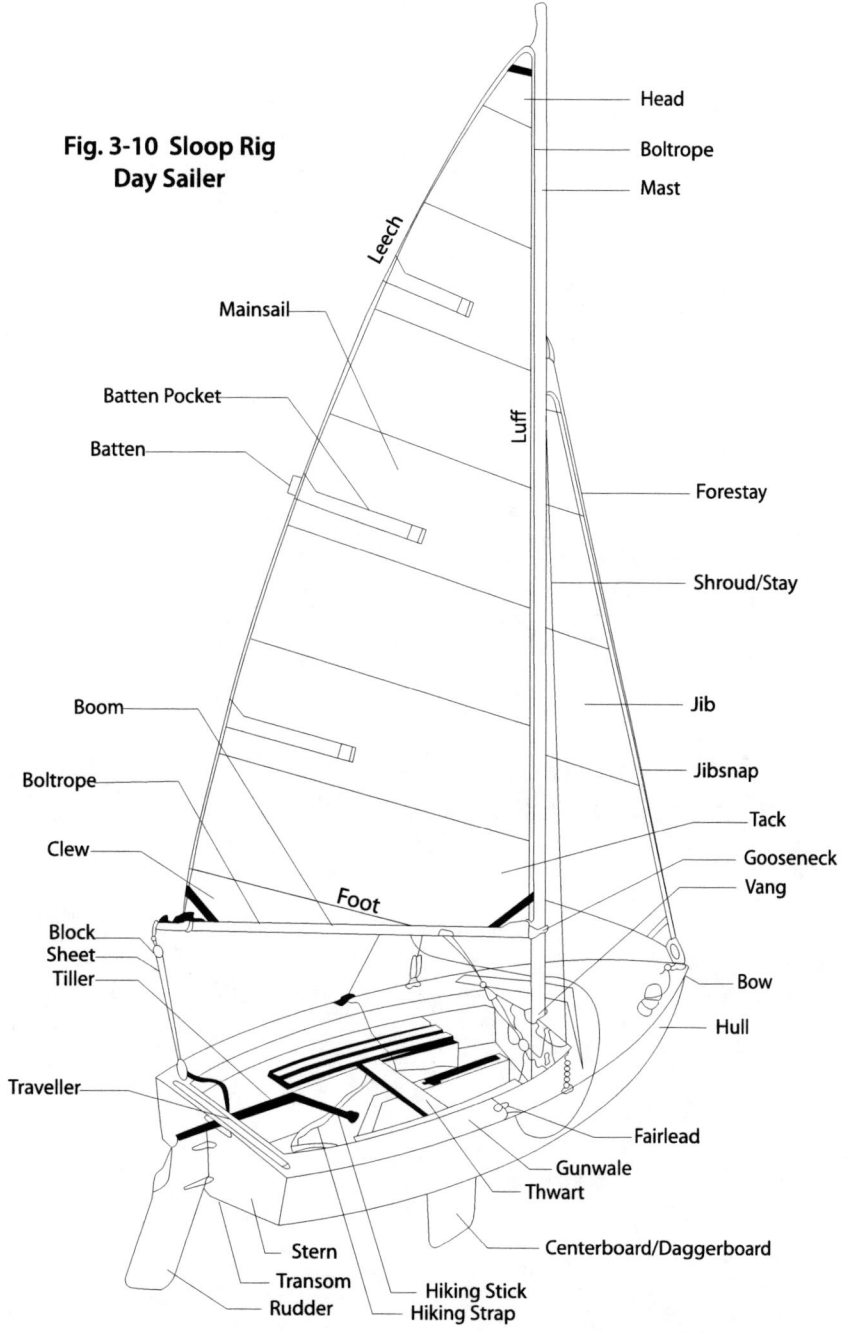

Figure reprinted with permission from Reekie, Shirley H.M. *Sailing Made Simple,* Leisure Press, 1986, p. 29.

F. Exercises and Review Questions

Complete Exercises and Review Questions for Chapter 3 in Appendix C *before* proceeding to Chapter 4.

Chapter 4
Laser and Sunfish

A. Laser

1. Description

The fiberglass Laser originated in 1970 and has become the most popular racing class sailboat. As of 2005, over 170,000 had been constructed. The International Laser Class Association (ILCA) hosts more events in more nations than any other one-design class sailboat in the world. One-design means that all boats of the class are identical. The ILCA works with the North American Regional office to provide racing events for sailors of all ages and skill levels from the Local club to the National Level. The International Sailing Federation recognized the Laser by awarding it Olympic status and making Laser class sailing a men's event at the 1996 Atlanta Olympics. The Laser Radial was selected as a women's Olympic event for the 2008 Olympics in Beijing China. Strict class rules guarantee that it is the sailor, not the equipment, that makes the difference. Laser racing is a true test of skill.

General boat specifications include length, beam, sail area, mast height, and hull weight. The length overall (LOA) of the Laser is 13' 10.5". The beam of the Laser is 4' 6". The sail area is 76 square feet, the mast height is 20' 1" and the hull weight is 130 pounds.

The Laser has a single mast, boom, and a triangular mainsail. It has a planing hull, meaning that it is designed to plane on the surface of the water when moving. This is in contrast to a displacement hull sailboat, which displaces the same volume of water whether it is anchored or moving through the water.

The Laser sailboat has been equipped with four different sail rigs. The standard Laser has a sail area of 76 square feet. Three other sail rigs have been produced for the Laser in order to make it easier to sail in heavy wind and also easier to sail by lighter and less experienced sailors. The Laser M sail rig (no longer in production) had a smaller mast and a sail area of 60 square feet. The Laser Radial has a shorter lower mast section and a sail area of 62 square feet and is recommended for those under 150 lbs. Finally, there is the Laser 4.7, which has a sail area of 51 square feet and is recommended for those under 120 lbs. This progression in sail rigs allows the sailor to use the same boat while changing mast/sail as the individual grows and/or improves in skill. The smaller sail plans are recommended for youth and those learning to sail. The Laser is an excellent boat for learning to sail because it is simple and, at the same time, has a design which permits "fine tuning" for racing. It can carry two adults; however, it is most efficiently sailed by one person.

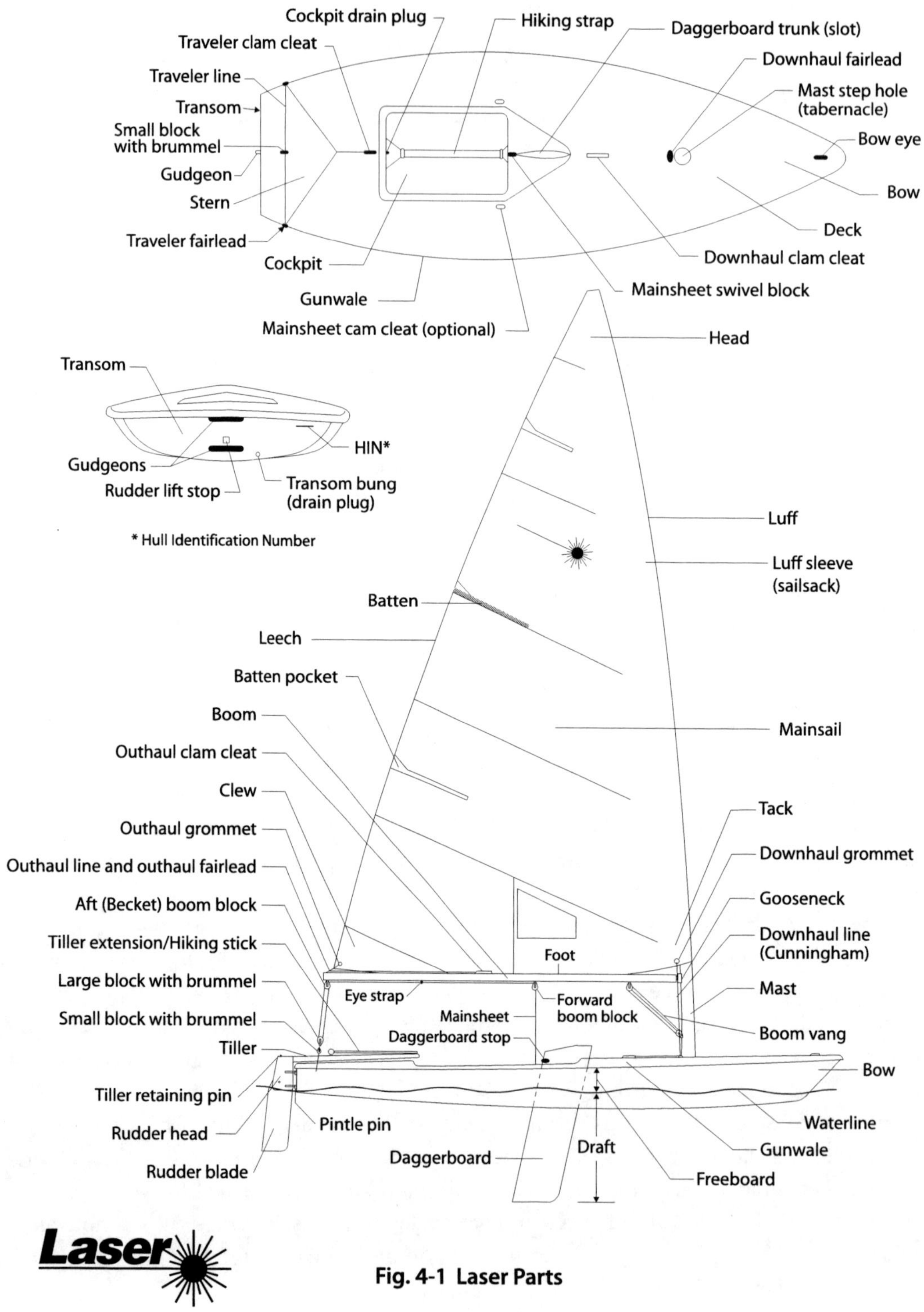

Chapter 4

Fig. 4-1 Laser Parts

Laser and Sunfish

Every part of the boat has its proper name. Use the labeled diagram of the Laser as a reference while reading this book and learning to rig the Laser. See the "Nautical Dictionary" in Appendix E for a definition/description of each term.

2. Rigging*

*Additional information, including parts diagrams, rigging, and tuning can be found by clicking on the Laser links at www.teamvanguard.com Since 2002 Lasers have been made with an improved Laser@vang. See the rigging instructions for this boom vang configuration at this web site.

The Laser is one of the more complicated small boats to rig. But, after learning to rig the Laser, you should be able to rig any board sailboat. The boat may be rigged on the beach or floating next to a dock. The following instructions are for rigging the boat at a beach. It is recommended that you follow the instructions *in order* to insure timely and problem free rigging. If possible, assemble all gear in a smooth uncluttered area near the water. A grassy area works well because it will minimize friction between the sailboat parts and the surface. Assembly on a hard surface (e.g. parking lot) or sand will tend to cause abrasion and wear on the equipment. See *Laser Sailing* by Tillman (Appendix A) for additional rigging possibilities as well as equipment options and controls for racing.

1. Position the hull near the water and turn it so that the *bow points directly into the wind*.

2. Put the two sections of the mast together and place it on the ground perpendicular to the direction of the wind with the gooseneck downwind.

3. Unfold the mainsail and slip the sail sleeve (i.e. sailsock) over the top of the mast being sure that the downhaul (Cunningham line) is on the gooseneck side. Remove any twists in the sleeve.

4. Insert the battens into the batten pockets. The short one goes in the top pocket; the other two are the same length and go in the second and third pockets. Be sure that the battens are in correctly and secured so they do not pop out while sailing.

5. Before stepping the mast, make sure the mast step hole (tabernacle) and mast butt (bottom of mast) are clean. Any sand or dirt in the mast step will grind into the gelcoat and eventually damage the boat. Also, be sure there are no wires overhead. To step the mast:

    Solo—Place the mast butt against a solid object, lift the top end, and walk toward the butt, raising it hand over hand until the mast stands vertical. Keep the butt in contact with the ground and the front of the mast pointed into the wind. Gain control of the ends of the downhaul and outhaul lines and hold them next to the mast. Face the wind behind the mast, place one hand high and the other low, and lift it. Continue to face the wind and walk the mast to the boat while keeping it vertical. You may have to walk forward, backward or sideways while lifting the mast to get it to the boat. *A vertical mast and proper alignment of the sail into the wind* (sail luffing downwind) will minimize the amount of force needed to lift, move, and step the mast. Place the bottom of the mast in the mast step hole and let it slide down into place. **Do not drop it**, as this may damage the step. Now, if necessary, reposition the hull so that the sail is luffing down the centerline of the boat. Also, remove any wraps in the sail sleeve.

With Partner—One person picks up the downhaul and outhaul lines and then the foot of the sail and holds them against and near the bottom of the mast. The other person bunches the top of the sail and holds it against and near the top of the mast. Both partners lift and carry the mast to the boat being sure not to drag the lines or sail along the ground. The butt of the mast is positioned so that the lower edge is in the mast step hole. The person at the bottom of the mast moves his/her hands so that one is high and the other is low (for control) and tells his/her partner to start walking the mast up to a vertical position. The individual at the top of the mast places his/her hands under the mast and starts pushing it up and into the wind while walking toward the boat. Both partners assist one another in rotating the mast to a vertical position, letting it slide into the mast step hole.

Last Resort—If the mast cannot be stepped solo or working with a partner; it can be stepped as follows. Point the bow of the boat into the wind and then roll it on its side. Now place the mast butt in the mast step hole and then roll the boat back to an upright position by lifting on the top of the mast and then walking it up to a vertical position.

6. Attach the boom to the gooseneck on the mast, exerting forward pressure to keep it in place. Continuing to exert forward pressure on the boom from the stern, run the outhaul through the outhaul fairlead at the back of the boom and then through the clam cleat on top of the boom. Pull the outhaul *toward the mast* as this is done to prevent the boom disconnecting from the mast at the gooseneck. Jam the outhaul in the clam cleat by pulling it taut, lowering it to boom level and then pulling it from the stern side of the cleat to lock it (jam it) in the groves of the clam cleat. Next, tie a figure 8 knot *close to the clam cleat.* The figure 8 knot ("stopper knot") will prevent the outhaul from slipping backwards through the clam cleat. If the outhaul were to slip backward, the pressure holding the boom to the mast at the gooseneck would be reduced and the boom could fall off. If there is excess outhaul line, wrap it around the boom and secure it with a clove hitch.

7. Take the downhaul (Cunningham line) through the fairlead on the boat hull, aft through the clam cleat and secure it. Now, tie a figure 8 knot in the line *close to the clam cleat.* Should the boat capsize, the downhaul will keep the mast in the mast step hole (i.e. tabernacle).

Laser and Sunfish

8. If you are using a clew tie-down, put it through the grommet in the clew of the sail and tie it around the boom. It should hold the clew tight against the boom but still allow it to slide forward and aft with outhaul adjustment.

9. The traveler should already be attached on the stern deck. If it is not, see your instructor or boat instructions. Attach the large traveler block from your sail bag to the small traveler block on the traveler by turning one perpendicular to the other and sliding the slots together. These fittings are called brummel hooks.

10. Rig the mainsheet *in the following order:*
    a. Place the neatly coiled mainsheet in the cockpit. Take one end of the mainsheet and run it forward through the mainsheet ratchet swivel block *against* the ratchet. Take the end up and through the front of the forward boom block leading it aft through the metal eyestrap on the bottom of the boom and then through the top of the Becket block (aft boom block) on the end of the boom.
    b. From an aft position, run the mainsheet forward through the large block attached to the small traveler block. Take the end up and through the front of the bottom of the Becket block running it aft until 8-10 inches of line are through. Secure the end of the mainsheet with a bowline.
    c. Tie a figure 8 in the end of the mainsheet lying in the cockpit. Be sure there are no kinks or tangles in the mainsheet.

11. To mount the Boom Vang, first make sure that the line is completely extended and all three parts are parallel. Place the end with the T-shaped pin in the slot on the underside of the boom. Remove the ring and then the pin from the block on the opposite end of the Vang being careful not to drop them, as they are small and easy to lose. Make sure the block is in a position so that the end of the line is coming out the bottom, or deck side, of the block where the v groove cleat is located. Use the pin and ring to secure the block to the bottom of the mast. Pull the Boom Vang line up, toward the cockpit, and then down to secure it in the jam of the block. A figure 8 should already be tied in the end of the line to prevent it from pulling backward through the block. See the Laser web site for instructions on rigging the new Laser@vang.

12. Place the rudder, with rudder blade up, on the stern of the boat by putting the pintles of the rudder into the gudgeons attached to the transom. Be sure the rudder lift stop snaps snugly into position on top of the bottom pintle strap, see Fig. 4.2. The rudder lift stop prevents the rudder from lifting and coming off the boat (e.g. when the boat capsizes).

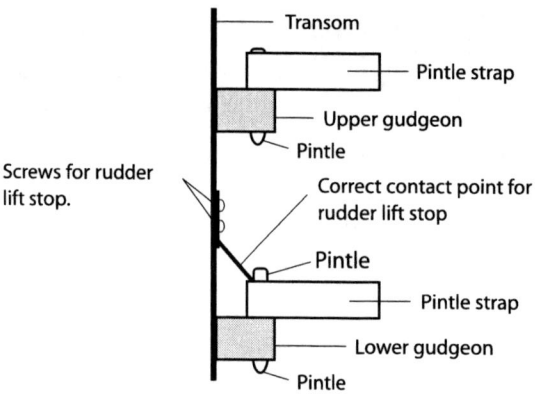

Fig. 4-2 Rudder Correctly Attached to Transom

13. With the tiller extension (hiking stick) on top, put the tiller *under the mainsheet traveler* and into the top of the rudder head. Secure the tiller in the rudder head with the tiller-retaining pin. The rudder line should be pulled up, through, and over the spacer of the top pintle and then under the traveler. It should be left loose until the boat is launched.
14. Place the daggerboard in the cockpit being sure it is not on top of the mainsheet.
15. Check that the two drain plugs (cockpit and hull) are in place and tight. The hull drain plug is also referred to as the transom bung and is used to empty water from the hull.

3. *Derigging (i.e. Unrigging)*

1. Reverse the above steps, *in order*, making sure that the outhaul and downhaul remain attached to the mainsail, the traveler is left attached to the hull and the boom vang parts and figure 8 are kept intact. Coil the mainsheet for storage.
2. Remove battens, accordion fold the sail (12-15 inch folds), and place it in its bag.
3. All gear should be clean and dry before being stored. If sailing in salt water, rinse all gear with fresh water and then dry before storing.

4. *Exercises and Review Questions*

Complete the labeling exercise for the Laser in Appendix C Chapter 4 *before* proceeding to Chapter 5.

B. SUNFISH

1. Description

The Sunfish originated in 1952 when two boat makers grafted a cockpit onto a crude proto-sailboard so their wives would have more foot room. The fiberglass Sunfish was the first off-the-beach sailboat and has become the most popular sailboat ever produced. Millions of people have learned to sail and enjoy the water on Sunfish. As with the Laser, there is an International Sunfish Class, which sanctions events throughout the world. The Sunfish has a length overall (LOA) of 13' 9", a beam of 4' 1", a sail area of 75 square feet, and a hull weight of 130 pounds.

The lateen rig of the Sunfish, with its equilateral triangular sail, and spars that are no longer than the boat, allow for easy set up and transport. It can be set up and sailing in five minutes. The v-bottom hull, low sail plan, and relatively wide beam make the Sunfish comparatively stable. It also has a kick-up rudder for beach landings and a self-bailing cockpit. The forgiving nature of the design, and a sail plan that requires just one line for control, make the Sunfish an ideal boat for children and those learning to sail.

Every part of the boat has its proper name. Use the labeled diagram of the Sunfish as a reference while reading this book and learning to rig the Sunfish. See the "Nautical Dictionary" in Appendix E for a definition/description of each term.

2. Rigging*

*For additional information, go to www.teamvanguard.com and click on the Sunfish links.

After learning the basics, the Sunfish can be rigged and sailing in a short amount of time. The boat may be rigged on the beach or floating next to a dock. The following instructions are for rigging the boat at a beach. It is recommended that you follow the instructions *in order* to insure timely and problem free rigging. If possible, assemble all gear in a smooth uncluttered area near the water. A grassy area works well because it will minimize friction between the sailboat parts and the surface. Assembly on a hard surface (e.g. parking lot) or sand will tend to cause abrasion and wear on the equipment.

1. Position the hull near the water and turn it so that the bow points directly into the wind.

2. Before stepping the mast, make sure the mast step hole (tabernacle) and mast butt are clean. Any sand or dirt in the mast step will grind into the gelcoat and eventually damage the boat. Also, be sure there are no wires overhead.

3. Lay the booms/sail on the deck of the boat with the bronze gooseneck over the mast step hole. Thread about half the halyard from the upper boom through the hole in the top of the mast and set the mast butt through the gooseneck and into the mast step hole. If necessary, reposition the hull so that the bow is into the wind and then raise

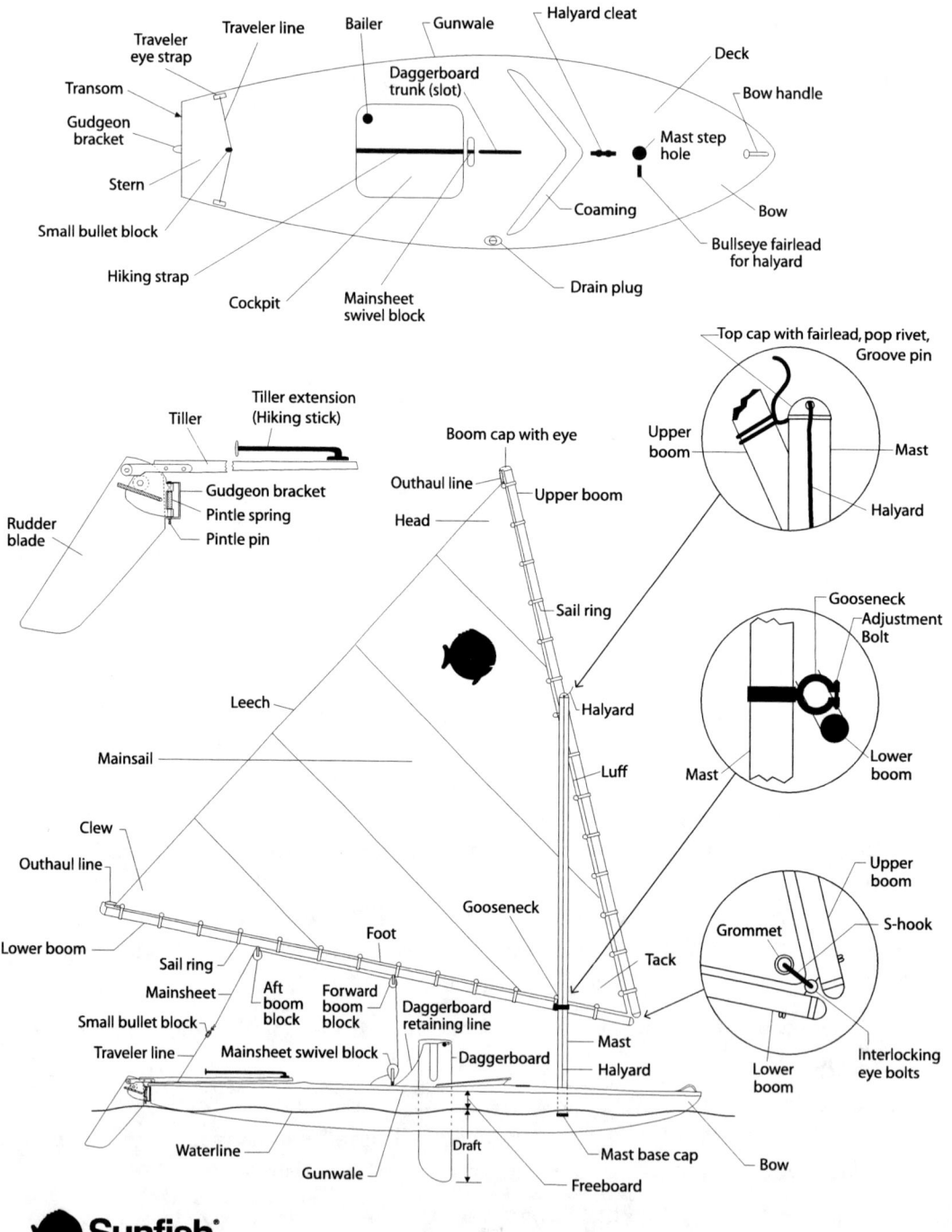

Fig. 4-3 Sunfish Parts

the sail by pulling on the halyard. Lifting the boom at the gooseneck, while pulling on the halyard, will assist in raising the sail. Pull the halyard until the upper boom is right against the mast. Feed the halyard through the main halyard bullseye fairlead and secure it to the main halyard cleat.

4. Place the neatly coiled mainsheet in the cockpit and attach the mainsheet hook to the traveler block. Thread the free end of the mainsheet forward through the aft boom block, the forward boom block and then down through the forward side of the mainsheet swivel block and into the cockpit. Take up the slack, making sure there are no kinks or tangles in the mainsheet, and then tie a figure 8 in the end of the line.

5. Lock the rudder in the up position and attach it to the boat by passing the tiller under the traveler and lining up the rudder pin with the pintles. Place the bottom groove into the bottom pintle and push down on the spring-loaded pin. Slide the top groove into the top pintle. Release the spring and lock the rudder in place. Make sure the rudder is securely connected to the boat at both top and bottom.

6. Place the daggerboard in the cockpit being sure it is not on top of the mainsheet.

7. Check that the drain plug is in place and tight. The bailer plug on the automatic bailer should be closed.

3. Derigging (i.e. Unrigging)

1. Reverse the above steps making sure that the sail remains attached to the booms and the halyard remains attached to the upper boom. Coil the mainsheet for storage.

2. All gear should be clean and dry before being stored. If sailing in salt water, rinse all gear with fresh water and then dry before storing.

4. Exercises and Review Questions

Complete the labeling exercise for the Sunfish in Appendix C, Chapter 4 *before* proceeding to Chapter 5.

Chapter 5
How a Sailboat Sails

A. Center of Gravity and Center of Buoyancy

Archimedes' Principle states that if the weight of an object is less than or equal to the weight of the volume of water it displaces, the object will float. Boats are constructed so that they will float, *even if capsized*, provided water does not enter the hull. Two concepts are important to understanding the buoyancy and balance of a boat—center of gravity and center of buoyancy. **Center of gravity (CG)** is defined as the weight or mass center of an object. It is an imaginary point around which all parts or molecules of an object balance. **Center of buoyancy (CB)** is the center of gravity of the volume of water displaced. For analysis purposes, it is helpful to consider the sum of the weight of all molecules of an object as exerting force through the CG. The direction of the CG force is toward the center of the earth, for practical purposes, it is considered to be perpendicular to the surface of the earth or water. The direction of the CB force is away from the center of the earth, for practical purposes, it is considered to be perpendicular to the surface of the water.

Consider a swimmer attempting to float in a horizontal position. Body weight is operating down through the CG of the swimmer. The buoyant force is operating up at the CB of the volume of water displaced. Most people cannot float in a horizontal position because their

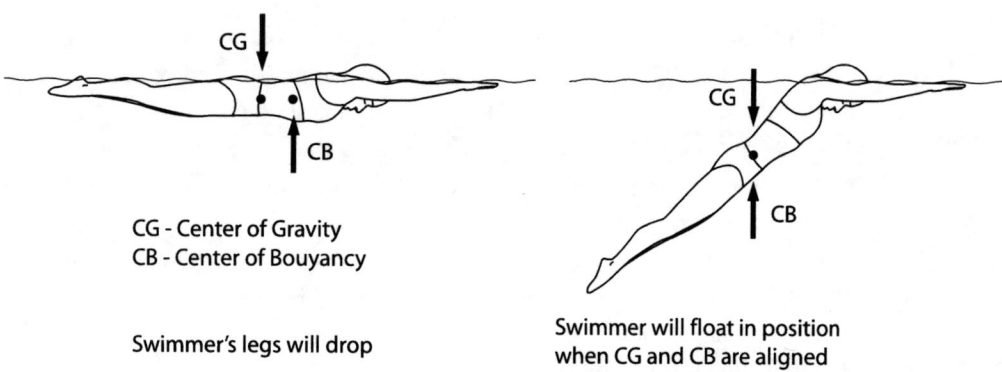

Fig. 5-1 Center of Gravity and Bouyancy Alignment

legs are heavier per unit volume than their trunk. As a result, the legs drop in the water until a point is reached at which the CG and CB lie along the same vertical line. If momentum is eliminated, the swimmer will float in this position.

Boats are constructed so that they will float level in the water when no one is onboard. However, when the weight of crew, equipment, or ballast is moved onto a boat, there will be a new CG representing the sum of all objects on the boat. If the new CG is off center, the boat will rotate until the CG and CB are aligned. For example, if a sailor moves aft, the stern will move down and the bow will rise. If a sailor shifts his/her weight to port, the port gunwale will go down and the starboard gunwale will move up.

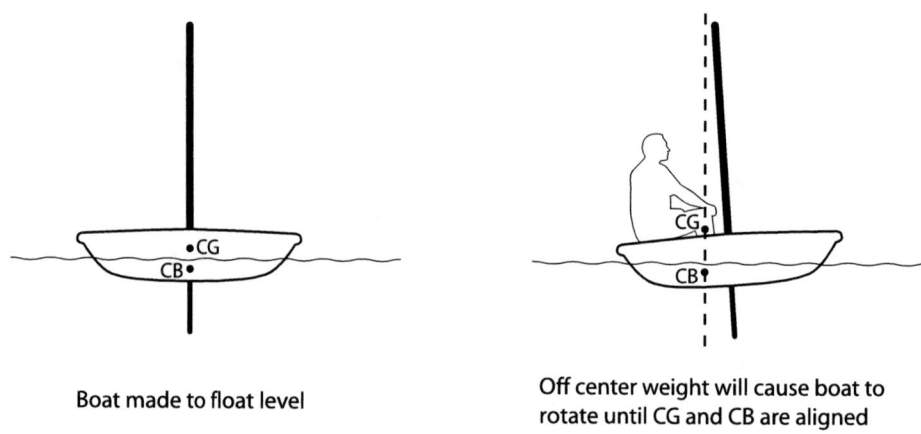

Boat made to float level

Off center weight will cause boat to rotate until CG and CB are aligned

Fig. 5-2 Boat Center of Gravity (CG) and Center of Bouyancy (CB) Alignment

B. Boat Axes

The rotational movements just described take place around major axes through the boat. Knowledge of these axes is helpful in understanding boat balance and movement. Three major axes pass through the CG of the boat and are at 90° to one another. In a balanced boat, the longitudinal axis runs from bow to stern and is identical to the centerline of the boat. Movement around the longitudinal axis is called **roll** (gunwales or sides of the boat move up and down). The bilateral axis runs side to side and is perpendicular to the longitudinal axis. Movement around the bilateral axis is called **pitch** (bow and stern move up and down). When an individual gets into (steps onto) a boat, body weight should be placed as close to the CG of the boat as possible (e.g. along the centerline close to the centerboard). The CG of the boat is where it is most stable. Placing weight near this point will minimize or prevent both roll and pitch. The vertical axis also passes through the CG. Movement around the vertical axis is called **yaw** (bow of the boat turns right and left or side to side).

How a Sailboat Sails

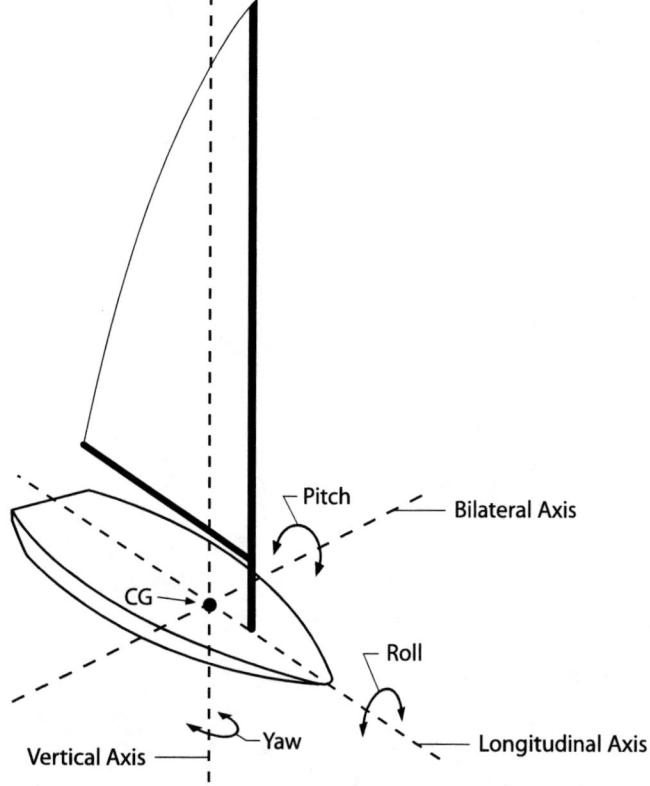

Fig. 5-3 Boat Axes and Movements

An example of controlled boat yaw is when the helmsman pushes the tiller to port (left) to turn the boat to starboard (right). The boat turns around a vertical axis through the CG (pivot point) of the boat. See Fig. 5-4.

C. Heeling

Another very important force affecting the balance of a sailboat is wind. The force of wind on a sail will cause a sailboat to rotate around its longitudinal axis. This boat rotation is termed **heeling**. As this happens the CB will shift to leeward and act to resist this movement. In the following figure, the force of the wind on the sail is clockwise and the resisting force of the CB is counterclockwise around the longitudinal axis through the CG of the boat. When the wind force on the sail stops, the force of the CB will cause the boat to return to its balanced position. This force is called the **righting moment** of the boat. The beginning sailor will soon learn that he/she should not fear the heeling (rolling) action caused by the force of the wind.

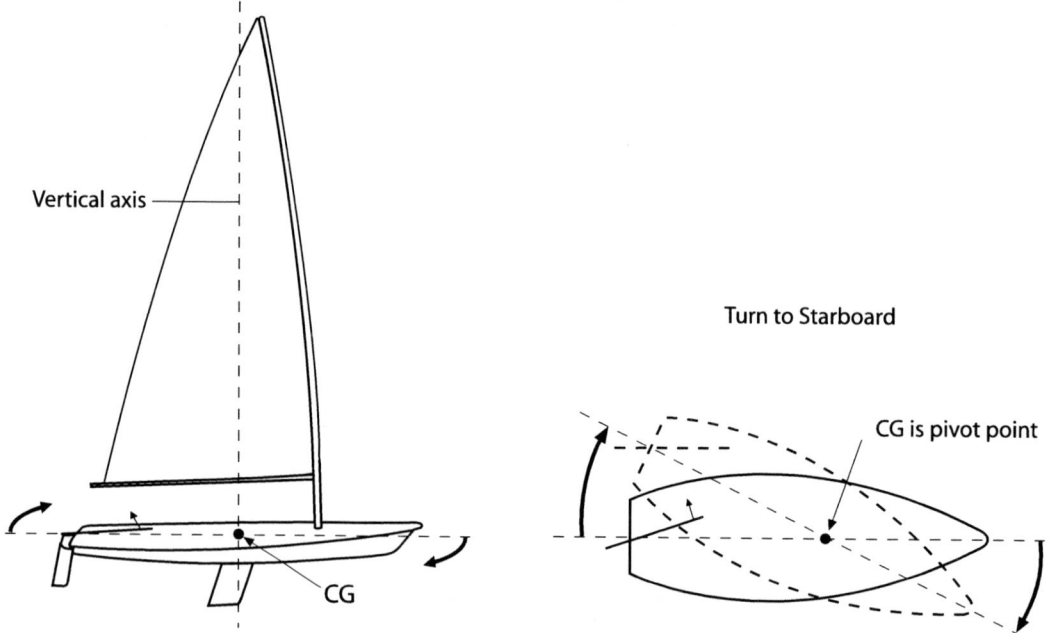

Fig. 5-4 Turning is Controlled Yaw Around a Vertical Axis Through the Center of Gravity (CG)

One of the exciting aspects of sailing is going fast. Most sailboats are designed so that they will go the fastest when they are upright or are heeling slightly to leeward. **Hiking** (shifting weight to windward) is a technique for resisting the rotational effect of the wind and keeping the boat balanced. Therefore, it can be used to promote speed. Hiking involves moving the body weight of the crew away from the longitudinal axis of the boat to counteract the force of the wind. In moderate wind, sitting on the upwind gunwale may be sufficient to balance the boat.

In strong wind the sailor will need to "hike out" to balance the boat. This is done by placing the feet under the hiking strap in the cockpit, moving the rear end over the gunwale and leaning back. The farther the sailor's CG can be moved away from the centerline of the boat, the greater the balancing (leverage) effect. The sailor needs to be alert to changes in the force of the wind and use his/her abdominal muscles to shift body weight away from or toward the centerline of the boat in order to keep it **on an even keel (e.g. balanced)**.

An intermediate skill possible in many catboats is being able to hike out in a strong wind and place the back of the head in the water—while controlling the tiller, mainsheet, and balancing the boat!

Other factors affecting stability of a boat are the size of the beam, shape of the hull, and height of the CG. The wider the beam or width of the boat, the flatter the bottom of the boat, and the lower the CG, the more stable the boat. For example, an outrigger on a boat will in-

How a Sailboat Sails

crease its effective width, a flatter bottom will decrease roll, and a weighted keel will lower the CG.

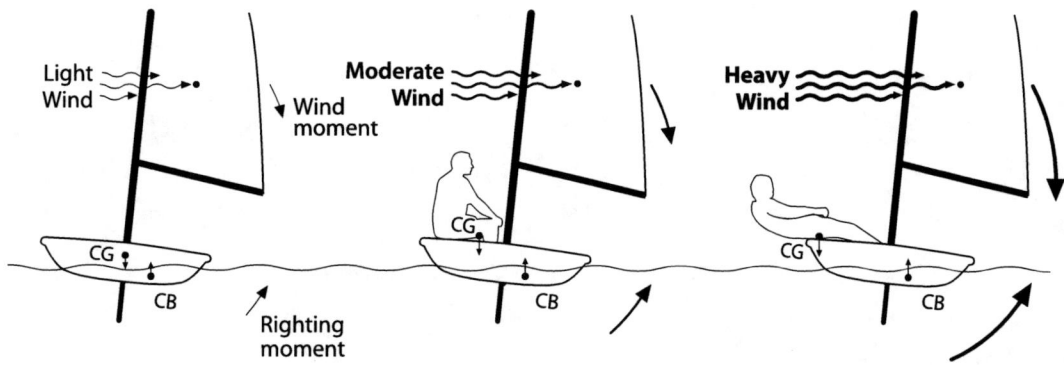

Fig. 5-5 Use Body Weight to Control Heeling

D. RUNNING

Consider an object floating in the water. In what direction will the wind blow it? The answer is, downwind. When a boat is being propelled downwind it is said to be on a **run**. The bow of the boat would be pointed downwind and the wind would be coming directly over the stern of the boat. To maximize speed sailing downwind, the sail would be positioned at 90° to the long axis of the boat, or to put it another way, perpendicular to the wind. The speed of the boat will always be less than the speed of the wind due to water resistance.

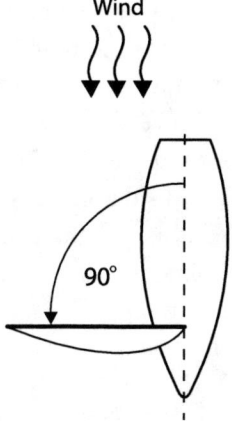

Fig. 5-6 Running

E. REACHING

Reaching is a term used to describe a boat sailing "across the wind." If boat direction is with the wind, but not running, the boat is said to be on a **broad reach**. If boat direction is perpendicular to the wind, the boat is said to be on a **beam reach**. That is, the wind is blowing directly on the side, or over the beam, of the boat. Finally, if boat direction is somewhat upwind (i.e. windward or toward the wind), the boat is said to be on a **close reach**. See Fig. 5-7.

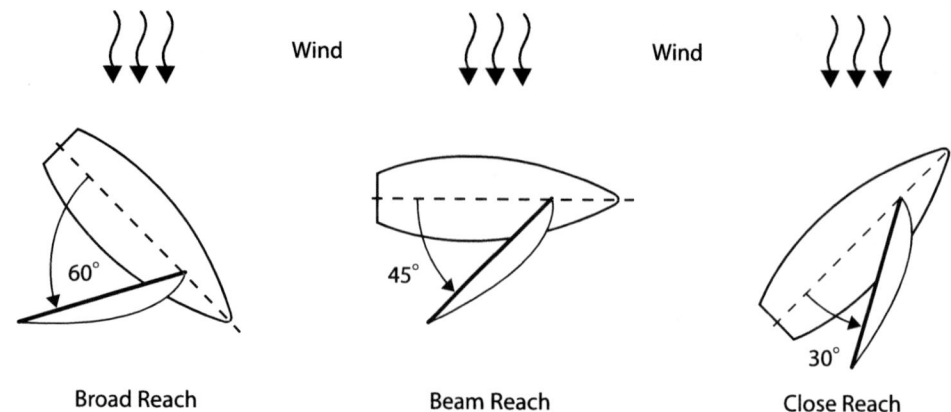

Fig. 5-7 All Boats are "Reaching" Across the Wind

F. Points of Sail

The beginner should *know and understand* the "Points of Sail" before going out on the water. **Points of sail are determined by the direction of the boat in relation to the direction of the wind.** It is helpful to consider these points in relation to a circle with the wind coming from the top, zero degrees, or twelve o'clock. A boat cannot sail into the wind. There is a segment of approximately 90° (45° on either side of the wind) which is called the No-Go zone. If a boat turns into this area it will stop and it is said to be caught **in irons**. It will be "dead in the water" with sail luffing. **Luffing** is a term used to describe the flapping of a sail from its luff edge when it is pointed into the wind.

The following figure shows the main "Points of Sail." Notice that the boats on the left side of the circle are on a **starboard tack**, that is, the wind is coming over the right or starboard side of the boat. The boats on the right side of the circle are on a **port tack**; that is, the wind is coming over the left or port side of the boat. Note that left and port both have four letters; it is an easy way to remember that the left side of the boat is the port side.

The run, broad reach, beam reach, and close reach points of sail have already been described. If a boat is on a close reach and sailing as close to the wind as it can, without going into the No-Go zone, it is said to be **close hauled** (i.e. sails are in tight) and on a **beat**. Some boats can beat at an angle of 35-40° off wind. Note that the position of the sail, in relation to the boat, is different for each point of sail. A good general guideline for the beginning sailor is to position the sail at 90° to the long axis of the boat when on a run, 60° when on a broad reach, 45° when on a beam reach, and 30° when on a close reach. Once this general adjustment is learned, then the sailor can learn to fine-tune the sail angle. This is done by first establishing the desired point of sail (i.e. direction of boat in relation to direction of wind), next letting out the sail until it begins to luff, and then tightening the sail enough to prevent luffing. The sail will then be near its optimum position. Maximum force is obtained when the air flows smoothly across both sides of the sail.

How a Sailboat Sails

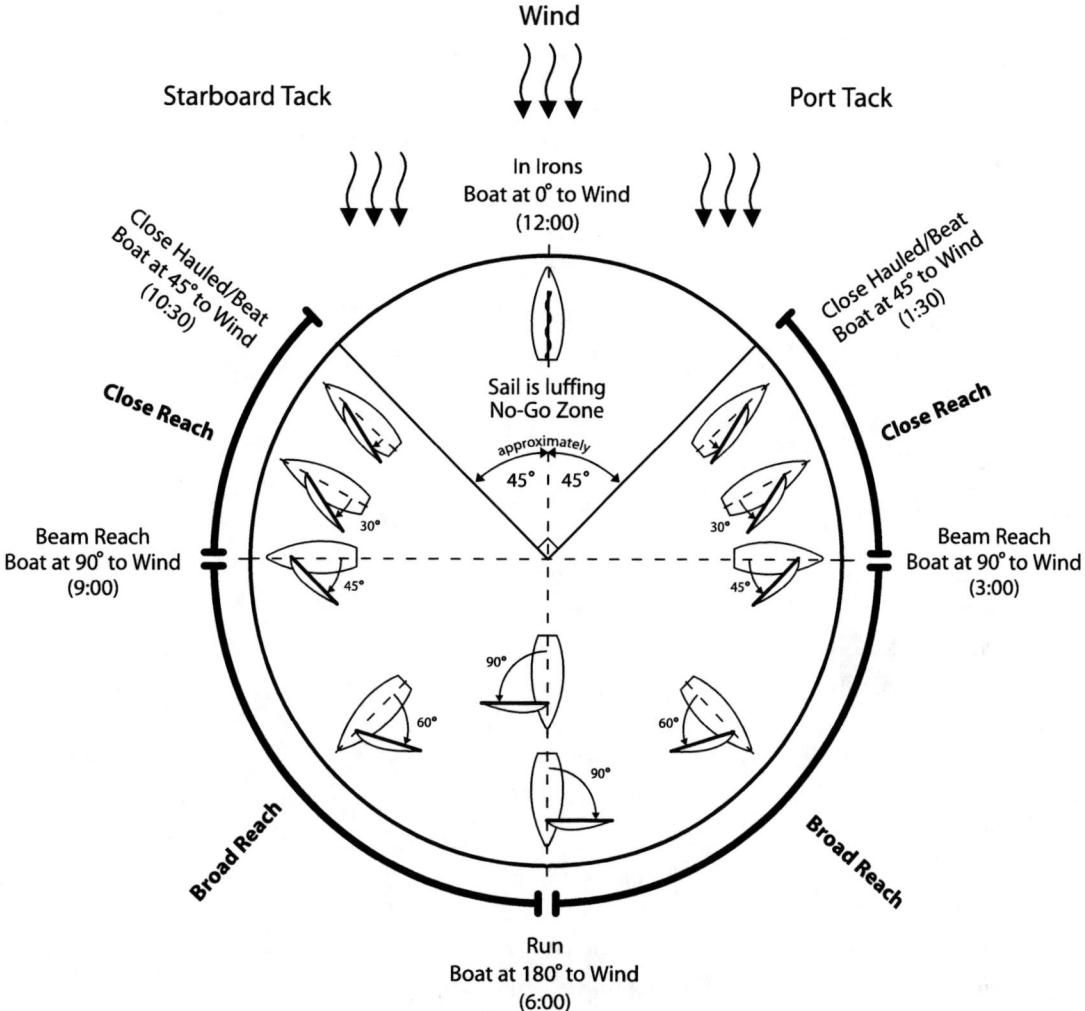

Fig. 5-8 Points of Sail

Some find it helpful to think of the face of a clock when determining point of sail. With the wind coming from the 12 o'clock position, 1:30 or 10:30 would be a close hauled position, 3:00 or 9:00 would be a beam reach, 5:30 or 7:30 would be a broad reach, and 6:00 would be a run.

Caution: Point of sail is determined by the direction of the boat in relation to the direction of the wind, *not* on the position of the sail in relation to the boat. For example, though not efficient or recommended, it is possible to sail on a broad reach with the sail in too tight or out too far. See Fig. 5-9.

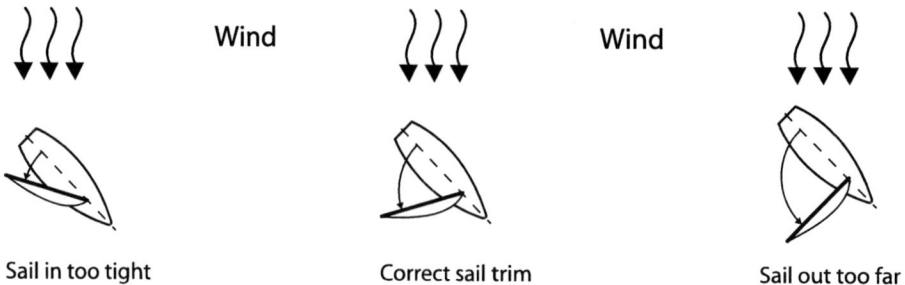

Fig. 5-9 All Boats are on a Broad Reach

G. Tacking

Recall that when a boat is sailing with the wind coming over its right side it is said to be on a **starboard tack**. When a boat is sailing with the wind coming over its left side it is said to be on a **port tack**. A boat **tacks** when it changes from a port tack to starboard tack (or vice versa). Changing tacks, sailing upwind or downwind, is called **tacking**.

A boat cannot sail directly into the wind. So, how can it get from point A in the middle of a lake to a dock that is directly upwind at point B? The answer is, tacking upwind. For example, first sailing on a close reach port tack and then a close reach starboard tack. Depending on distance and conditions, the captain may tack once or several times to reach his/her goal. Even though you cannot sail directly upwind from point A to point B, you can still get there!

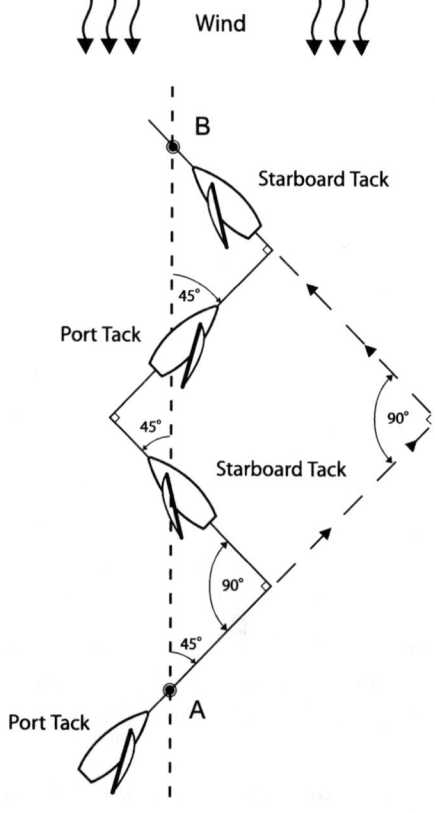

Fig. 5-10 Tacking to Reach Upwind Goal

How a Sailboat Sails

H. Terms Related to Boat Movement and Direction

A boat moving in any direction is said to have **way on**. A boat moving forward is said to have **headway**. A boat moving backward is said to have **sternway**. Note: A boat can only be steered if it is moving, whether that movement is forward *or* backward.

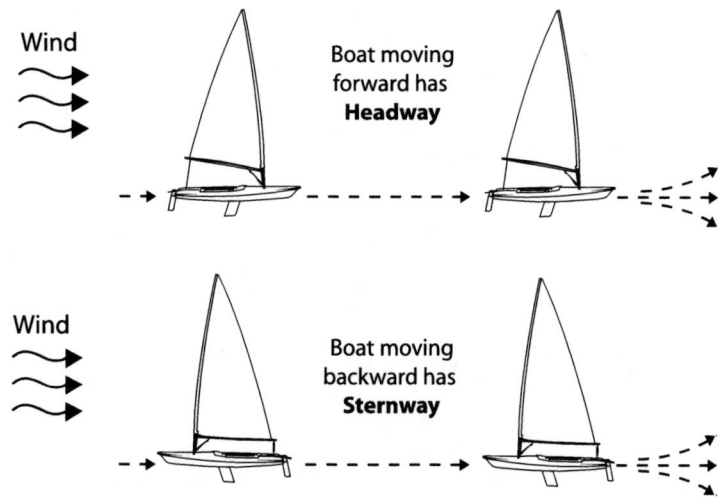

Fig. 5-11 Only Boats with "Way-On" (Moving) Can be Steered

Sideways slippage of a boat in the direction the wind is blowing is called **leeway**. Fig. 5-12 (next page) shows the relationship between the course steered (heading) and the course made good for a boat with (1) centerboard up—large leeway, boat is blown downwind, (2) centerboard down—moderate leeway, result of boat moving through a fluid medium, and (3) centerboard down and boat steered to adjust for leeway—course steered and leeway combine resulting in the course made good being in the desired direction.

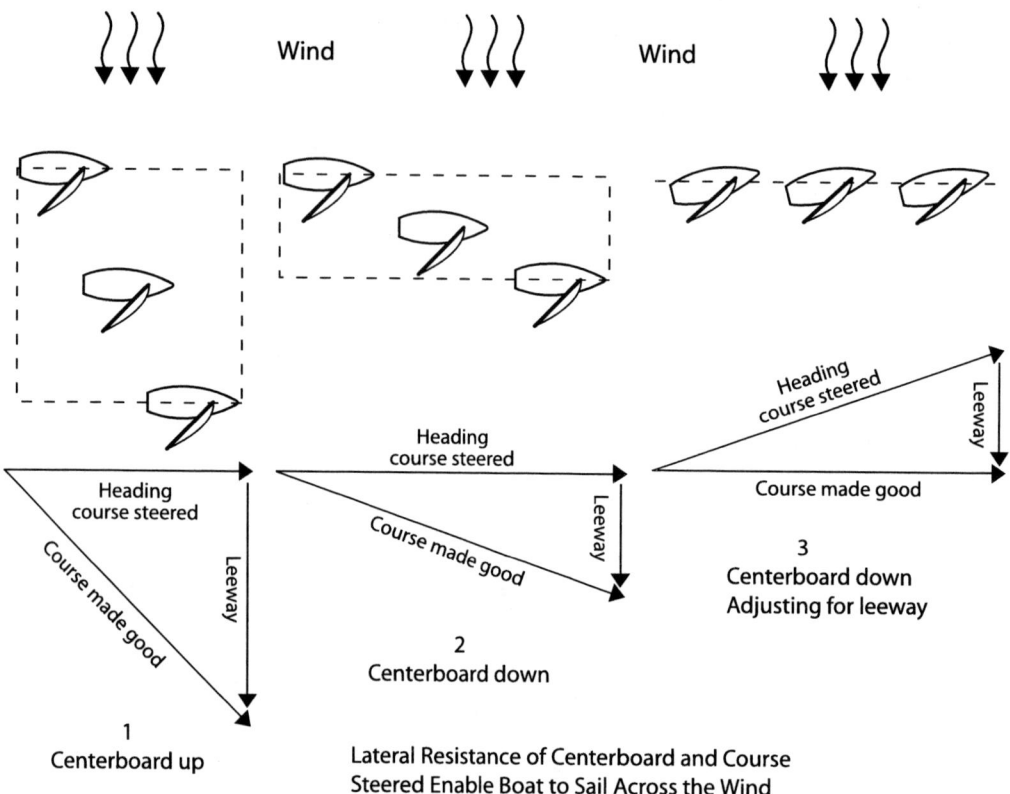

Fig. 5-12 Leeway

The **heading** of a boat is the direction the bow points. It can be described in relation to the point of sail (i.e. run, broad reach, beam reach, close reach, or close-hauled) or in relation to compass direction (e.g. "heading due east"). Changes in heading are given in relation to the wind. **Head-up** means to point the bow more into the wind. **Fall-off** (head-off or bear-off) means to point the bow farther away from the wind. If given the direction "fall-off," don't fall off your boat (as one of my beginners once did!). Rather, turn the bow of your boat away from the wind! After heading up or falling off, adjust your sail for the new direction of your boat (new point of sail).

How a Sailboat Sails

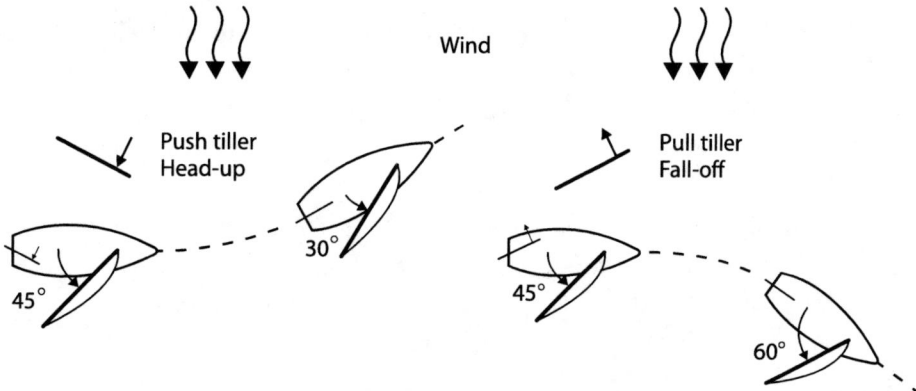

Fig. 5-13 Adjust Sail After Heading-Up or Falling-Off

Examine the above figure. For a boat on a port tack (wind coming over the left side of the boat), pushing the tiller to starboard (right) will cause the boat to turn to port (left) and pulling the tiller to port will cause the boat to turn to starboard (right). Also, notice that in moving a boat from a beam reach to a close reach the sail is trimmed in and when moving from a beam reach to a broad reach the sail is let out.

The following are some additional directional terms. The direction toward the wind is called **upwind or to windward**. The direction away from the wind is called **downwind or to leeward** (sailors pronounce it "loo-ard"). The weather or windward side of the boat is the side the wind is blowing on (i.e. upwind side). The lee or leeward side of the boat is the side away from the wind (i.e. downwind side). Note that the boom and sail are always on the leeward side.

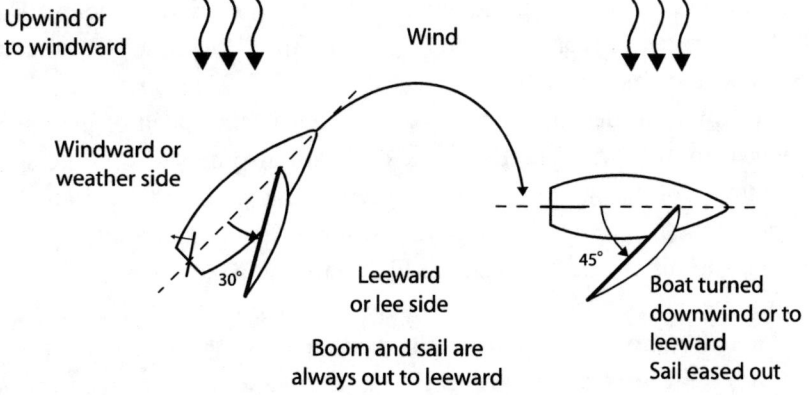

Fig. 5-14 Upwind/Windward/Weather Side is Opposite of Downwind/Leeward Side

As a boat moves through the water it creates both bow and stern waves and leaves a wake. A line through the middle of the wake is called the **track of disturbance**. The direction of the track of disturbance will usually be the same as the course made good.

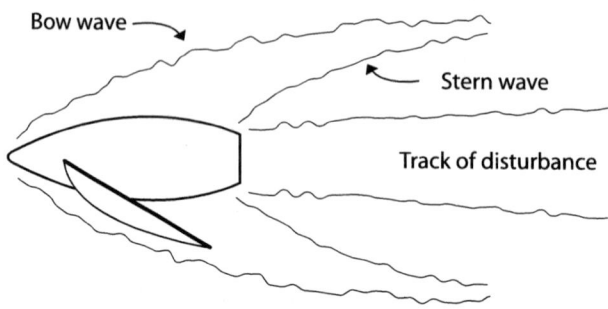

Fig. 5-15 A Moving Boat Creates Waves

I. THEORY OF SAILING

How is it possible for a boat to sail to windward or even on a beam reach without being forced downwind? The answer lies in a combination of sail aerodynamics and boat lateral resistance.

1. Sail Aerodynamics

To understand the principles involved, it is helpful to compare the aerodynamics of a sail to those of an airplane wing. The airplane wing is designed so that air molecules moving over the top of the wing will move faster than those moving under the bottom of the wing. The result is an area of low pressure on top of the wing and an area of high pressure under the wing. This combination produces a "lift" force on the wing. The aerodynamics related to the production of this lift force were first presented and explained by Swiss scientist Daniel Bernoulli in the 18th century and became known as "Bernoulli's Principle." This same aerodynamic effect occurs on a sail as a boat moves across the wind.

The **wind force** on a sail depends on the size of the sail, the speed of the wind, and the orientation of the sail to the wind. The **lift force** on a sail also depends on the speed of the wind and the orientation of the sail to the wind. Speed of the wind and orientation of the sail to the wind determine the magnitude of the high and low pressure zones on opposite sides of the sail. The greater the difference between the high and low pressure zones, the greater the lift force. The lift force can be resolved into two components, a **forward component of the lift force** and a **lateral component of the lift force** that are at 90° to one another. The forward component of the lift force acts to propel the boat forward. The lateral component of the lift force acts in the same direction as the wind force to cause the boat to rotate around its longitudinal axis. Therefore, the **total rotational force** on a sail is a combination of the wind force and the lateral component of the lift force.

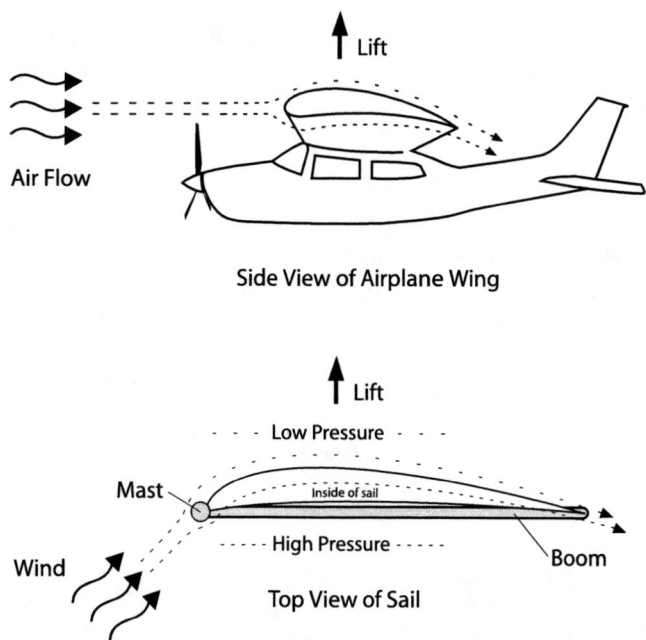

Fig. 5-16 Difference in Pressure Creates Lift Force

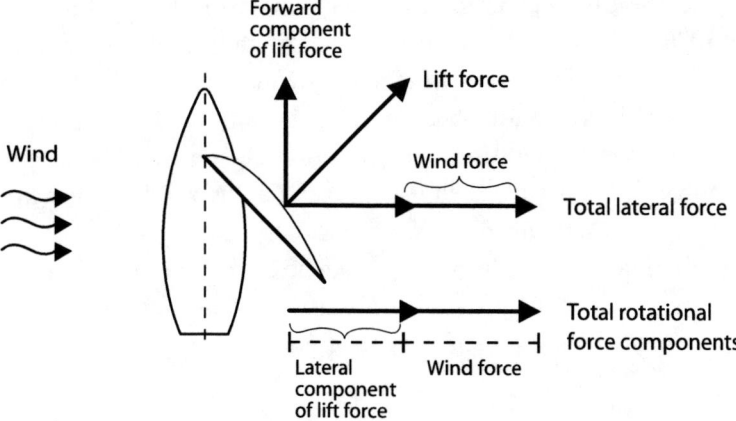

Fig. 5-17 Lateral Component of Lift Force + Wind Force = Total Lateral (Rotational) Force

When a sailboat is on a run the motive force comes entirely from the wind pushing on the sail and the various surfaces of the boat that are facing windward (e.g. stern). The wind force is maximum and the lift force is zero. However, as the boat is directed first on a broad reach, then a beam reach, and finally a close reach, the trimming of the sail to the wind produces an increasing aerodynamic effect. The more the luff edge of the sail is pointed toward the wind the higher the pressure on the inside of the sail verses the back of the sail and the greater the lift force. In the figure below, the arrowhead indicates direction while the length of the arrow represents the magnitude of the lift force (L). Note how the lift force increases going from a run (L = 0), to a broad reach (L1), to a beam reach (L2), and to a close reach (L3). Remember, there are other forces acting on the boat at the same time (e.g. wind pushing on the boat and sail and lateral resistance). The combination of all forces will determine the direction and speed of the boat.

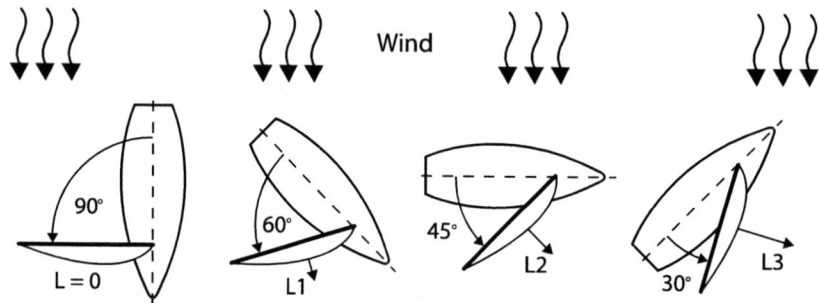

Fig. 5-18 Lift Force (L) Increases as Boat and Sail are Pointed Toward the Wind

Interestingly, as the lift force is increasing moving from a broad to a beam to a close reach, the force of the wind on the windward side of the sail is decreasing. The point of maximum total force (wind force plus lift force) is usually reached when on a beam reach with optimum sail trim. Therefore, the beam reach is usually the fastest point of sail for a catboat. As the boat continues to turn into the wind to a close reach and then becomes close-hauled, the total force decreases and then reaches zero as the sail luffs and the boat goes into the No-Go zone at a point approximately 45° to windward.

Boats such as the sloop rig are designed to take advantage of and maximize the lift force. The jib sail not only provides more total surface area, its position directs more air over the leeward side of the mainsail thereby increasing the lift force (Fig. 5-19).

How a Sailboat Sails

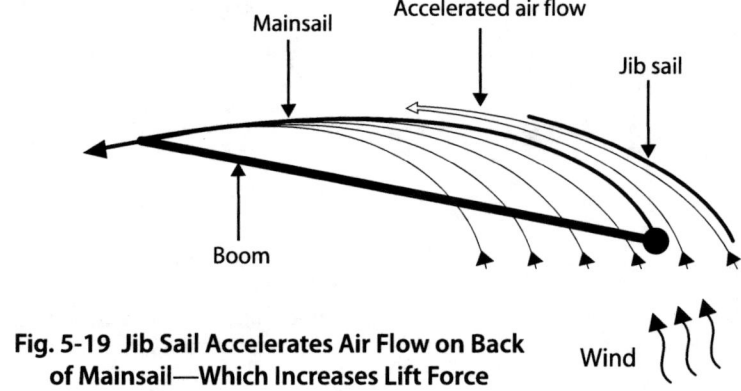

Fig. 5-19 Jib Sail Accelerates Air Flow on Back of Mainsail—Which Increases Lift Force

2. Boat Lateral Resistance

Boat lateral resistance is the resistance to lateral or sideways movement in the water. The amount of boat lateral resistance depends on the total lateral surface area of the hull, rudder, and daggerboard that is in the water.

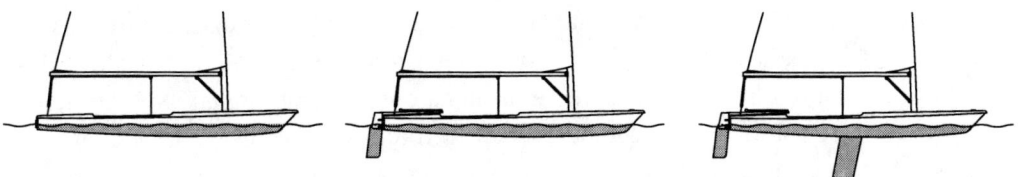

Fig. 5-20 Lateral Resistance = Lateral Surface Area of Hull + Rudder + Daggerboard

If a boat attempts to sail on a beam reach (sail halfway out) without the daggerboard and rudder in the water, it will move forward somewhat but it will mainly be blown downwind. See Fig. 5-21 (next page). With the daggerboard and rudder in place the boat has sufficient lateral resistance to sail across the wind. In fact there is enough lateral resistance to sail about 45° into the wind!

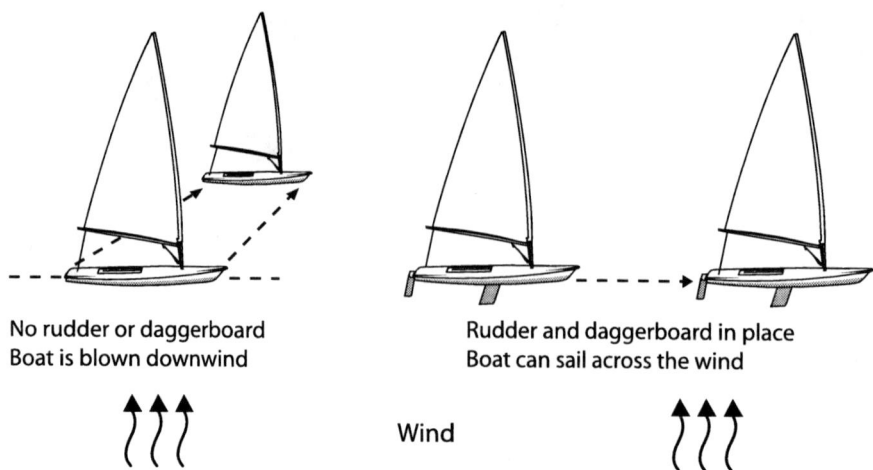

Fig. 5-21 Hull, Rudder and Daggerboard Provide Enough Lateral Resistance to Sail Across the Wind

Examine the following figure: (1) a counterclockwise force at the top of the pencil produces counterclockwise movement at the bottom of the pencil. This movement occurs around a pivot point at the fingers; (2) the counterclockwise force of wind on a sail results in counterclockwise force being exerted by the underwater lateral surfaces (hull, rudder, and daggerboard) of the boat on the water. This force occurs around a longitudinal axis through the CG of the boat (pivot point); (3) the counterclockwise force is resisted by an equal and opposite (clockwise) force from the water on the lateral surfaces of the boat.

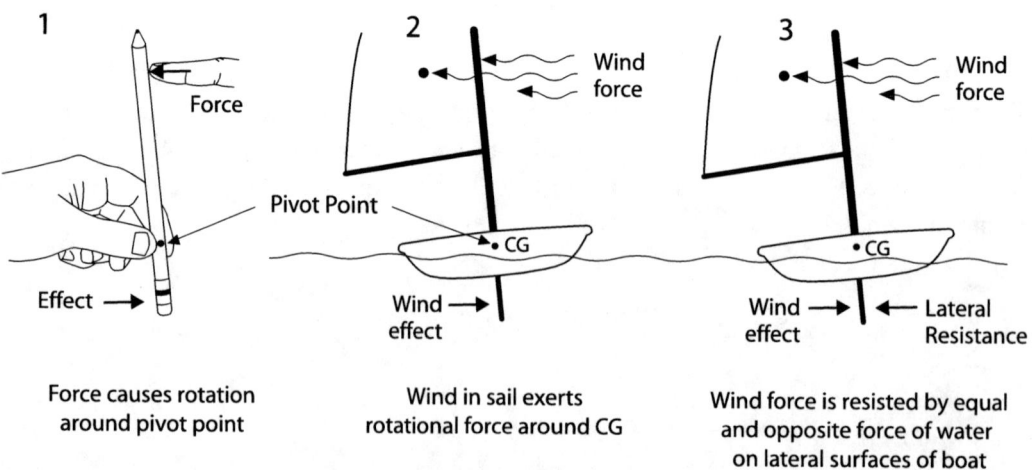

Fig. 5-22 Wind Force Produces Equal and Opposite Lateral Resistance Force from Water

How a Sailboat Sails

Because of the streamlined shape of the hull, equal and opposite forces on the underwater surfaces of the boat cause it to be "squeezed" forward. The forces are produced by the wind and the equal and opposite force of the lateral resistance of the water. This is similar to what happens when one squeezes a wet watermelon seed from both sides—it shoots forward along the path of least resistance!

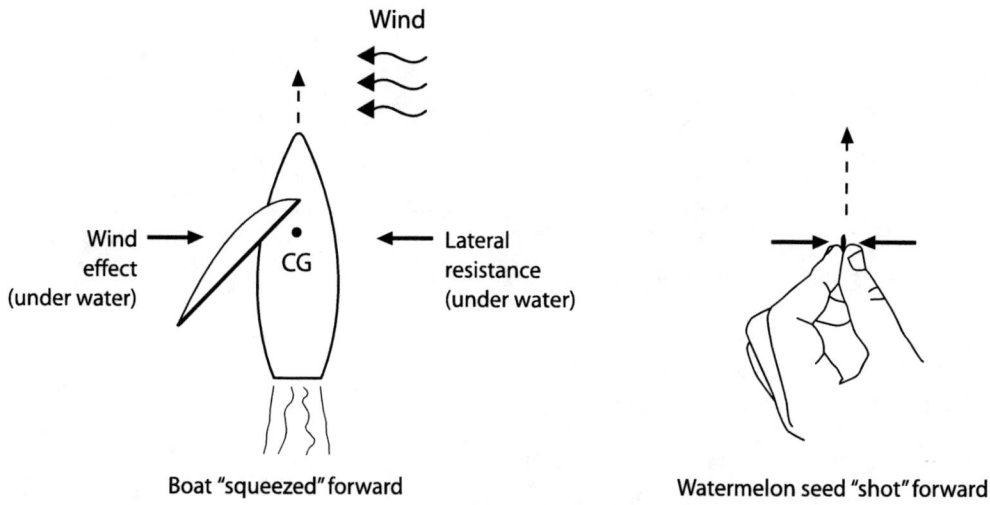

Fig. 5-23 Streamlined Boat and Watermelon Seed Move Forward as a Result of Equal and Opposite Lateral Forces

3. *Sail Center of Effort*

The point on a sail where the wind can be said to be concentrated is termed the **center of effort (CE)**. The concept of CE is similar to that of center of gravity (CG) and center of buoyancy (CB). For a triangular sail, the CE is located 1/3 up on a line from the center of the foot to the head of the sail. If a jib sail is part of the sail plan, the CE of the mainsail/jib combination can be found as follows. Draw a straight line from the CE of the mainsail to the CE of the jib sail. The combined CE of the two sails is located on this line at a point that represents the proportional surface areas of the two sails. If the jib is 1/3 of the total sail area, the CE moves 1/3 the length of the line toward the jib (Fig. 5-24).

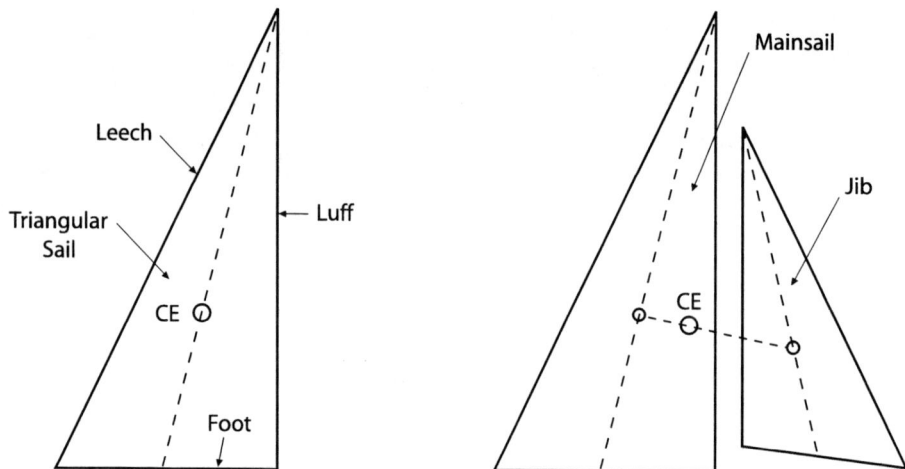

Fig. 5-24 Center of Effort (CE) of a Triangular Sail and a Mainsail/Jib (Sloop) Sail Plan

4. Center of Lateral Resistance

The **center of lateral resistance (CLR)** of a boat is represented by a vertical line that bisects the lateral resistance. In other words, there is the same amount of lateral resistance fore and aft of this line. If the CE of a boat is aft of its CLR it will tend to turn into the wind, thus, it is said to have a **weather helm**. Most sailboats are built so that they will have a weather helm. That is, if the boat is rigged, floating, and unoccupied, it will turn into the wind. This is good news for the sailor who falls off his/her boat, because, when the tiller is released, the boat will tend to point up into the wind and stop. However, in a good breeze, the boat will still be blown downwind. Therefore, if you find yourself off your boat, get back to it as soon as possible to prevent chasing it downwind.

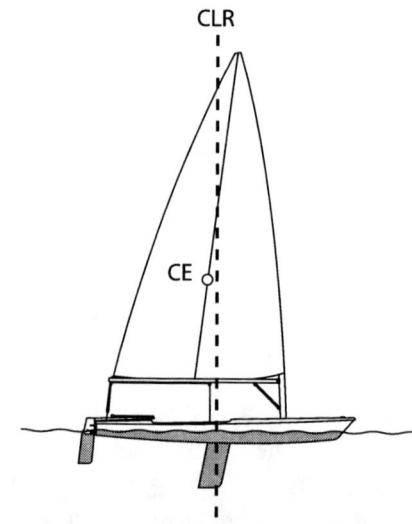

Fig. 5-25 Boat with Weather Helm—
The Center of Effort (CE) is Aft of the Center of Lateral Resistance (CLR)

If the CE of a boat is forward of its CLR it will tend to turn away from the wind, thus, it is said to have a **lee helm**. The position of weight in a boat will not only affect balance but will also affect the location of the CLR. A boat will sail best and be easiest to control when it is in a balanced position. Placement of body weight is very important in bringing the CE and CLR in alignment. This is an efficient position for sailing because it will minimize the effort

How a Sailboat Sails

required to steer the boat. If a boat has either a weather or a lee helm, it will require more force on the tiller to keep the boat on course. Also, from a racing standpoint, the boat will not be as fast. Put another way, stay out of the "ends" of the boat. Ideally, the boat should float on the same line with or without a sailor on board. Two people on a small boat will require that they work together for optimum balance.

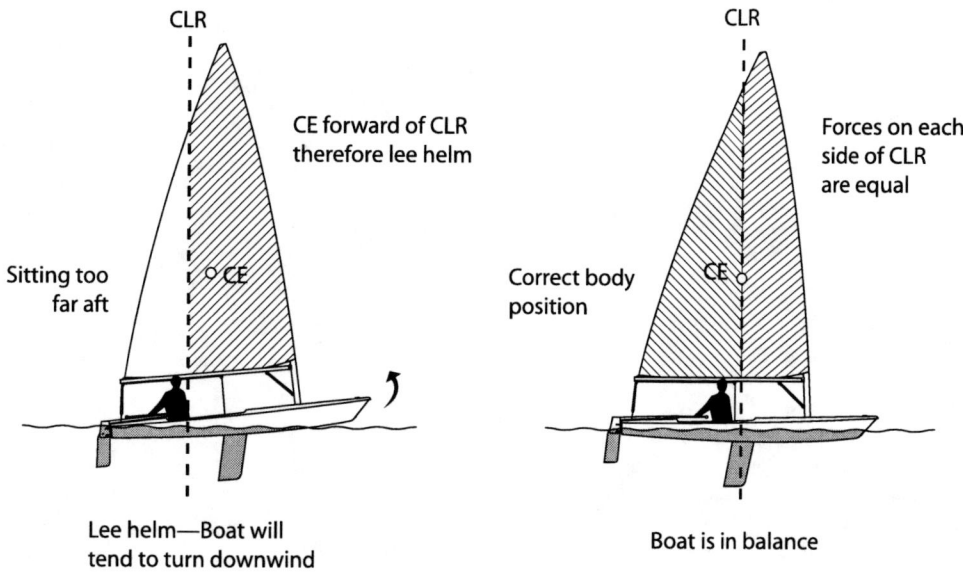

Fig. 5-26 Use Bodyweight to Balance Boat

Hopefully, the sailor will never break or lose the rudder. However, if this happens, body weight can be used to produce a weather or lee helm in order to help steer the boat in the desired direction. Move body weight forward to produce a weather helm and the boat will turn toward the wind. Move body weight aft to produce a lee helm and the boat will turn away from the wind. For a sloop rigged boat, the mainsail could be furled to produce a lee helm to help sail downwind, or the jib could be furled to produce a weather helm to help sail upwind.

J. EXERCISES AND REVIEW QUESTIONS

Complete Exercises and Review Questions for Chapter 5 in Appendix C *before* proceeding to Chapter 6.

Chapter 6
Sailing Techniques

A. INTRODUCTION

The best way to learn to sail is with private lessons from a certified instructor. A certified sailing instructor will provide safe, clear, and efficient instruction. Group instruction from a certified instructor is also very effective. Another possibility is self-study and sailing with a knowledgeable and skilled sailor—provided that person is patient and a good teacher.

Learning to sail is not difficult provided the individual is motivated and takes responsibility for the learning process. The beginner wants to get out and sail and that's a positive attitude to have. However, the place to start is the beginning of this book. There is a good deal of information the beginner needs to know *before* he/she is ready to set foot (or backside) in a boat. The following "off water" study and practice tasks are the place to start:

- know the information in the "Sailing Safety" chapter
- practice and be able to tie the knots necessary to transport and rig your boat
- practice properly rigging your boat—know your boat
- read/study the "How a Sailboat Sails" and "Sailing Techniques" chapters—read for understanding and carefully examine each figure and illustration
- after reading each chapter, do the exercises and answer the review questions presented in Appendix C
- re-read/study the parts of the "Sailing Techniques" section you plan to practice right before your next sail
- watch learning to sail videos and online video clips (see Appendix A, Resources and References)
- practice skills onshore (e.g. maintaining tiller and mainsheet control when coming about)
- visualize performing skills in your mind before attempting them on the water—mental practice works
- practice sailing techniques following the progression outlined in the next section
- re-read/study the parts of this book that will help you understand and therefore perform each basic sailing technique

B. PROGRESSION

First, complete the "off-water" study and practice described above. Next, follow the progression of information and practice the skills presented in this chapter.

- determine the direction of the wind
- rig the boat
- plan for launch and initial point of sail
- launch
- sail on a beam reach
- basic boat controls
- adjusting to force of wind
- safety position and stopping the boat
- getting out of "irons"
- coming about
- righting a capsized boat
- landing

Once the above can be performed with some confidence, the individual is ready to move on to other points of sail. It is now time to gain further control of the boat and be able to sail confidently in any direction.

- close reach and broad reach
- run
- jibing
- practice (e.g. triangle course)

Following a logical progression will optimize learning. Resist the temptation to try more advanced skills until you understand and can perform the basic ones. After the skills in this chapter have been mastered, the sailor is ready to move on to Intermediate Sailing Skills (Chapter 7).

C. WIND SPEED AND DIRECTION

1. Wind Speed

The speed or velocity of the wind can be obtained from a weather report, a wind gauge, or judged based on observation. Feeling the force of the wind on one's face and body, observing trees, flags, waves, etc. will give a good indication of wind speed. The Beaufort Force Scale, developed in 1805 by Admiral Sir Francis Beaufort of the British Navy, is another way to judge wind speed. It rates wind speed from 0 (none) to 12 (hurricane, >64 knots or 74 mph [1 knot = 1.15 mph]). Beaufort included a description of the wind as well as water surface conditions with his scale. Table 1 presents the Beaufort Force Scale in conjunction with a description of how wind speed can be used to rate conditions for learning to sail. Note, only conditions relevant to the recreational sailor are included (Beaufort Force Scale ratings of 0-6). Know the highest wind speed (and related conditions) at which you can sail safely. DO NOT SAIL at higher wind speeds.

Force	Wind Speed (Knots)	Wind Speed (mph)	Description	Water Surface Conditions	Conditions for Learning to Sail
0	0	0	Calm	Smooth, like a mirror	Stay home
1	1–3	1–3	Light air	Small ripples	Fair, practice rigging, balance, launching, capsizing, landing
2	4–6	4–7	Light breeze	Short small wavelets with no crests	Excellent for learning basics
3	7–10	8–12	Gentle breeze	Larger wavelets with crests	Excellent for practicing skills
4	11–16	13–18	Moderate breeze	Longer, small waves, some with white caps	Good if comfortable with basic skills
5	17–21	19–24	Fresh breeze	Moderate waves with many whitecaps	Not for beginners; experienced sailors will enjoy speed
6	22–27	25–31	Strong breeze	Large waves, extensive whitecaps	Only well-prepared and skilled sailors

Table 1. Adapted from the Beaufort Force Scale established in 1805 by Admiral Sir Francis Beaufort of the British Navy.

When rigging a boat, the mainsail should be adjusted for wind speed. Sail shape is important to efficient and controlled sailing. A general statement will be helpful to the novice sailor.

"Use a full sail shape in light to moderate winds and a flat or tight sail shape for higher wind conditions."

Sail shape is controlled by the tension in lines attached to the sail and standing rigging (e.g. halyard, downhaul, outhaul, and/or boom vang). Determine wind conditions and then adjust these lines accordingly when rigging the boat. Use light tension on these lines in light wind and heavy tension in heavy wind. Additional information on sail shape and trim is presented in the section titled Sail Shape in Chapter 7, Intermediate Sailing Skills.

2. *Wind Direction*

The sailor must constantly monitor and be aware of wind direction. When arriving at a body of water, determination of wind direction and speed is the first thing the sailor will do. The boat will be pointed into the wind to be rigged and a plan will be formulated to launch the boat and start sailing. The direction the wind is blowing *from (not to)* is designated as the direction of the true wind.

There are many ways to determine wind direction. Face the wind, and then turn your head until the wind is felt evenly on both ears—your nose will point to the wind. Check the direction of smoke coming from smokestacks. Drop some grass and see which way it moves. Look at the ripples or waves on the water. Note the direction that flags or pennants are blowing. Examine the direction of **telltales** (small lengths of wool, nylon, or other lightweight material) attached to standing rigging or a masthead fly. Also, boats tied to moorings will point into the wind.

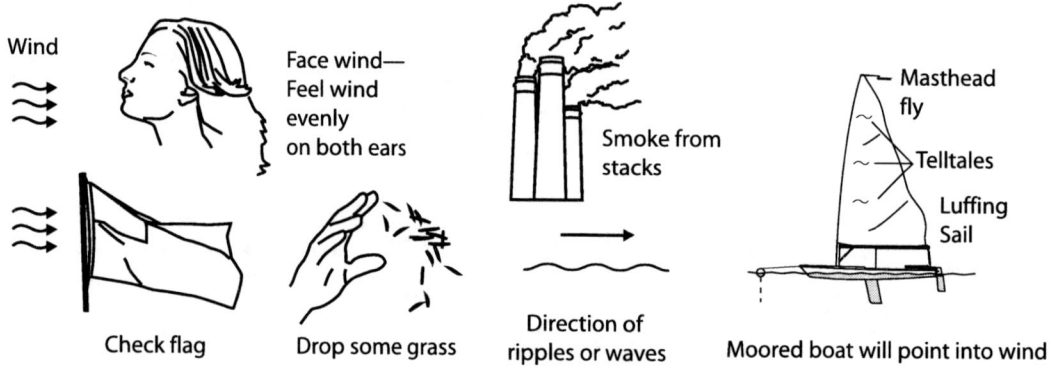

Fig. 6.1 Determining Direction of True Wind

When the boat is rigged, the sail provides an excellent means of determining wind direction. Point the bow of the boat somewhere toward the wind. Allow the sail to move with the wind and it will act like a flag and line up so that the luff edge points in the direction of the true wind.

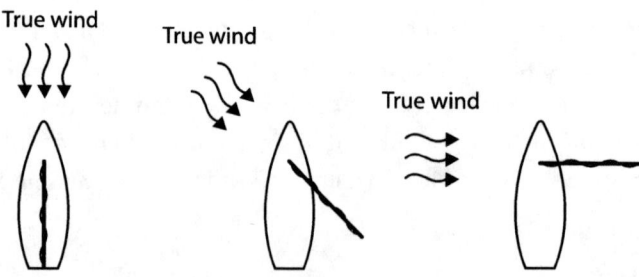

**Fig. 6-2 Boats at dock or stopped in water
Sails are luffing—Sail points in direction of true wind**

Sailing Techniques

The methods just described will help in determining the "**True Wind**," that is, the direction from which the wind is blowing. The air movement due to the speed of a boat is called the "**Motion Wind**." It is the same as the wind you "feel" when you are running or riding a bicycle. The force of the Motion Wind is directly related to your speed. When a boat is moving across the water, the wind felt on a sailor's face is a combination of the True Wind and the Motion Wind—it is called the "**Apparent Wind**." The Apparent Wind will "feel" stronger when sailing upwind and less strong when sailing downwind. If on a run, and the boat is moving at a speed that approximates the true wind velocity, it may "feel" like there is no wind. When the boat is moving, the telltales on the rigging and masthead fly will indicate the direction of the apparent wind. The sail is always trimmed to the apparent wind direction.

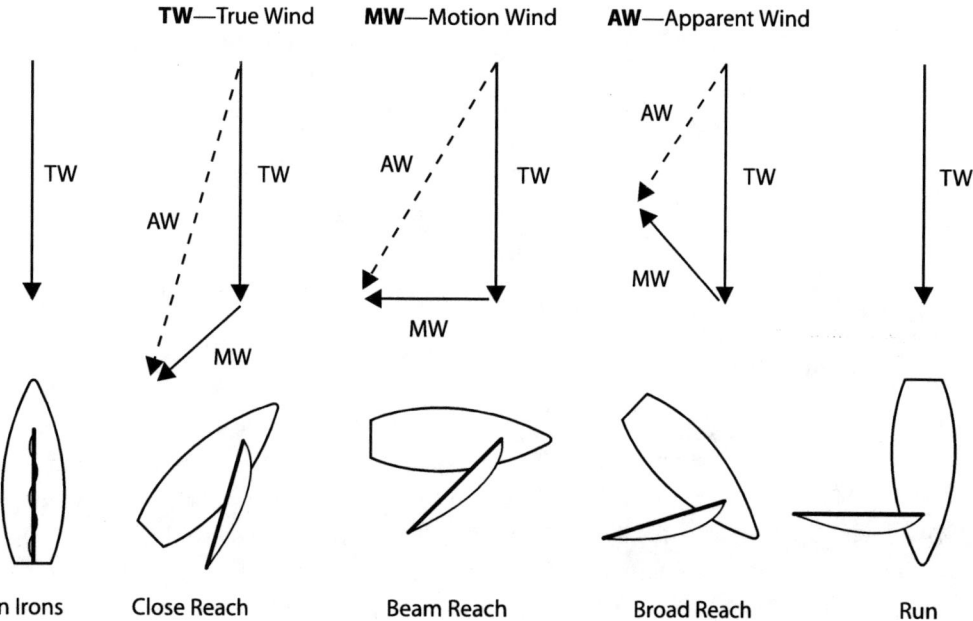

Fig. 6-3 Apparent Wind is the Wind you "Feel" While Sailing

It is important that the sailor know the direction of the true wind when establishing a point of sail. It is helpful to picture the points of sail diagram in one's mind and superimpose it on the water where the boat is sailing. The 0° or 360° position (i.e. top of the Points of Sail Circle, 12 o'clock) is pictured to be at the point that the true wind is coming from. If available, identify a landmark (e.g. dam, tower, tall tree, flagpole, building, rock outcrop, dock, etc.) at this point. The landmark can then be used as a reference when sailing.

The wind does not always blow from the same direction, it shifts. Therefore, the sailor needs to monitor the wind and adjust his/her imaginary points of sail circle as the direction of the wind changes. If it is not clear where the wind is coming from, or if the boat is on an open body of water where there are no landmarks, turn the boat toward the wind, stop, and let the sail luff. The sail (e.g. flag) will indicate the direction of the true wind.

Also, the wind is not always constant. There will be puffs (brief increases in wind speed) and lulls (decreases in wind speed). Look for darker areas on the surface of the water—they indicate the location of puffs. Consider sailing to these areas to increase speed of the boat.

High winds will produce high waves. Waves will build up and crash on the windward side of anything (e.g. island, point of land, rocky shore, dock, etc.) in their path. The sailor should avoid these areas. At the same time, the area on the leeward side of wind obstructions can provide a calm and protected area from heavy seas.

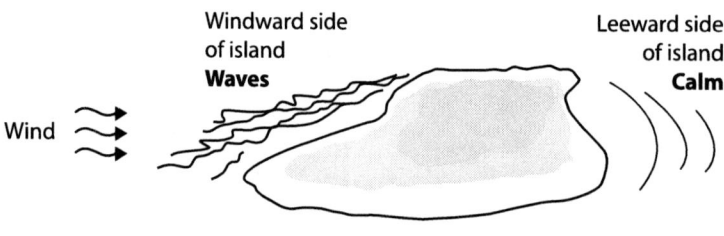

Fig. 6-4 Island

D. LAUNCHING

1. From Beach

The procedures described will be for two people launching a boat. The boat is on the beach near the water, is properly rigged (has been checked, e.g. plugs are secure), and is pointed into the wind. The daggerboard is lying in the cockpit, not obstructing the mainsheet in any way, and the rudder is in the up position. The daggerboard should not be on the deck as it could slide off during launching and float away. Before starting, one individual is identified as the captain or helmsman and the other the crew. The captain is the person who will control the helm (i.e. tiller and rudder) and the crew on a small boat is the person who will control the line (e.g. mainsheet or jib sheet). Therefore, the crew person on a small boat is called the linesman. The linesman also has the important tasks of helping to balance the boat and keeping a lookout for other boats and obstacles.

The linesman goes to the bow of the boat and the captain to the stern. Together, they move the boat off the beach into the water while keeping the bow pointed into the wind. Keeping the boom down the centerline of the boat will ensure that the boat is pointed into the wind. The boat has to be moved into the water far enough so that the rudder and daggerboard can be put in without hitting the bottom. It is the linesman job to keep the boat pointed into the wind. The captain next moves to the side of the boat, takes up any slack in the mainsheet (makes sure it is running freely to the traveler), and takes the daggerboard out of the cockpit. The linesman now moves the bow slightly off wind (boom moves away from centerline) so

Sailing Techniques

that the captain can easily place the daggerboard in the daggerboard trunk. The daggerboard can be put down all the way or only part way depending on the depth of the water. However, it must always be put in far enough so that the top is below and does not interfere with movement of the boom.

The captain now goes to the stern of the boat to put down the rudder. The captain should be sure the rudder is secure when it is put down. [On the Laser, this involves taking the rudder line, **_under the traveler,_** and putting it around the jam cleat on the tiller. The rudder line should not be tied to the tiller (e.g. knot) as this will interfere with releasing it when landing.] The Sunfish rudder will snap into place when pushed down.

For boats that do not have a pop up rudder, the rudder is placed in the cockpit when rigging and then attached to the boat when it is in shallow water.

The captain is in charge of the boat and gives "orders" which are followed by the crew. **Before launching**, the captain decides on the first point of sail. The direction of the wind, the location of the boat in relation to other objects and areas, and where the captain wants to go, determine what that point of sail will be. For example, the location of other boats, docks, buoys, swim areas, fishermen, shallow areas, etc. will influence the starting point of sail.

The wind may be coming from off-shore, cross-shore, or on-shore. In each case there will be directions and places the boat can sail (Go zones) and others it cannot or should not sail (No-Go zones). Given the wind direction and obstacles, the captain decides if the initial point of sail will be a starboard or port tack. The captain then moves to what will be the upwind or windward side of the boat while keeping it pointed into the wind. He/she then directs the

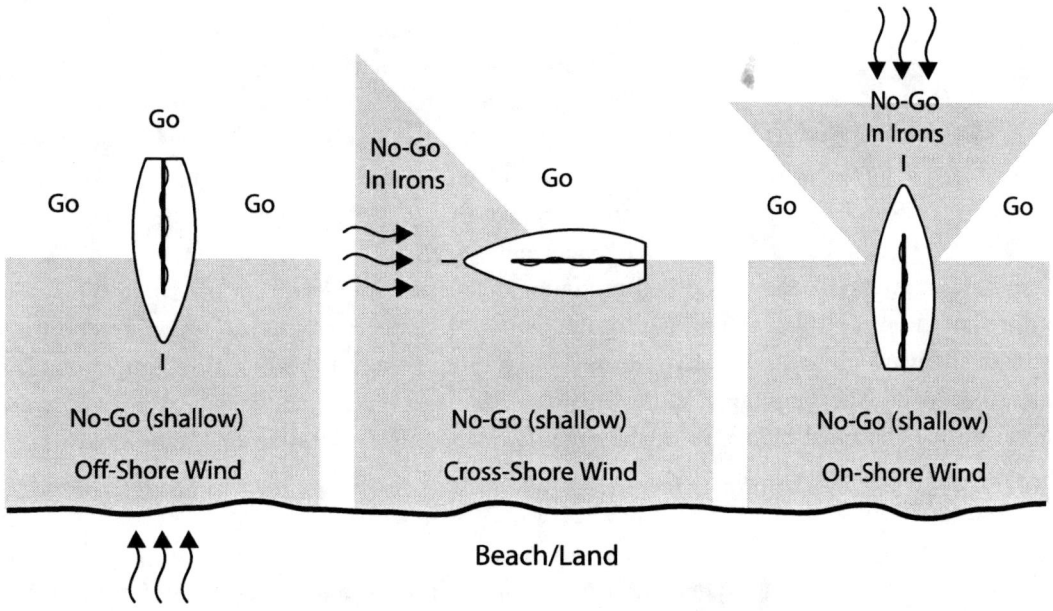

Fig. 6-5 Go and No-Go Zones When Starting to Sail

linesman to release the bow and get into the boat from the opposite side (i.e. what will be the downwind or leeward side of the boat when starting to sail). When getting in, the linesman should keep body weight as close to the center of gravity (CG) of the boat as possible. The captain helps balance the boat while the linesman gets in.

When the linesman is settled and has control of the mainsheet, the captain turns the boat so that it falls-off the wind more than 45°. The linesman allows the sail to move out and luff as the boat falls-off the wind. The captain gets in the boat as the linesman assists with balance. The captain takes control of the tiller and then directs the linesman to pull in the mainsheet until the wind fills the sail. The boat will slowly pick up speed and start to sail. The captain and linesman use their body weight to balance the boat fore and aft (bow should be slightly higher than stern) as well as side to side. Good balance will make it easier to turn the boat when coming about. The captain should be positioned far enough forward so that the tiller can be moved 180°. The tiller needs to be moved freely and *should not* hit the captain's leg or butt. This is done by using a palm down grip on the tiller extension (hiking stick), holding it in front of the body, and moving the hips forward in the boat. The beginner should learn early on to use the tiller extension to control the rudder. Body position is also important. The hips and shoulders should be kept parallel to the long axis of the boat.

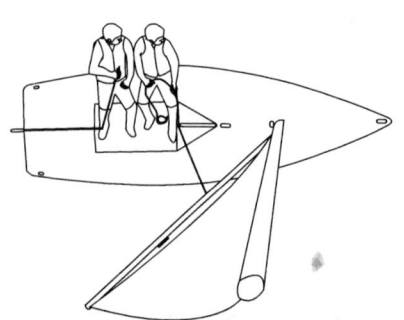

Fig. 6-6 Body Position

Assuming sufficient wind, the captain and linesman should be sitting on the upwind gunwale perpendicular to the long axis of the boat. This position will make it easy for the crew to bend forward or lean back to balance the boat (control the amount of heel). The captain looks forward toward the front of the boat and uses landmarks to help keep the boat on course. Captain and linesman constantly survey the area looking for other boats and obstacles. Both need to regularly check the blind spot behind the sail by looking through the sail window and under the boom. In light air, the captain and linesman may have to sit on opposite sides in order to balance the boat.

Some caution is needed if a beginning sailor is launching with an off-shore wind. The sailor should be careful not to go out too far as it will be necessary to sail upwind to return to the launch site. Sailing upwind requires tacking (coming about to change direction upwind) to make progress. The beginning sailor will often have some difficulty sailing to windward; therefore, he/she must be aware of the potential problem and realize that additional time is necessary to make progress upwind.

The same difficulty can arise if there is a cross-shore wind. The beginning sailor should be able to easily sail out and back on a beam reach; however, he/she should be aware that sailing downwind will require tacking back upwind to return to the launch site. Consequently, it is recommended that the beginning sailor sail out and somewhat upwind when there is a cross-shore breeze. It should then be an easy task to sail back to the launch site.

Sailing Techniques

Launching Solo: The procedures and steps described in launching a boat with a partner also apply when launching solo. The major difference is in control of the boat. The sailor must constantly be aware of wind direction and *keep the boat pointed into the wind with the boom down the centerline of the boat.* The boat should be controlled and moved into position from the bow end. The only exception would be pulling the boat off the beach from the stern when there is an off-shore wind. In this case, the sailor should move to the bow for control as soon as the boating is floating in the water.

After the boat is in position, pointed into the wind, and floating in at least waist deep water, the sailor carefully moves to the side of the boat that will become the upwind side when launched. This is accomplished by moving the hands (underhand grip) down the gunwale to control the boat and keep it pointed into the wind. The sailor then turns the boat far enough off wind to allow for easy placement of the daggerboard into the daggerboard trunk. [On the Laser, the top of the daggerboard should be forward as it is placed into the daggerboard trunk on an angle.]

The sailor then turns the bow back into the wind and moves to the stern while working the hands (underhand grip) down the gunwale for boat control. The rudder is secured in the down position and the sailor then moves forward to prepare for launch. The boat is then turned about $60°$ off wind allowing the boom and sail to be blown downwind from the boat. While maintaining control, the sailor gets in the boat and takes control of the tiller. When in position, slack is taken out of the mainsheet. As the mainsheet is pulled further, the sail comes under power and the boat starts to move. The mainsheet and sail are then adjusted to the point of sail. A common error for beginners is to get into the boat while it is still pointed into the wind (not turning it off wind); as a result, they get caught in irons. As a sailor becomes skilled at solo launching, he/she can get in the boat while it is being turned off wind, take control, and start sailing immediately.

As a general guideline for recreational sailing, the captain should sail upwind after launching the boat in a cross-shore breeze. It will be more work to sail on a close reach but will make it easier to return to the launching location. Also, the wind could drop while out sailing requiring a long time beating to get back to the launch site if downwind.

2. *From Dock*

A sailboat can be partially rigged then placed in the water or rigged while floating next to a dock. If the boat is rigged ashore and then carried to the dock or launched from a trailer, do not hoist the sail [for Laser—do not attach sail to boom] until the boat is properly positioned at the dock. A turn or two of small line or a bungee strap can be used to hold the sail in place.

In launching a boat from a dock, the first concern is the position of the boat in relation to the wind and the dock. Position the boat so that the bow is pointed into the wind and it is on the downwind (leeward) side of the dock. This will facilitate the final steps in rigging, hoisting the sail, and sailing away from the dock. When the boat is in the water, a **painter** (line attached to bow) is used to move it and hold it in place at the dock.

When getting into a boat, always step as close to the centerline and center of the boat as possible. Also, stay as low as possible with both hands out to the side and holding on to the boat to maintain at least three points of contact. This will minimize rotation of the boat (e.g. heeling) and possible loss of balance. Keep weight balanced in the boat (captain and crew) while adjusting rigging and preparing to sail. Review the previous section on launching from a beach for a description of related procedures, Go and No-Go zones, as well as the role of captain and crew (linesman).

Leaving a dock is called **shoving off**. Untie and coil the painter and then push away from the dock so that the boat falls-off the wind. If sailing with captain and linesman, the linesman secures the painter and pushes off while the captain controls the tiller. When the boat is turned onto a reach, the linesman pulls in the mainsheet to power the sail and the captain adjusts the tiller for the desired point of sail.

In Fig. 6-7, note how the boat is pushed off hard from a crowded dock. The rudder is initially kept straight, then the rudder is turned and the boat steered with sternway until it is off the wind. If more force is needed, the boom may be pushed forward to create additional backward momentum. After turning the boat off the wind, the sail is then trimmed to start sailing.

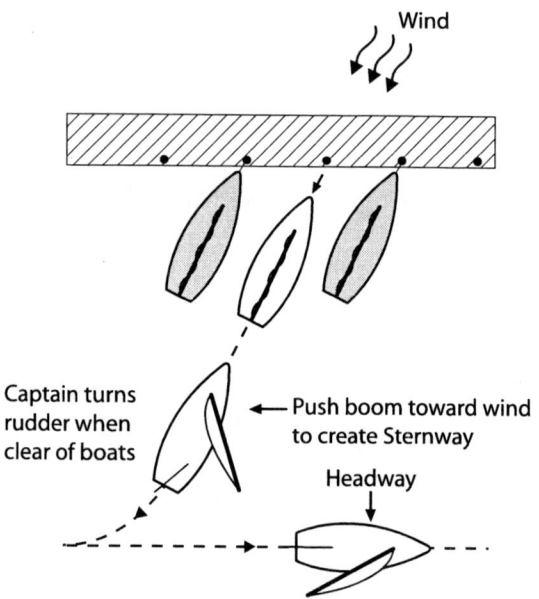

Fig. 6-7 Shoving off from Dock

E. Beam Reach

Once launched, move the boat onto a beam reach, this is the easiest point of sail for beginners. The sailor must constantly be aware of the three things that determine how (and if) a sailboat moves. They are: (1) the direction of the wind, (2) the direction of the boat in relation to the wind (point of sail), and (3) trim of the sail (correct angle of boom and sail in relation to centerline of boat). Always think of these in order. First, know the direction of the wind. Second, know your point of sail and head the boat in the desired direction. Third, correctly trim the sail for the boat heading. Sail back and forth on a beam reach while practicing the skills in the following sections, i.e. basic boat controls, stopping the boat and safety position, getting out of "irons," adjusting to force of wind, and capsize-recovery.

Sailing Techniques

In practicing the beam reach, it is helpful to identify one landmark (e.g. buoy, flag, building, dock, tree, etc.) that is 90° clockwise from the wind and another that is 90° counter-clockwise from the wind. The task is then to sail back and forth across the wind using the landmarks as guides for boat direction. Be aware that wind direction can change. If it is not clear where the true wind is coming from, put the boat in irons, let the sail luff (flap like a flag), and the luff edge of the sail will point toward the true wind. Now reference landmarks can be reestablished. Backwind, and start sailing on a beam reach. As a general guideline, the boom should be at an angle of about 45° to the long axis of the boat (about half way out) when on a beam reach.

Another way of setting course to a beam reach is to first find the wind direction and then move the boat onto what is believed to be a beam reach. The sail is then trimmed to a position 45° out from the centerline of the boat. Next, slowly push the tiller to leeward to head the boat up into the wind until the sail just starts to luff. Now, fall-off the wind (pull tiller slightly) until the luffing stops. The boat is now on a beam reach. Look for a landmark straight ahead to use as a reference in maintaining the beam reach. This same method can be used for other points of sail.

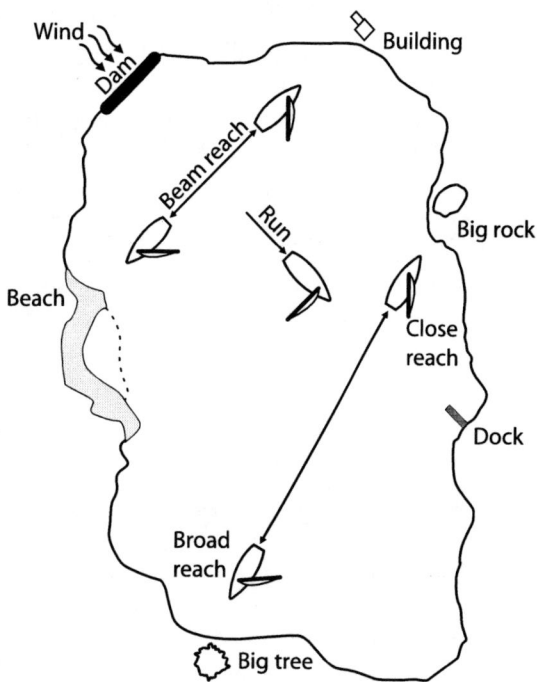

Fig. 6-8 Use Landmarks to Help with Boat Direction and Points of Sail

F. Basic Boat Controls

The first task of the beginner is to become familiar and comfortable with basic boat controls. The tiller controls the rudder and therefore the direction and turning of the boat. The mainsheet controls the boom and sail angle and therefore the speed of the boat. Practice using these controls as follows:

While sailing on a beam reach with good sail trim:
1. First, maintain length of the mainsheet and slowly turn the boat a little toward the wind (push tiller toward the sail) and then somewhat away from the wind (pull tiller away from the sail)—use small/controlled movements of the tiller. Notice how moving the tiller in one direction turns the boat in the opposite direction. For example, when sailing on a port tack (i.e. wind coming over the left or port side of

the boat), push the tiller to starboard (right side of boat) to make the boat turn left or to port. Pull the tiller to port (left side of boat) to make the boat turn to the right or starboard. Practice pushing and pulling the tiller *slightly* to starboard and then port to get a feel for how the boat responds and the direction the bow turns. Also, notice how the boat slows down when turning toward the wind then speeds up when turning away from the wind. Recall that turning toward the wind is called **heading-up** and turning away from the wind is called heading down or **falling-off**.

2. Next, keep the tiller steady and slowly ease out then trim in the mainsheet. Notice how the boat slows when sheeting out (sail starts to luff) and then speeds up when sheeting in.

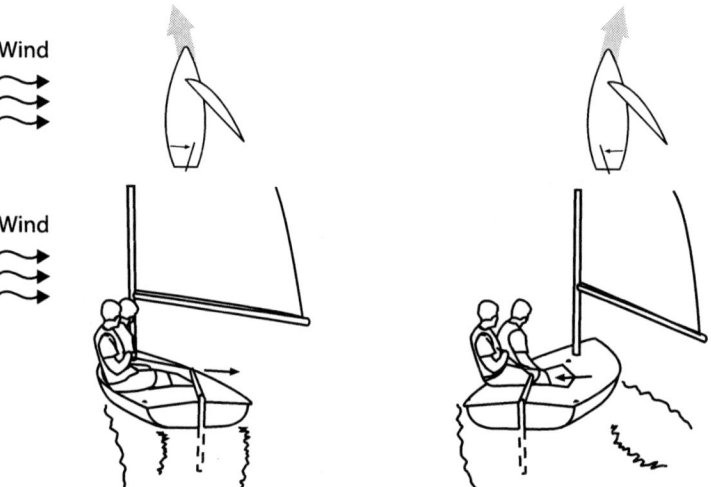

Fig. 6-9a Push Tiller to Head-Up   Fig. 6-9b Pull Tiller to Fall-Off

General Rule for Correct Sail Trim: While maintaining point of sail, ease out the sail until it starts to luff, then trim it in just enough to stop the luffing.

G. ADJUSTING TO FORCE OF WIND

Wind speed and force could increase gradually or a gust of wind might hit suddenly. The sailor needs to be prepared to react and adjust to each situation. As force on the sail increases, the boat will tend to heel. See Chapter 5 "Heeling." The simplest and most efficient way to handle this is to use body weight as a counterforce to balance the boat. Sit perpendicular to the centerline of the boat so that leaning straight back will produce the greatest balance

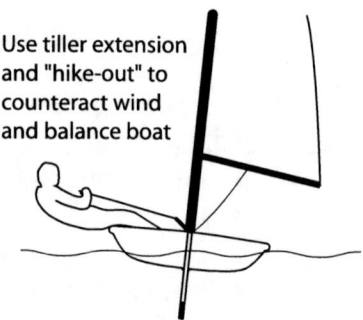

Use tiller extension and "hike-out" to counteract wind and balance boat

Fig. 6-10 Hike Out to Balance

Sailing Techniques

effect. As wind force increases, sit further from the centerline. In heavy winds, place feet under the hiking strap, put butt over gunwale and lean back (hike out) while holding the tiller extension (i.e. hiking stick) and mainsheet.

If a gust of wind strikes and it cannot be countered by hiking out, adjust by temporarily heading up into the wind (be careful not to turn into irons). If necessary, also let out the mainsheet to reduce some of the wind force. A good guideline for beginners is, "When in doubt, ease it out." When the gust passes, return to the desired course and trim sail.

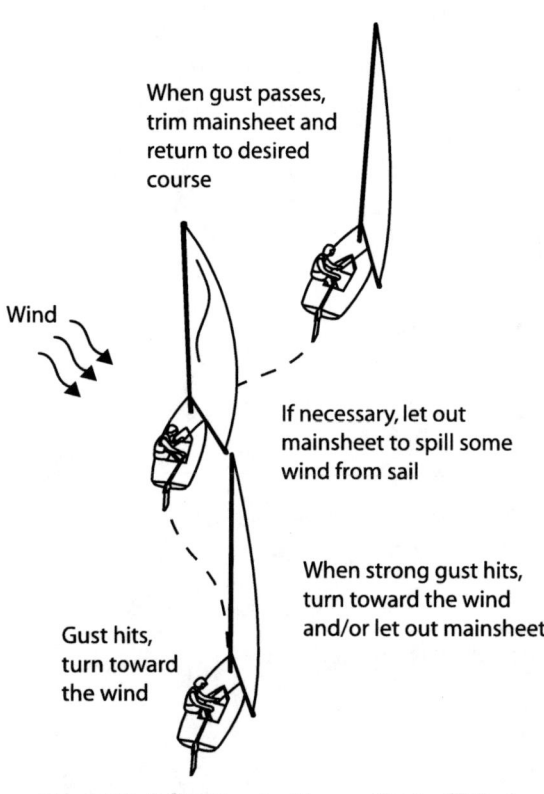

Fig. 6-11 Adjusting to Strong Gust of Wind

Sailing with speed is one of the exhilarating aspects of the sport. The sailor attempts to optimize point of sail, boat position, and sail trim for maximum speed. However, there are times when the sailor would like to slow the boat to increase control and safety. Control is needed in turning the boat, moving around obstacles, landing, and docking. Also, it might be necessary to slow the boat to prevent capsizing or a collision.

There are three ways to slow a boat. First, maintain the same course but let out the mainsheet to "spill" some wind. Second, maintain the tension on the mainsheet but change course by turning the boat toward the wind. Third, both actions could be done at the same time. All three methods will decrease force on the sail and slow the boat. As a general guideline, if the wind is tending to blow the boat over and you feel you are losing control—let out the mainsheet (be prepared to balance the boat with your body weight).

H. SAFETY POSITION AND STOPPING THE BOAT

The next skill the beginner should practice is putting the boat into the safety position. When in the safety position, the boat is stopped and the sail is luffing. The easiest and most obvious safety position is to turn the boat into irons (into the wind), it will stop. The safety position can also be achieved while on a close reach or beam reach by letting out the mainsheet. Simply let out the mainsheet until the sail luffs and the boom is pointed directly downwind. The boat will stop—this is also a safety position. When stopped, the sailor(s) can adjust lines and equipment, change positions in the boat, or just relax.

When ready to start sailing, if in irons, use the "backwind technique," to turn the boat off wind and start sailing. See the next section—getting out of irons.

If ready to start sailing and the boat is in a close reach or beam reach position—shift body weight to windward as you slowly pull in the mainsheet. The sail will "catch" the wind and the boat will start to move. As the boat accelerates, first the tiller and then the mainsheet (i.e. boom and sail) are adjusted to the desired point of sail.

The safety position is not possible when on a broad reach or run because the boat is still powered by the wind even when the mainsheet is all the way out. Therefore, first move to a beam reach or preferably a close reach before going into the safety position.

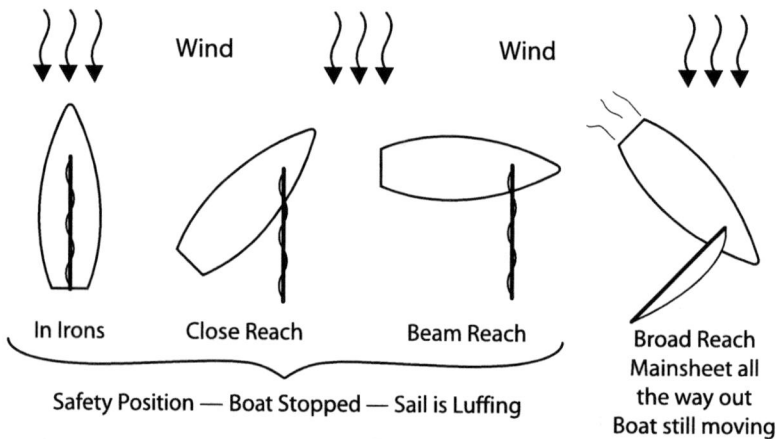

Fig. 6-12 Safety Position is Possible when Bow is Pointed 0° to 90° Off-Wind

Stopping the boat when and where you want is an essential skill. You must stop the boat when landing or docking. Also, you may need to stop the boat to prevent a collision, perform a rescue (e.g. man overboard), to change positions with another person in the boat, or to adjust gear or rigging. As with slowing a boat, there are three ways to stop a boat. First, turn the boat directly into the wind (i.e. put it in irons). Second, let out the mainsheet until the sail luffs (safety position). This will work on a close reach or beam reach. It will not work on a broad reach or run because the figure 8 stopper knot in the end of the mainsheet will not permit the sail to move downwind and luff. Third, turn the boat into the wind and let out the mainsheet at the same time.

In an emergency, turn the boat into the wind and let out the mainsheet at the same time. This will stop the boat as quickly as possible. Be prepared to balance the boat with your body weight as this occurs!

Sailing Techniques

I. Getting Out of "Irons"

You will get "caught in irons." You need to know how to get out! **Backwind** is a technique for getting out of irons. Balance the boat with your weight and push the boom into the wind to the side you want to turn (starboard or port)—the wind will exert force on the back of the sail. This is one of the few times when it is permissible to hold on to the boom! The boat will start to move backwards (sternway). Now, push the tiller in the same direction you want to turn. Be sure to turn the boat *more than 45°* off-wind. After the boat is turned off-wind, straighten the tiller and then pull in the mainsheet slowly to start the boat moving.

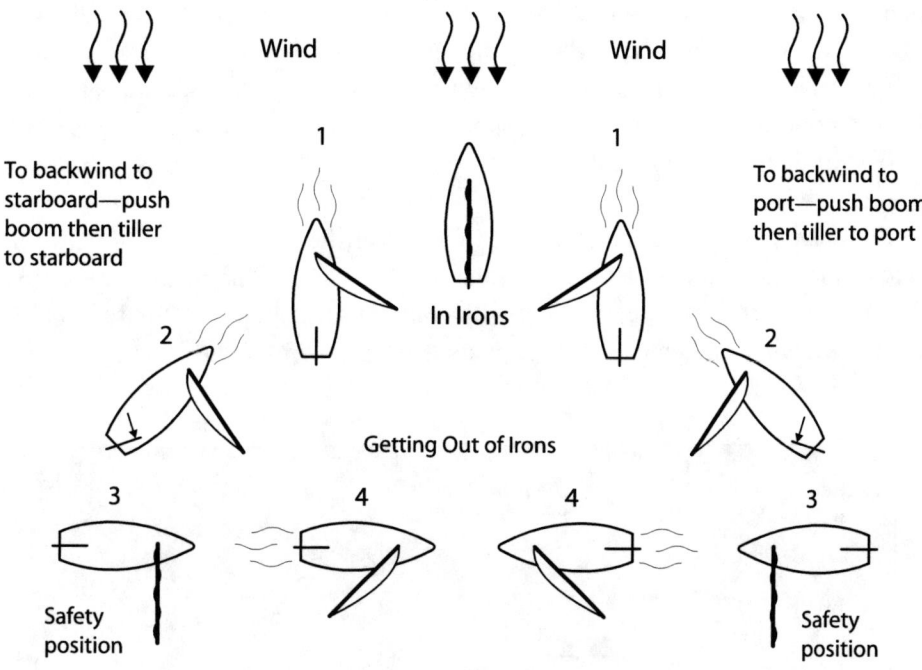

Fig. 6-13 Backwind Technique

Backwind steps: (1) push boom out to produce sternway, (2) push tiller to produce turn, (3) backwind more than 45° off-wind and (4) pull in mainsheet to start sailing.

J. Coming About

After reaching out across the water the sailor will want to head back. There are two methods to turn the sailboat around, "coming about" and "jibing" (will be reviewed later). Changing a boat's course, so the bow crosses the wind and the sail fills on the opposite side, is called **coming about**. This is the easiest and safest way to turn a boat around. The boat will move from a port tack to a starboard tack or from a starboard tack to a port tack, therefore, this maneuver is also called **tacking**. In preparing to come about, the beginner should first move the boat to a close reach (preferably a close-hauled position) *and then* execute the turn.

There are set commands that are used in coming about. When the captain is ready to turn, he/she gives the command **"Stand By To Come About"** or **"Ready About."** The crew immediately gets ready to turn and responds **"Ready."** The captain then gives the command **"Hard-a-Lee," "Tacking"** or **"Coming About"** as the tiller is pushed to the lee side (i.e. downwind or sail side) of the boat. The tiller should be pushed forcefully, held in the out position until the bow is turned 90°, and then straightened when the boat is on the new tack. The captain faces forward throughout the turn and passes the tiller behind his/her back. This helps the captain keep oriented throughout the turn so the boat is not turned too much or too little. As the boat turns up and crosses the wind, the captain and linesman *duck their heads under the boom* as it swings by and shift their weight to the opposite side of the boat. The sailor(s) should be conscious of boat movement and use their body weight for dynamic balance. "Feel" the shift of force in the sail and boat and time body movement to correspond to this change.

The linesman should take the slack out of the mainsheet as the boom comes toward the centerline of the boat and then let it out on the opposite side as the boat moves onto the new tack. When the turn is complete, the boat will again be sailing close-hauled but on the opposite tack. The captain can then change boat course (and sail trim) to the point of sail desired.

Coming About—See Fig. 6-14 Positions 4 and 6

Sailing Techniques

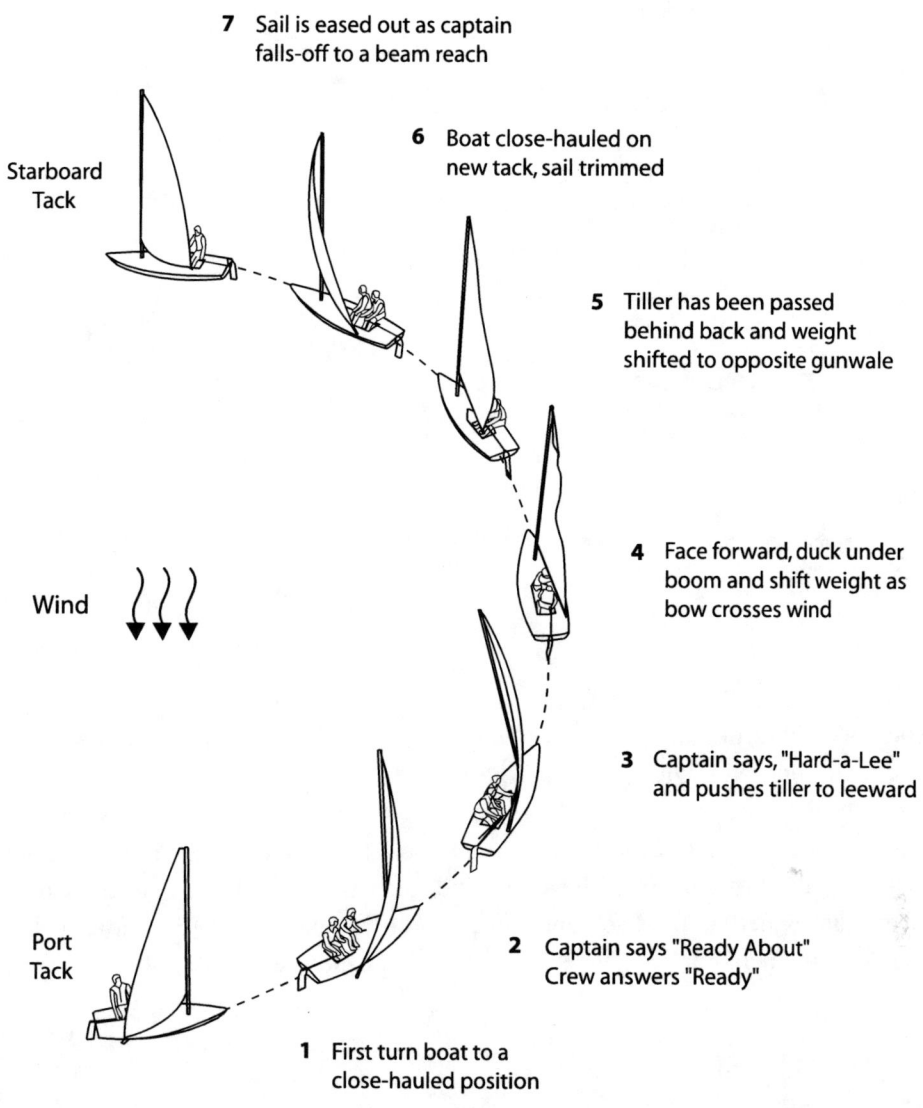

Fig. 6-14 Coming About

It may be helpful to use a landmark when coming about. First, be sure the boat is sailing close-hauled. Next, identify a landmark that is dead abeam (90° to the current course). When the boat is brought about, it should be headed toward this landmark. See Fig. 6-15.

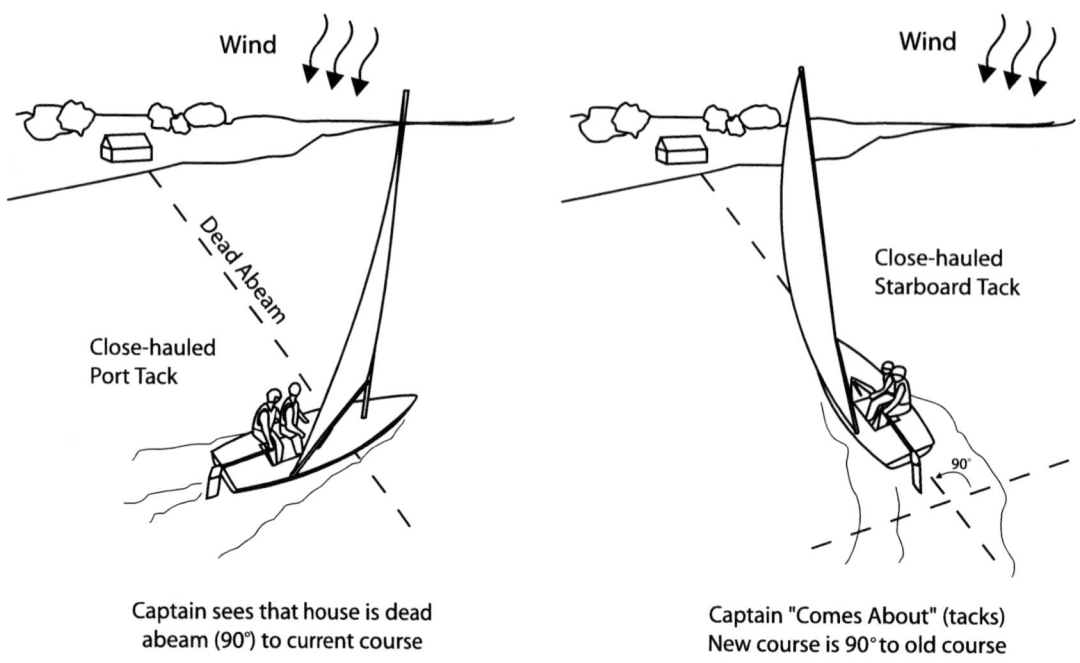

Captain sees that house is dead abeam (90°) to current course

Captain "Comes About" (tacks) New course is 90° to old course

Fig. 6-15 Using Landmarks

Solo: The key to turning the boat when sailing solo is to always have control of both the mainsheet and tiller. **Never let go of the mainsheet or tiller!** This is accomplished by using the tiller extension when tacking. Use the palm down grip on the tiller extension and start by pushing it toward the sail (leeward side). As the boat turns across the wind, rotate your body so it is facing the bow, balance the boat, and keep the head low. The hand holding the mainsheet reaches behind the back and grasps the tiller extension. The mainsheet and tiller extension are now being held by the same hand. The hand previously holding the tiller is re-

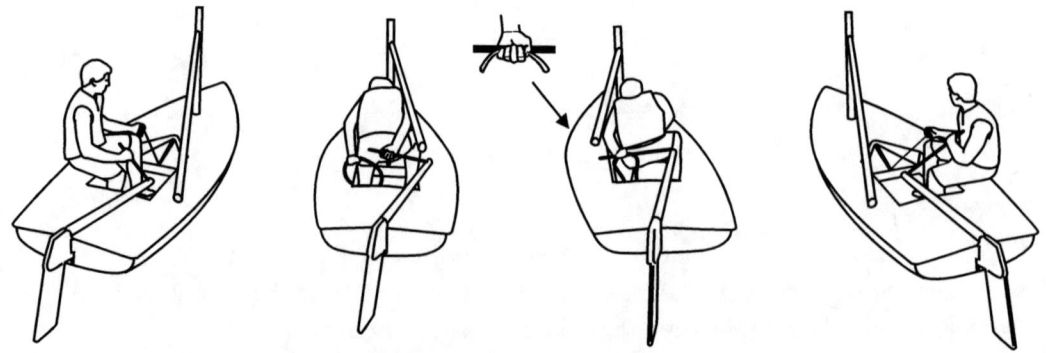

Fig. 6-16 Coming About—Changing Hands on Tiller Extension Behind Back While Controlling Mainsheet

Sailing Techniques

leased as the body continues to turn and weight is shifted to the opposite side of the boat. The free hand grasps the mainsheet (it is then released by the hand on the tiller), the tiller extension is pivoted to its new position, and the sail is adjusted for the new tack.

Helpful Hints When Sailing Solo: It is easy to let out the mainsheet and still have control by letting it slide through the hand. However, in the absence of a cam cleat, taking in the mainsheet is more difficult. The mainsheet can be easily pulled in one arm length. But, what if it needs to be brought in more? A good way to handle this situation is to temporarily hold the main sheet with the same hand that is holding the tiller extension and then reach forward with the opposite hand to re-grasp the mainsheet and pull it to a tighter position. This can be done as many times as is necessary to get the sail to the desired position.

There is a second method for bringing in the mainsheet that works on some boats. The tiller is controlled with the back of the knee of the leg closest to the stern while sheeting in the mainsheet with a hand over hand action. When the desired sail position is reached, the hand closest the stern returns to control the tiller. Again, *always maintain control of both the tiller and mainsheet.*

Common Errors in Coming About—Resulting in Boat Being Caught In Irons:

- Attempting to come about from a broad reach or beam reach and not having enough momentum to cross the wind. For the beginner, the boat should be on a close reach before coming about.
- Not having enough speed (i.e. momentum) to make the turn. The boat must have sufficient headway (speed) for the tiller to turn the boat across the wind.
- Releasing tension in the mainsheet *before* the tiller is pushed hard to leeward. This will release the force of the wind, which is needed to power the turn.
- Not pushing the tiller out far enough. The turn will be too slow and the boat will tend to stop.
- Straightening the tiller before the bow has crossed the wind and the sail starts to fill on the new tack. This will stop the turning momentum of the boat and point it into the wind.

In good wind, the tiller should be pushed out forcefully when coming about. However, in light wind, if the tiller is pushed way out, the rudder will act as a brake more than turn the boat. Therefore, in light wind, push the tiller out and turn slowly. Also, minimize tacking in light wind because with each tack you lose headway.

Go to www.ussailing.org Getting Started—Online Education—Small Boat Course—Turning the Boat—Tacking, to see a video on how to Come About.

K. Capsize Recovery

Small boats are prone to **capsizing** (turning over). This is a good reason to *always* wear a life jacket! Beginners should expect to capsize often as they practice various sailing skills. The boat may turn over on its side with the sail on the water or might turn completely over so it is upside down in the water, in which case the boat is said to be **turtled**. One of the first skills a sailor should practice is righting a boat that has been capsized.

1. Standard Capsize Recovery Technique

1. First, make sure that all crewmembers are OK and free of sails and lines. Swim to the boat, hang on to it, and be sure the mainsheet is not cleated or tangled. **Turn the bow of the boat directly into the wind.**
2. If there is a captain and linesman, the linesman should hold the bow of the boat into the wind as the captain rights the boat. Turning the bow of the boat into the wind is *very important*. If the boat is perpendicular to the wind, and an attempt is made to right it, the boat could be blown over on top of the individual(s) who are attempting to right it. If the daggerboard came out, it will have to be reinserted. If the boat is turtled and the daggerboard will not stay in due to a loose daggerboard trunk, it can be partially inserted from the bottom of the boat, used as

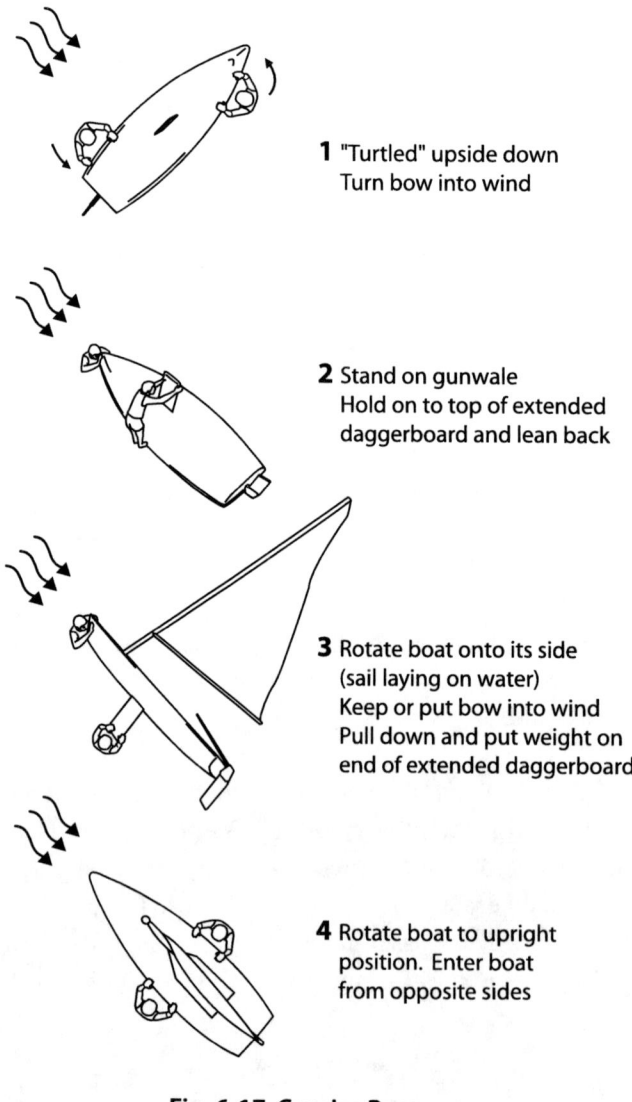

1 "Turtled" upside down
Turn bow into wind

2 Stand on gunwale
Hold on to top of extended daggerboard and lean back

3 Rotate boat onto its side (sail laying on water)
Keep or put bow into wind
Pull down and put weight on end of extended daggerboard

4 Rotate boat to upright position. Enter boat from opposite sides

Fig. 6-17 Capsize Recovery

Sailing Techniques

a lever to right the boat, taken out, and reinserted correctly when the boat is righted. To prevent the daggerboard from coming out when the boat capsizes, attach the top to a daggerboard retaining line when rigging the boat. To right a turtled boat, climb up on the bottom, extend and hold on to the bottom of the daggerboard, stand on the underside of the gunwale, and lean back.

3. When the boat is on its side and the sail is laying on the water, **be sure the bow is pointing into the wind**. Make sure the daggerboard is sticking out all the way and pull down on the end in order to obtain as much leverage as possible. It may be necessary to boost yourself up and put all of your weight on the end of the board or even stand on it to exert enough force. As the boat comes up, reduce the force (turning effect) so that the boat stops in the upright position. If the captain does not weigh very much, the linesman can help right the boat as long as it is kept pointed into the wind.

4. If there are two sailors, take turns entering the boat from opposite sides. One person keeps the boat balanced as the other enters. If a person is having difficulty getting in the boat, the other individual can allow the boat to rotate in the direction of the person who is attempting to enter. This will decrease the distance between the gunwale and the water and make it easier to get in the boat. The key is for one person to counterbalance the boat as the other enters. The boat is now floating "in irons," i.e. pointed into the wind. All rigging should be checked. Is the rudder down? Are all lines attached properly? Is the drain plug in? Are the mainsheet and traveler lines free? If the answers to these questions are yes, then you are ready to backwind, sail off and have fun!

2. Scoop Capsize Recovery Technique

The "scoop capsize recovery" technique can be used when sailing with two people. It can also be used to help an individual who is tired, injured, or heavy get into the boat. From the capsized position where the boat is on its side and the bow is pointed into the wind, the individual "to be scooped" gets in position on the deck side of the boat near the daggerboard. While that person is holding on to a stationary part of the boat, with the hips as high in the

Fig. 6-18 Scoop Capsize Recovery

water as possible, the person doing the recovery gets up on the fully extended daggerboard sticking out of the bottom of the boat. While standing on the end of the daggerboard and holding on to the gunwale, the sailor leans back and rotates the boat into the upright position. As the boat comes up, the person on the deck side is "scooped" into the boat.

Knowing how capsizes occur can help prevent them. Common causes of capsizing to windward include (1) not adjusting to a sudden lull or heading shift in the wind, and (2) letting go of the mainsheet and/or tiller when hiked out. Common causes of capsizing to leeward include (1) not adjusting to a gust of wind, and (2) bearing away too rapidly. If the boat heels to the point that the boom end is dragging in the water, it is likely to capsize.

L. LANDING

1. At Beach

The objective in landing at a beach is to stop the boat in waist deep water directly opposite the point where the boat will be pulled up on the beach. ***Do not*** run the boat up on the beach. This could cause boat or equipment damage and at the very least will cause unnecessary wear on the boat. As in launching, there may be obstacles (e.g. other boats, swim areas, shallow areas, etc.) that the sailor must avoid in landing. The captain should have a plan to avoid obstacles and stop the boat in the desired location *before* the approach to the beach. The plan should be communicated to the crew.

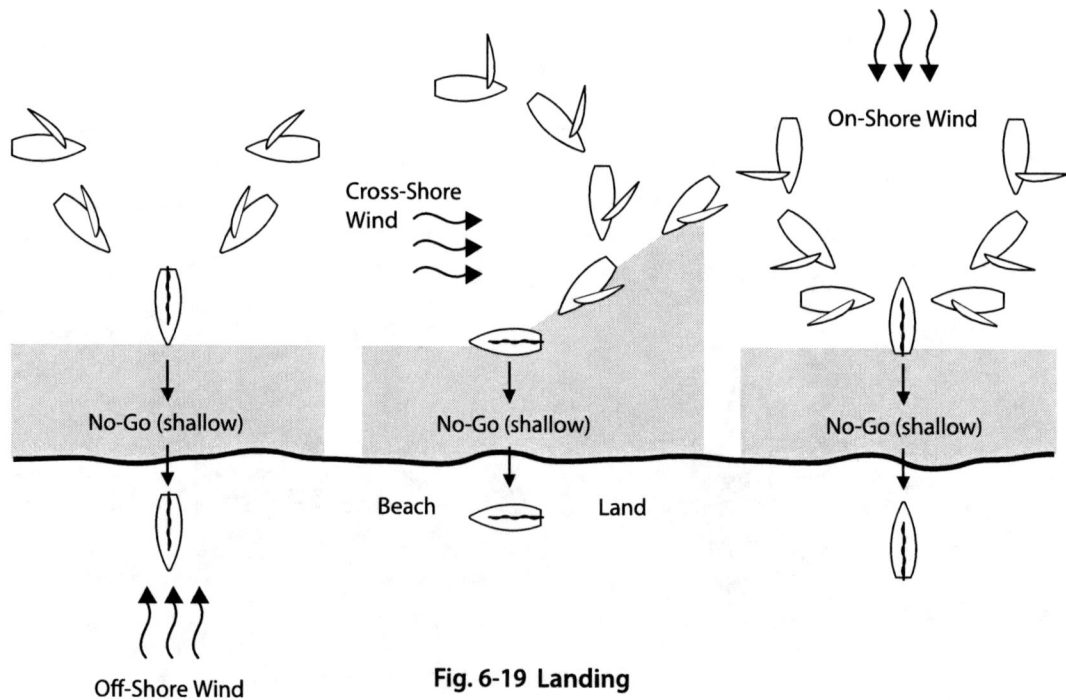

Fig. 6-19 Landing

Sailing Techniques

The approach toward the beach will depend on the boat's current location, wind direction, obstacles, and the desired stopping point. The wind may be coming from off-shore, cross-shore, or on-shore. In each case there will be directions and places the boat can sail (Go zones) and others it cannot or should not sail (No-Go zones).

When stopping, the captain will turn the boat into the wind (put it in irons) at the desired location. This is most easily accomplished if the boat is on a close reach before it is turned into the wind. Therefore, the captain should maneuver the boat onto a close reach before the final turn. Also, it is advisable to let out the mainsheet somewhat on the approach in order to slow the boat and increase control.

Steps to be followed by captain and linesman when landing a boat:

- Captain plans approach and communicates plan to crew.
- Captain releases the rudder line well before turning into irons (e.g. Laser). This allows the rudder to pop up should it hit the bottom. The Sunfish does not have a rudder line but does have a pop up rudder. Boats that do not have a pop up rudder must stop in water that is deep enough to prevent the rudder from hitting bottom.
- Captain moves the boat toward or onto a close reach.
- Linesman releases the mainsheet somewhat to slow the boat for more control.
- Linesman pulls daggerboard part way up *(keep top below boom)* so that it will not hit bottom as the boat approaches shore, turns into irons, and stops. See Fig. 6-20.
- Captain gives command "Prepare to Stop" and then the command "Hard-a-Lee" as the tiller is pushed to leeward turning the boat into irons. The captain straightens the tiller as the boat turns into the wind. If the tiller is kept out, the boat will come about!
- Linesman removes daggerboard and places it in the cockpit (not on deck)
- Both captain and linesman step out on what was the upwind side of the boat, i.e. the side opposite the sail. This is much easier and safer than attempting to duck under the boom.
- Both sailors control the boat and keep it pointed into the wind as the linesman moves to the bow and the captain moves to the stern.
- Captain removes rudder and places it in cockpit.
- Keeping the boat pointed into the wind, the boat is moved onto the beach. If the rudder has not been removed and there is a cross-shore or on-shore wind, it is important to lift the rudder as the boat is moved onto land. This will prevent rudder damage and problems moving the boat should the rudder hit the ground.
- The boat should now be on the beach, pointed into the wind.

See Fig. 6-20, if the daggerboard is down too far, it will hit the bottom. This could result in daggerboard and/or daggerboard trunk damage. If the daggerboard and/or daggerboard trunk is damaged, the daggerboard will not fit snugly in the daggerboard trunk. A loose daggerboard will not stay in position. Also, it will tend to fall out if the boat is capsized and turtles. If the daggerboard will not stay up due to previous damage, then the linesman will have to hold it in the up position until the boat is stopped. When sailing solo, the sailor will have to remove the daggerboard while turning into irons or put the boat into irons in deeper water and then remove the daggerboard.

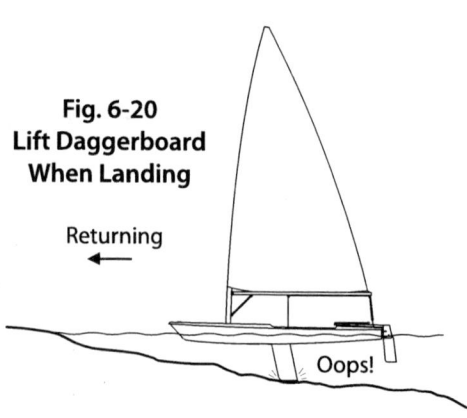

**Fig. 6-20
Lift Daggerboard
When Landing**

Alternative landing method: Follow the steps outlined above, approach slowly, and point the boat as much into the wind as possible. However, instead of the captain putting the boat in irons, the mainsheet is released before the desired stopping point, the sail luffs, and the boat glides to a stop. Step out of the boat *and turn the bow into the wind*. The bow to wind position is necessary for boat control. The daggerboard and rudder are now removed and placed in the cockpit and the boat is moved onto shore.

This procedure can work well in an off-shore or cross-shore breeze. When landing in an on-shore breeze an additional step is needed. The figure 8 stopper knot is removed from the end of the mainsheet as the boat approaches shore. Just before reaching the predetermined stopping point, the mainsheet is allowed to run through the mainsheet block. This will depower the sail and allow it to move out in front of the boat. Again, step out of the boat and *turn the bow into the wind* and then move it onto shore.

Landing Solo: The procedures and sequence of events are the same for landing solo as when landing with captain and linesman. Of course, the solo sailor must handle all boat and equipment adjustments. On the Laser, the solo sailor holds the mainsheet and tiller extension (i.e. hiking stick) in the forward hand while releasing the rudder line from the jam cleat on the tiller. An alternate method is to hold the tiller behind the knee of the back leg while releasing the rudder line. When approaching shore, the mainsheet is held by the rear hand against the tiller extension as the sailor reaches forward to lift the daggerboard with the forward hand. After the daggerboard is raised, the forward hand again grasps the mainsheet and the rear hand remains on the tiller extension. The sailor is now ready to turn the boat into irons or use the alternative landing procedure described above.

Sailing Techniques

Summary

1. Release the rudder line when still well out in the water (Laser).
2. Raise the daggerboard part way well before reaching the stopping point.
3. Turn the boat into irons in waist deep water.
4. Get out on the side of the boat opposite the sail and be sure the bow is pointed into the wind.
5. Remove the daggerboard and rudder and place them in the cockpit.
6. Keep the boat pointed into the wind while moving it up onto shore.

2. *At Dock*

The guidelines and procedures in approaching a dock are similar to those involved in approaching and landing at a beach. One advantage in landing at a dock is that the sailor does not have to be concerned with the daggerboard or rudder hitting bottom. Therefore, both can be left in the down position. Also, the sailor need not get wet! On the other hand, the sailor does need to be concerned about where to land at the dock and the possibility of running into the dock (and perhaps hitting other boats that are nearby).

Set up the approach and plan to land in a specific position on the leeward side of the dock. Landing on the leeward side will prevent the wind and waves from banging the boat against the dock. Also, the boom and sail will be blown away from the dock instead of across it. This position will make it easy to step off the boat and secure it to the dock. Some possible docking positions are illustrated in Fig. 6-21.

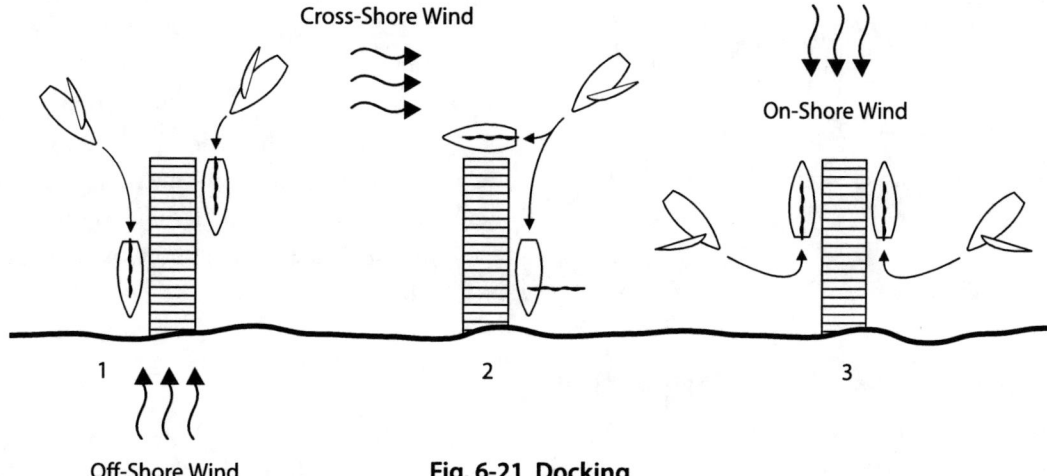

Fig. 6-21 Docking

(1) from a close reach, the boat is put in irons at the dock; (2) from a close reach, the boat is put in irons at the end of the dock or steered to the leeward side of the dock as the mainsheet is released to luff the sail and stop the boat, and (3) from a broad reach, the boat is quickly turned onto a beam reach, a close reach and then is put into irons as it is steered to a position along side the dock. (Alternate 3) approach dock on a broad reach or run, remove figure 8 from end of mainsheet, allow mainsheet to run out and sail to move in front of boat to depower sail and stop boat next to dock.

The sailor uses the tiller to control direction while controlling speed and momentum with the mainsheet (sail). The sailor must learn to judge the momentum of the boat in order to bring it up softly against the dock. "Fenders" or "bumpers" may be used to protect the boat from chafing against the dock.

In stepping out of the boat onto the dock, remember Newton's Law which states that for every action there is an equal and opposite reaction. If you push off the boat in a direction away from the dock, the boat will move in that direction—you could end up in the water! Also, if you step on the gunwale, the boat will roll in the direction of that force—with perhaps the same unwanted result! Take control of the painter (or mooring line) and, from a position along the centerline of the boat, carefully step onto the dock with balance. A boat hook or extension (e.g. paddle) can be used to help with balance. Secure the boat to the dock and then begin the derigging procedure.

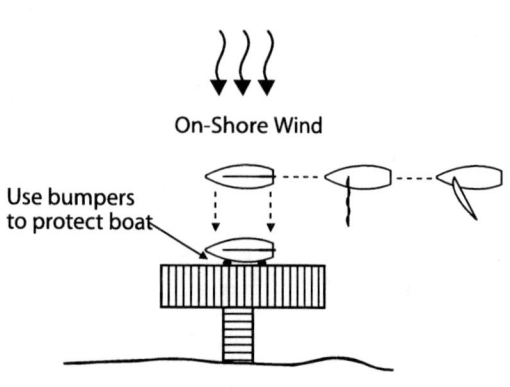

Fig. 6-22 Docking in On-Shore Wind

Even though it is not recommended, there may be times when it is necessary to land on the upwind side of a dock. One procedure is to approach on a beam reach and stop the boat in a position parallel to and some distance from the dock by allowing the sail to luff. The sail is then lowered. If sailing a Laser with the sailsock over the mast, the outhaul is released and the boom placed and secured along the center of the boat. In both cases the wind pushing against the side of the boat will move it into the dock. It is recommended that bumpers be used to protect the boat as the wind pushes it against the dock.

M. CLOSE REACH AND BROAD REACH

Once comfortable sailing on a beam reach, the beginning sailor should next practice sailing alternately on a close reach and a broad reach (figure 8 pattern). Come about when changing from one reach to the other. Know the direction the wind is coming from and

Sailing Techniques

identify a landmark to be used as a reference when changing direction and then steering on the new course. When first learning, turn slowly and be aware of the different points of sail.

Examine Fig. 6-23. Start with the boat that is sailing on a close reach port tack. It is using the dock as a landmark. As it approaches the dock, it comes about and is then sailing on a close reach starboard tack. The boom is just off the back corner of the boat at an angle of approximately 30° to the long axis of the boat. Next, the captain slowly pulls the tiller to cause the boat to fall-off the wind and move from a close reach to a beam reach. As the boat goes onto the beam reach, the tiller is straightened and the mainsheet is eased out causing the boom to move to a position where it is at an angle of about 45° to the long axis of the boat. The captain then slowly pulls the tiller again, causing the boat to fall-off the wind further and move from a beam reach to a broad reach. As the boat goes onto the broad reach, the captain straightens the tiller and again eases the mainsheet so that the boom moves out to a position

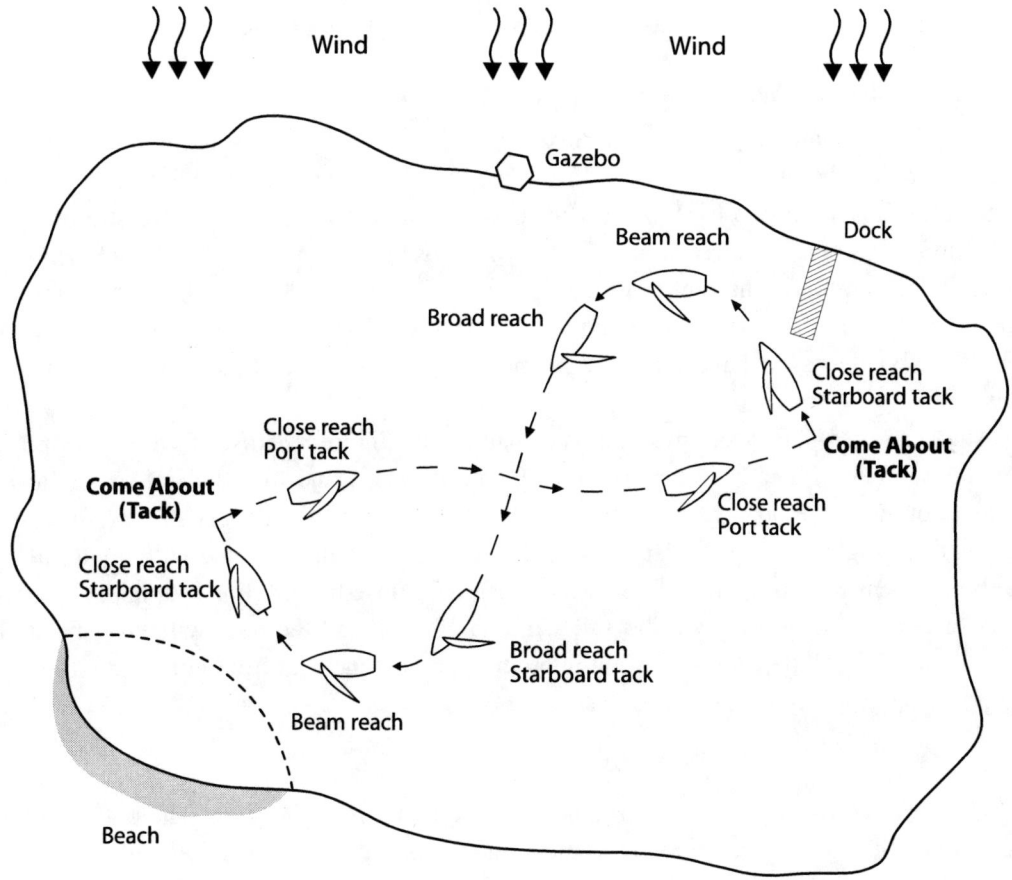

Fig. 6-23 Figure 8 Practice

where it is at an angle of about 60° to the long axis of the boat. The boat is then sailed toward another landmark—the beach.

As the boat approaches the beach, it is turned toward the wind. First the captain slowly pushes the tiller to move the boat from a broad reach to a beam reach. As the boat goes onto the beam reach, the captain straightens the tiller and pulls in the mainsheet so the boom moves in to a position where it is at an angle of about 45° to the long axis of the boat. Next, the captain slowly pushes the tiller again to turn the boat from a beam reach to a close reach. As the boat goes onto the close reach, the captain straightens the tiller and pulls in the mainsheet so the boom moves to a position close to the stern where it is at an angle of approximately 30° to the long axis of the boat. The boat then comes about again, changing from a close reach starboard tack to a close reach port tack and heads back toward the dock.

Whenever you change course—readjust the sail
1. Ease the mainsheet till the sail starts to luff
2. Harden the mainsheet till the luff is gone
3. The sail is now trimmed correctly for the course heading

The boat will move in a figure 8 pattern as it goes from a close reach to a broad reach on the opposite tack, sails for a time, and then comes about again to move from a broad reach to a close reach on the original tack. As skill improves, the sailor will be able to move directly from a close reach on one tack to a broad reach on the opposite tack. It is also possible to move directly from a broad reach on one tack to a close reach on the opposite tack. However, the beginner may find it helpful to go from a broad reach to a close reach on the same tack, make sure the boat has sufficient speed and momentum, and then come about onto the new tack. If the boat does not have sufficient momentum when coming about, it will get caught in irons.

Another way to adjust sail position when sailing the Figure 8 course toward the windward (upwind) landmark, is to head the boat up 45° into the wind and trim the sail so it is just off the rear corner of the boat. Next, push the tiller slowly until the sail just starts to luff. Now, pull the tiller slightly until the luffing stops. The boat is now close-hauled with good sail trim. The boat is sensitive to small shifts in wind when it is close-hauled. For example, if the wind shifts further ahead of the boat, the sail will start to luff and the boat will lose speed. The captain must fall-off the wind somewhat in order to prevent the boat from going into irons.

N. RUN

The boat is on a run when the wind is coming directly over the stern. The optimum boom and sail position is out at a 90° angle to the long axis of the boat. The sail could be out on either the port or starboard side of the boat. The run is the most unstable point of sail. This is because the centerboard does not provide lateral resistance to the wind when sailing directly downwind. For example, the boat will be much more susceptible to rolling. Body weight

Sailing Techniques

should be kept low in the cockpit and used to balance the boat. Control the rudder using a palm down grip on the tiller extension and face forward while balancing the boat. The boat should be kept balanced fore-aft as well as side-to-side. A heavy wind will tend to push the bow down when on a run; therefore, body weight will need to be kept aft to balance the boat.

The beginning sailor may lose track of wind direction and not trim the sail properly. The following figure presents one example of this situation and how it could lead to capsizing. The boat in the figure is on a run; however, the captain has the sail trimmed as though it is on a close reach (out 30° from the long axis of the boat). The boat will sail (though very inefficiently) in this position. However, if the wind shifts as little as 45° (not unusual), the sail will be pushed to the opposite side of the boat. That is the side that the sailor(s) is sitting on! The unexpected swing of the sail from one tack (e.g. starboard) to the opposite tack (i.e. port), as the boat is moving downwind, is called an accidental or "Slam" jibe. This is an example where improper trim of the sail could result in the boom hitting the crew and/or capsizing the boat.

The beginner need not be concerned with optimizing speed; however, this is important for the racer. One way of increasing speed on a run is to raise the centerboard. Since it is not needed for lateral resistance, it can be raised to affect a small decrease in water resistance to forward movement of the boat. See "Daggerboard Adjustments" in the next chapter on intermediate sailing skills.

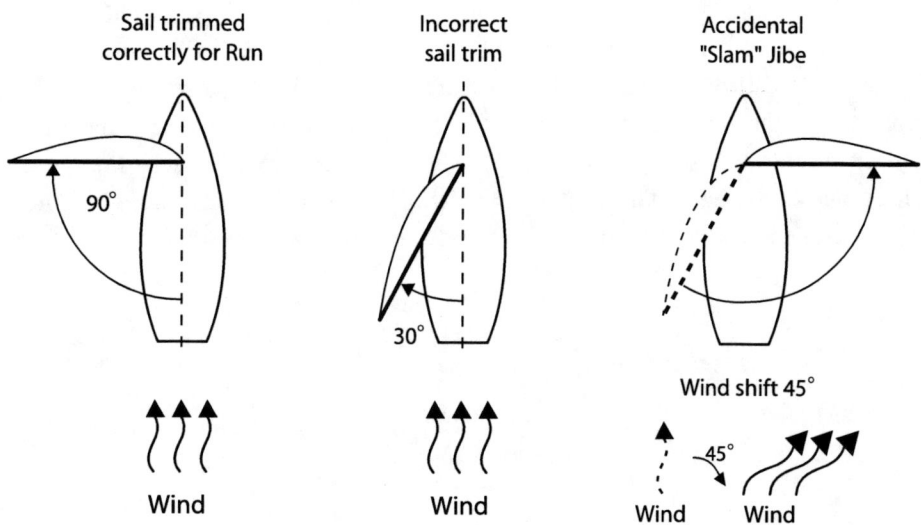

Fig. 6-24 Incorrect Sail Trim Can Result in an Accidental or "Slam" Jibe

O. JIBING

There are two ways of changing tack and crossing the wind, coming about and jibing. Coming about is changing tacks when sailing upwind (bow crosses wind). **Jibing** is changing tacks when sailing downwind. Jibing is accomplished by bringing the sail in on one side and letting it out on the other. One of the problems in jibing is that the wind is always coming from behind the boat. That means that the wind is exerting force on the sail throughout the maneuver. Jibing can be dangerous and should not be attempted by beginners in heavy wind.

To become proficient at jibing requires a thorough understanding of procedures as well as practice under various wind conditions. Jibing is one of the more difficult skills in sailing. It requires knowledge of correct technique, a sense of wind direction, and good coordination. More problems arise when jibing than at any other time sailing. Jibing (tacking downwind) can be performed: (1) while on a run or (2) from a broad reach.

1. Jibing While on a Run

In light wind, the easiest and safest way to jibe is from a run. First, point the bow downward (i.e. wind is dead astern). If you have wind indicators (e.g. pennant, or masthead fly) check them—they should be streaming in front of the boat. The captain gives the command "**Ready to Jibe**" or "**Stand by to Jibe.**" Both captain and crew immediately get ready to jibe. After a brief pause (to be sure the linesman is ready), the captain gives the command "**Jibe Ho**." The linesman takes in the mainsheet in a hand over hand fashion while balancing the boat and preparing to duck under the boom and shift weight to the opposite side. The linesman pulls the boom across the centerline and the sail fills on the opposite side as body weight is shifted to the other side of the boat. As the sail fills on the new tack, the linesman lets out the mainsheet rapidly but with control. It is important that the linesman keep tension on the mainsheet throughout the jibing procedure so it does not get caught on the back corner of the boat. The captain switches hands on the tiller behind his/her back as the boom crosses and also uses body weight to balance the boat.

Sailing Techniques

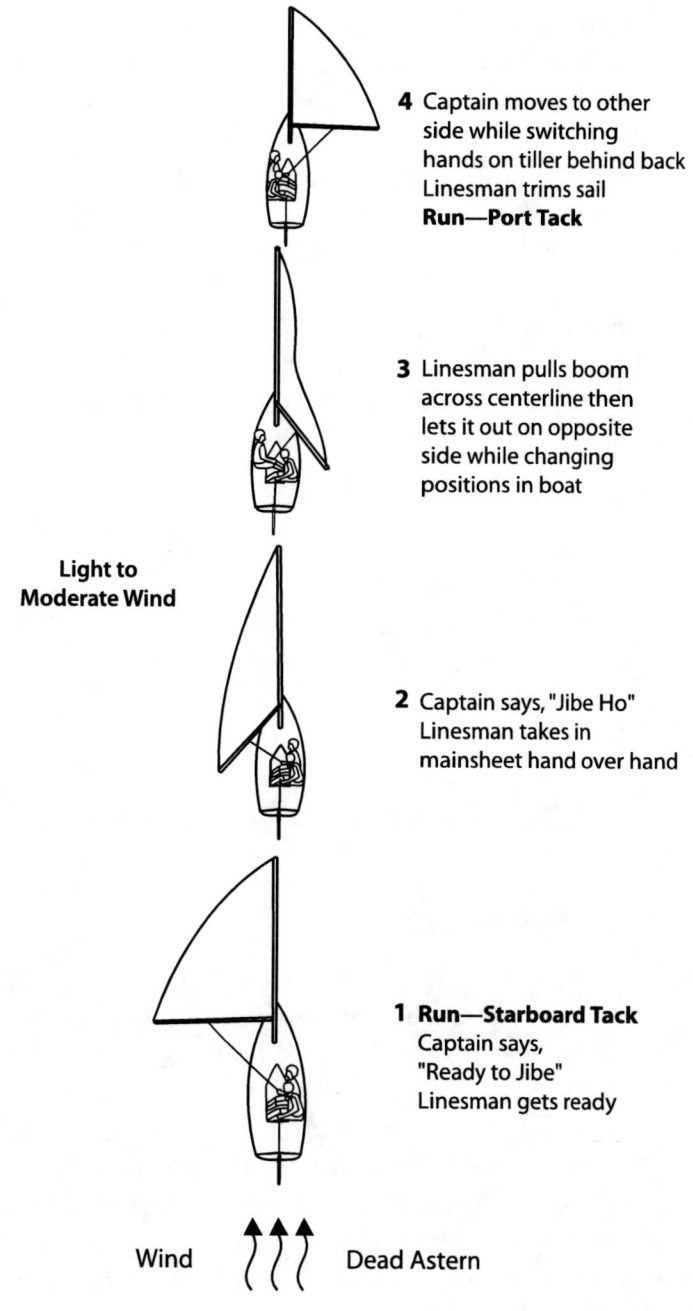

Fig. 6-25 Jibing from Run

Solo: The basic procedures for jibing solo are the same as those for jibing with captain and crew. Of course, the solo sailor must control both the mainsheet *and* tiller at the same time **(do not let go of either)**! While in a balanced position, bring in the mainsheet and hold it with the hand that is on the tiller; then reach forward and sheet in again, repeat until the boom and sail approach the boat. Next, reach forward and grab the mainsheet as far toward the mainsheet block as possible and give it a quick pull (say to yourself "Jibe Ho"). Duck your head as you pull the boom and sail across to the opposite side of the boat. Immediately, grasp the tiller behind your back with the hand that pulled the mainsheet and hold the mainsheet on the tiller. Now release the opposite hand and use it to reach forward and grasp the mainsheet as you shift your body weight to balance the boat. You can now release the mainsheet from the tiller hand. You have changed hands on the tiller behind your back. Allow the mainsheet to pay out under control and center the tiller.

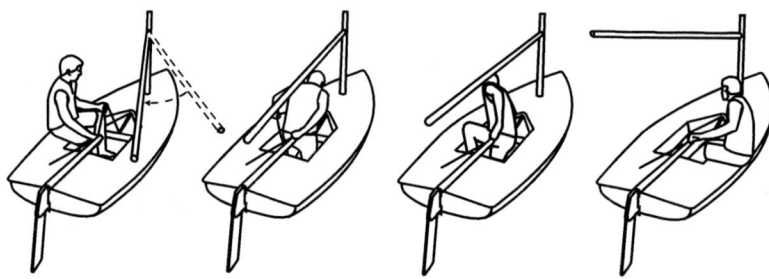

Fig. 6-26 Tiller/Mainsheet Control—Jibing

2. *Jibing From a Broad Reach*

In moderate to heavy winds, it is recommended that the jibe be performed from a broad reach on one tack (e.g. starboard) to a broad reach on the opposite tack (i.e. port). If available, the captain identifies a landmark that will be used for the new course heading following the jibe. The captain gives the command "**Ready to Jibe.**" The linesman brings in the sail about half way. After a brief pause, the captain gives the command "**Jibe Ho**" as he/she *pulls* the tiller to change tack. The linesman takes in then lets out the mainsheet, while shifting weight to the opposite side of the boat. As the boom crosses the centerline, the captain changes hands on the tiller behind the back, centers the tiller, and moves to the new upwind side of the boat. The key to a smooth and controlled jibe is to have the boom along the centerline of the boat exactly when the stern is in the wind's eye. The captain and crew need to stay low and keep their heads below the boom. As the sail fills on the new tack, the linesman lets out the mainsheet with control. Note: The stern has crossed the wind; see Fig. 6-27. It is important that the linesman keep tension on the mainsheet throughout the jibing procedure. If the mainsheet is slack as the boom swings across, it could get caught on the rear corner of the boat and lead to capsizing. Following the jibe, the captain adjusts the tiller and boat to the desired heading.

Sailing Techniques

5 Linesman trims sail for **Broad Reach—Port Tack**
Captain steers boat on new course.

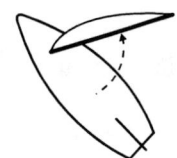

4 Linesman moves to opposite side of boat while letting mainsheet pay out under control
Captain changes hands on tiller behind back and moves to the opposite side of the boat

3 Boom should be along centerline as stern crosses wind
Both Captain and Linesman balance boat as they duck under boom

2 Captain says, "Jibe Ho" and **pulls** tiller to windward
Linesman takes in mainsheet hand over hand

1 **Broad Reach—Starboard Tack**
Captain says, "Ready to Jibe"
Linesman brings in boom about half way

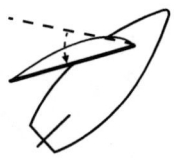

Wind

Fig. 6-27 Jibing from a Broad Reach

Go to www.ussailing.org Getting Started—Online Education—Small Boat Course—Turning the Boat—Jibing, to see a video on how to Jibe.

Solo: From a broad reach begin by pulling the sail in half way. Next, slowly pull the tiller toward the upwind gunwale and move toward the center of the cockpit. This will cause the boat to turn downwind. Take in the mainsheet as the boat turns. As the wind comes dead astern—say to yourself "Jibe Ho" and pull the boom across the boat. Turn forward and duck as the boom moves across and change position to the opposite side of the boat. As the stern crosses the wind, change hands on the tiller behind the back and grasp the mainsheet with the opposite hand. Pay out the mainsheet with control while quickly adjusting the rudder to the new point of sail.

Common Errors in Jibing—Could Result in Boom Swinging Violently across the Boat and/or a Capsize.

- Jibing in a gust. Wait for steady wind.
- Not pulling in the mainsheet and keeping tension on it throughout the jibe. If it is slack, it can get caught on the corner of the boat during the jibe.
- Not centering the tiller as soon as the boom crosses the centerline of the boat. The boat will continue to turn and may capsize downwind.
- Not easing the mainsheet smoothly after the boom has swung over.
- Failing to balance the boat as the boom swings over to the opposite side.

One way of avoiding problems is to prevent them from happening. For example, sailing by the lee is not recommended because it can lead to an accidental jibe. An accidental (or unintentional) jibe is dangerous because the boom swings unexpectedly across the boat and can hit the sailor(s) and/or capsize the boat.

Sailing by the lee is when a boat is sailing with the sail on the wrong side of the boat. What makes this dangerous is that a change in wind direction (or sail adjustment) could result in the wind unexpectedly shifting from one side of the sail to the other causing the boom to swing forcefully across the boat—an accidental or **"Slam" jibe**.

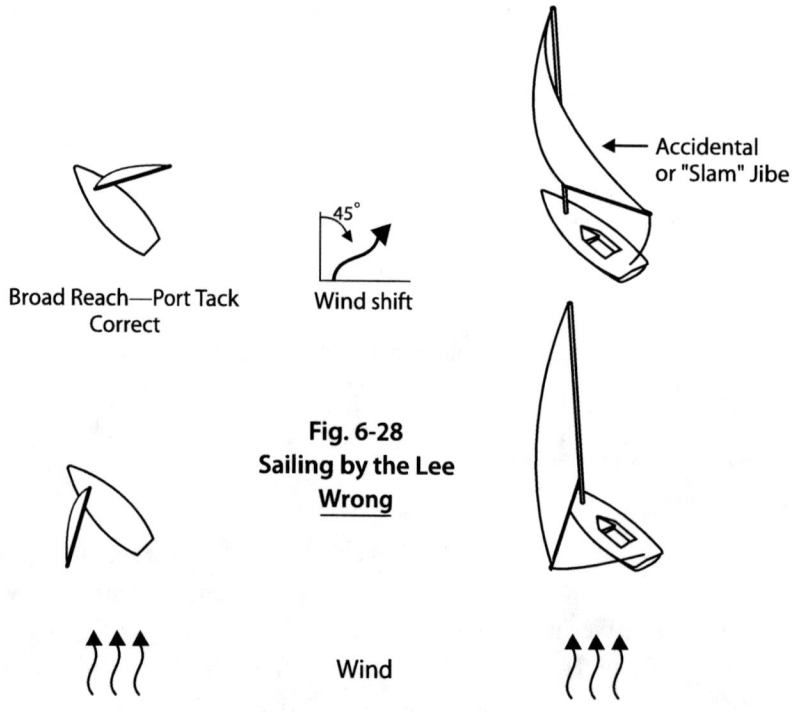

**Fig. 6-28
Sailing by the Lee
Wrong**

Sailing Techniques 103

P. Practice

The old adage "practice makes perfect" applies to sailing. A good way to practice all points of sail is to sail around two markers (e.g. buoys) that are arranged for an upwind-downwind course or three markers that are set out in a triangle course that has one leg upwind.

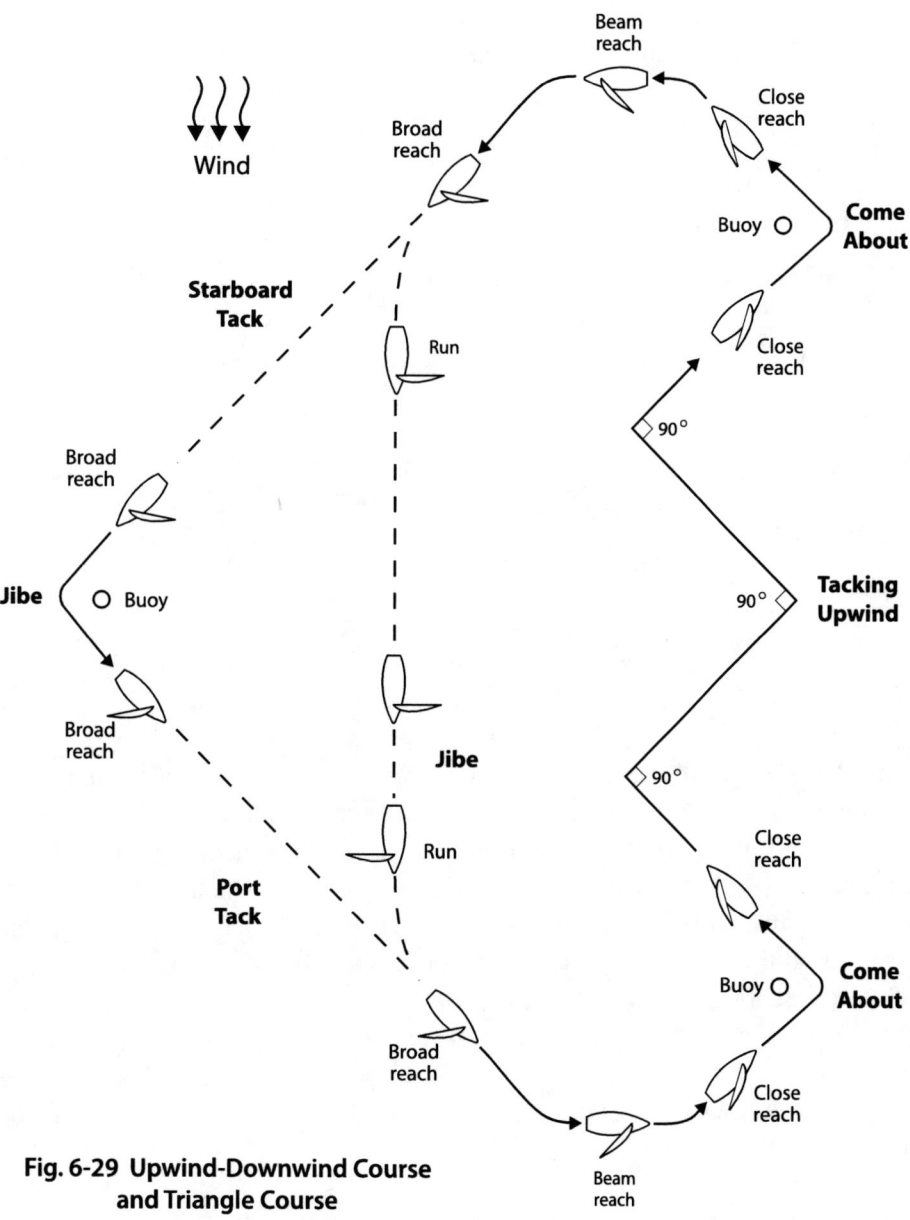

Fig. 6-29 Upwind-Downwind Course and Triangle Course

Upwind-Downwind Course—concentrate on each point of sail while sailing the course. When tacking upwind, make clean 90° turns. When turning around the windward (upwind) marker (e.g. buoy), do it in stages to emphasize boat position and sail trim for first the close reach, then the beam reach, then the broad reach, and finally the run. Do a controlled jibe when running downwind and round the downwind marker (e.g. buoy) in stages. First, move from a run to a broad reach, then to a beam reach, and then to a close reach. Trim the sail to its "ideal" position with each change in course. This is accomplished by slowly letting out the mainsheet until the sail starts to luff and then pulling it in enough to stop the luffing. This procedure will place the sail in its optimum position for the course being sailed.

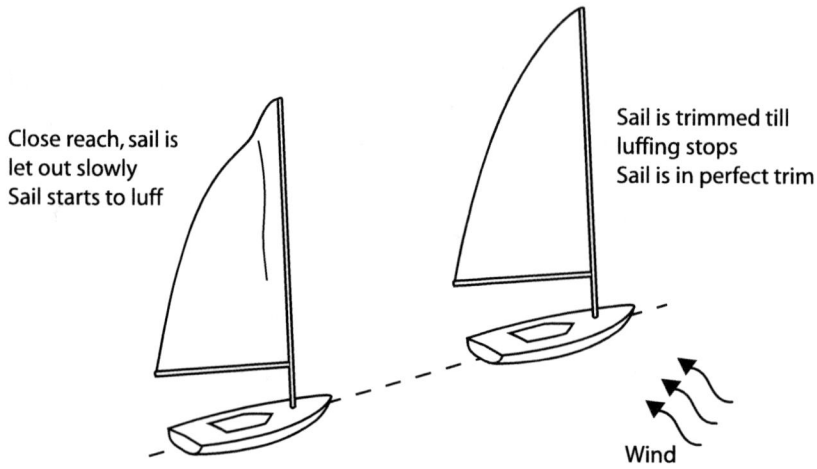

Fig. 6-30 Adjusting Sail

Triangle Course—after tacking to the windward marker (e.g. buoy), round it by moving the boat from a close reach to a beam reach and then to a broad reach heading toward the next marker (e.g. buoy) of the triangle. Perform a jibe around this marker, moving from a broad reach on one tack (e.g. starboard) to a broad reach on the opposite tack (e.g. port). Continue to the downwind marker (e.g. buoy) of the triangle and round it moving from a broad reach to a beam reach and then to a close reach. Now perform one or more tacks to get to and around the windward marker.

If there are heavy winds and the sailor feels uncomfortable jibing when on a run or broad reach, he/she can turn the boat back upwind and come about to change tack—see Fig. 6-31, "In Heavy Wind Come-About Instead of Jibing" on the next page. The rest of the course would be sailed in the same way.

Sailing Techniques

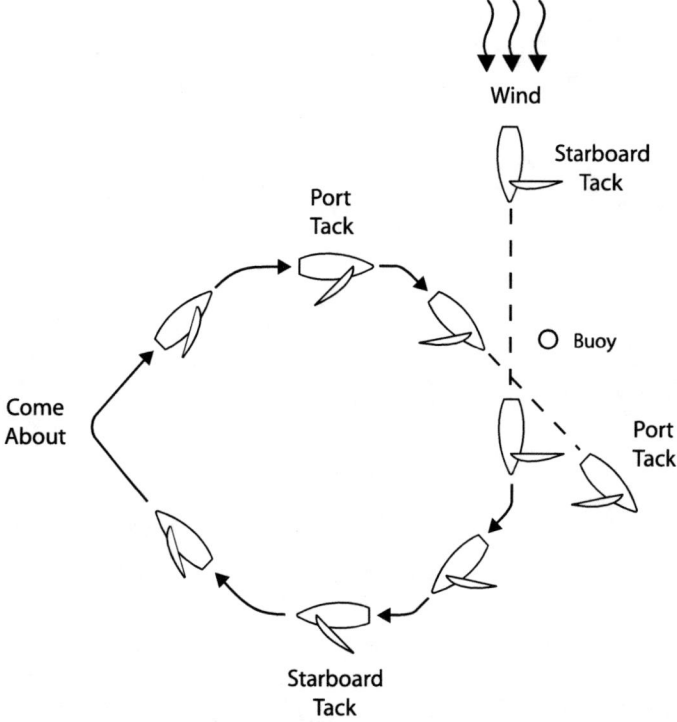

Fig. 6-31 In Heavy Wind Come-About Instead of Jibing

When the sailor knows how to sail around a triangle course (clockwise and counter-clockwise) and can do it in a reasonable amount of time—he/she is no longer a beginner! Of course the time to sail the triangle will depend on its size and the speed of the wind. The individual now "knows how to sail" and is ready to move on to intermediate sailing skills.

Q. EXERCISES AND REVIEW QUESTIONS

Complete Exercises and Review Questions for Chapter 6 in Appendix C *before* proceeding to Chapter 7.

Chapter 7
Intermediate Sailing Skills

A. INTRODUCTION

This chapter is for the individual who wants to develop sailing skills beyond the beginning level. It presents information on sailing techniques that can be used to improve skills and equipment adjustments that can be used to fine tune the sailing rig. The objective is to sail more efficiently. As the sailor refines skills, he/she will feel greater control and therefore be more comfortable in the boat. At the same time, it is a truism that greater knowledge and ability results in greater enjoyment of the sailing experience.

B. SAILING EFFICIENTLY

1. Telltales

As described earlier, telltales are small lengths (4-6 inches long) of wool, nylon, or other lightweight material that are attached to the sail or standing rigging to indicate wind direction. Telltales attached to a sail indicate the flow of air across the sail and are used as a reference to correct sail trim. Telltales can be placed on the upper third, middle, and lower third of the sail about one-third the distance between luff and leach. It is helpful to place the telltales on the starboard side of the sail about one to two inches above the corresponding telltales that are on the port side of the sail. This will help distinguish the windward and leeward telltales when the sun is behind the sail.

When the sail is in proper trim, telltales on both sides of the sail will be flowing smoothly aft. Fluttering telltales indicate turbulent air flow. If the sail is sheeted in too tight, turbulent air flow along the leeward side of the sail will cause the telltales on the leeward side of the sail to flutter. If the sail is sheeted out too far, turbulent air flow along the windward side of the sail will cause the telltales on the windward side of the sail to flutter. In both cases the sail needs to be adjusted for optimum air flow and power. See Fig. 7-1.

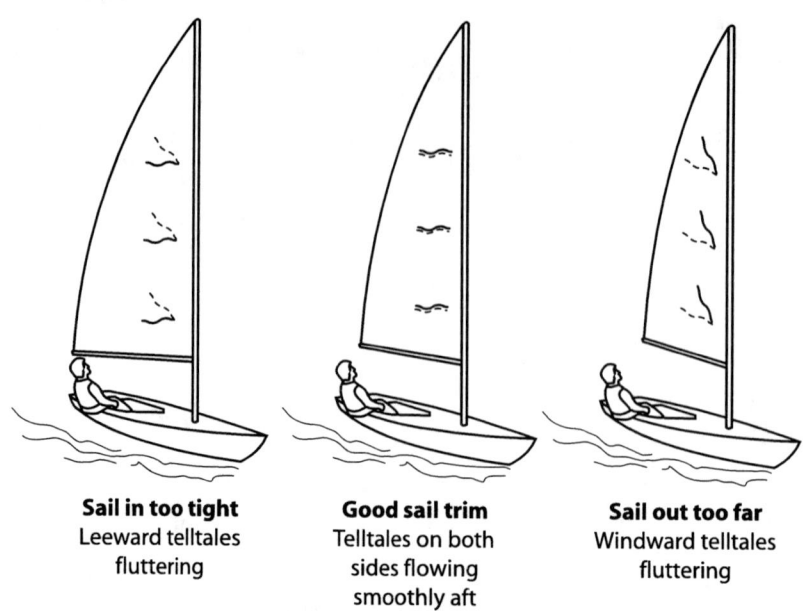

Sail in too tight
Leeward telltales fluttering

Good sail trim
Telltales on both sides flowing smoothly aft

Sail out too far
Windward telltales fluttering

Fig. 7-1 Using Telltales

2. *Sailing Upwind*

"Sailing on the Wind" refers to sailing to windward or upwind. A boat can sail up to 45° into the wind to reach an objective without changing course. However, if the objective (e.g. buoy, beach, dock, etc.) is more than 45° into the wind the boat will have to tack at least once to reach the desired point. If the objective is directly upwind and some distance away, the sailor will need to perform a series of tacks along a zigzag course in order to reach the destination. To do this efficiently, the boat is sailed close-hauled first on one tack (e.g. starboard) and then the other (e.g. port). Sailing **close-hauled** is sailing as close as possible to the wind without the sail luffing. The sail is hauled in close to or just over the rear corner of the boat. Sailing as close to the wind as possible on one tack and then the other to make progress upwind is called **beating**.

The boat is steered along a relatively narrow lane as it makes progress to windward. When starboard and port telltales are flowing smoothly aft the boat is sailing efficiently in the lane and the boat is said to be "In the Groove." If the boat is steered too high in the lane the windward telltales will start to flutter or stall and the boat will lose speed. If the boat is steered too low in the lane the leeward telltales will start to flutter or stall and the boat will pick up speed but will not be making good progress upwind.

Intermediate Sailing Skills

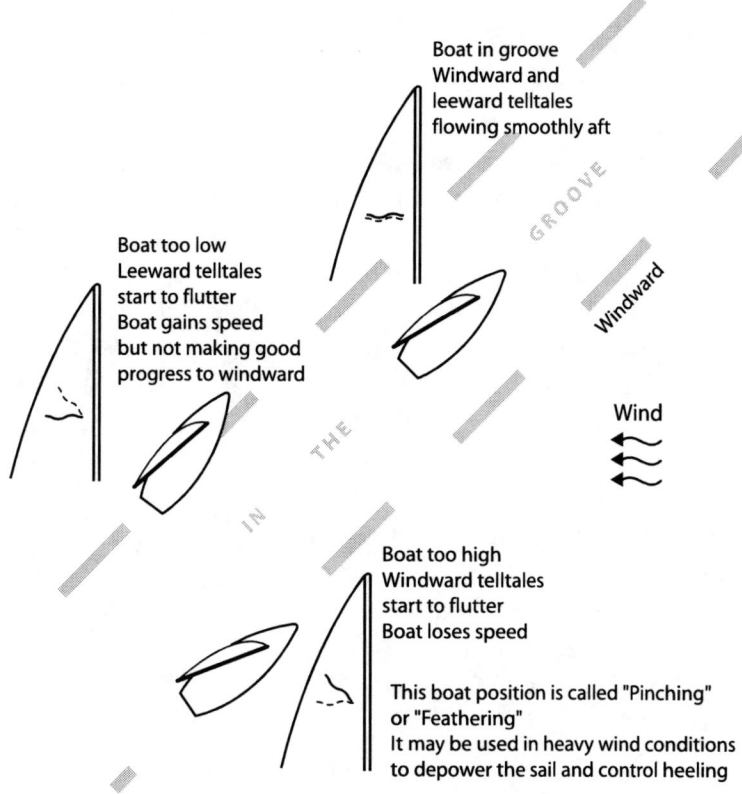

Fig. 7-2 Sailing Efficiently Upwind

3. Pinching

When sailing upwind under high wind conditions or when a puff hits, it may be difficult to maintain the boat in a level position—"on an even keel." The sailor can and should hike out to counter the force of the wind. The mainsheet can also be eased to spill some wind and reduce heeling, however, there will be less progress upwind. Another technique that can be used is pinching. **Pinching** (also called feathering) is sailing on the windward side of the groove when beating. From a close-hauled position the captain steers slightly closer to the wind. This will result in a slight flutter (luff) in the front of the sail. Also, the telltales on the windward side of the sail will flutter or stall. This is as close to the wind as can be sailed without going into irons. The advantage of this technique is that the sailor can keep the boat stable while making good progress upwind under heavy wind conditions.

C. Using Body Weight

1. Boat Balance

The importance of positioning body weight to keep the boat balanced side to side and fore-aft has already been emphasized. The boat will usually sail fastest when on or near a balanced position. However, there are some exceptions. When sailing in light air the sailor should move toward the front and leeward side of the boat. Allow the boat to heel about 5-10 degrees and lift the stern slightly out of the water. This will reduce the wetted surface area of the boat and allow it to move through the water with less resistance. Also, moving body weight closer to the CG (pivot point) of the boat will help it turn faster and prevent stalling (stopping in irons) when coming about.

The skilled sailor can also decrease hull resistance and rudder drag when sailing on a run (or broad reach) by using body weight to heel the boat. When on a run, there is a big lever effect due to the center of effort (CE) being some distance from the center of gravity (CG) of the boat. Fig. 7-4

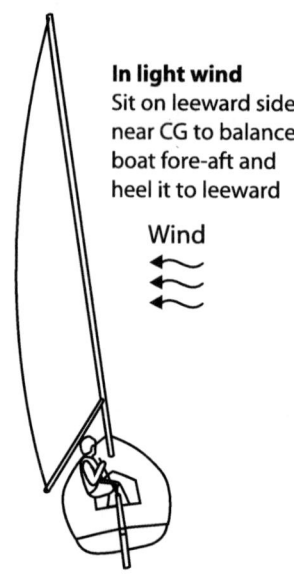

Fig. 7-3 Sailing in Light Wind

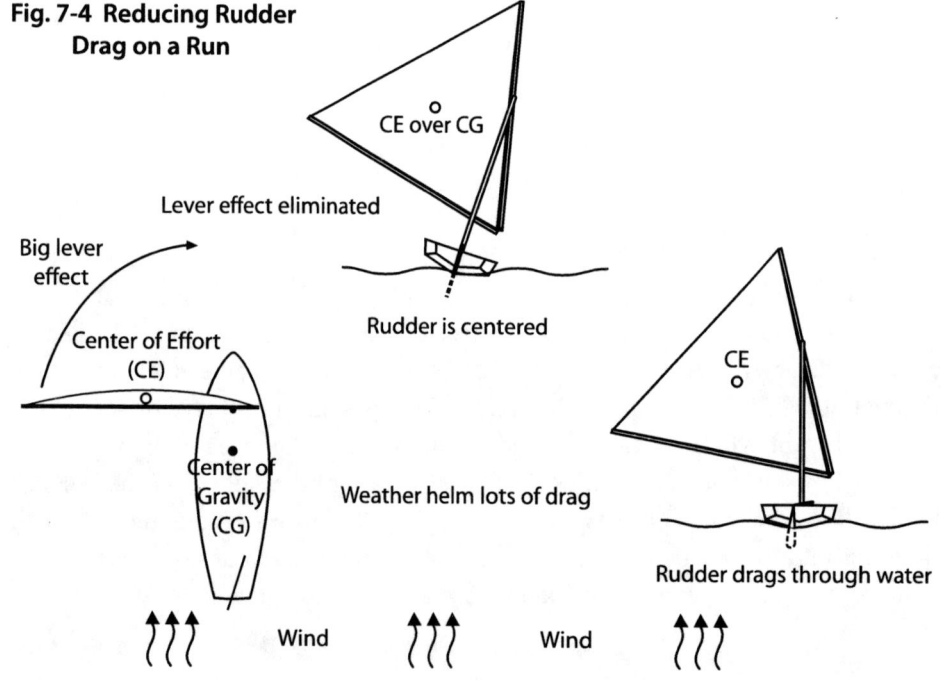

Intermediate Sailing Skills

shows how this results in a weather helm and a good deal of rudder drag. Body weight can be used to heel the boat and bring the center of effort over the center of gravity. As a result, the big lever effect is eliminated and the rudder can be centered reducing rudder drag.

2. *Steering Boat*

Body weight can be used to steer the boat. Practice this technique from a reach when the boat is in a balanced and controlled position. While maintaining tiller (and therefore rudder) position, lean toward the leeward or sail side of the boat. Notice how the boat heels to leeward and turns toward the wind. Return the boat to a balanced and controlled reach and then lean away from the sail. Notice how the boat heels to windward and turns away from the wind. Using body weight to turn the boat toward the wind and away from the wind is a good way to sense how changing body position affects both balance and boat movement. The sailor will gain an appreciation for the importance of body weight in controlling the boat.

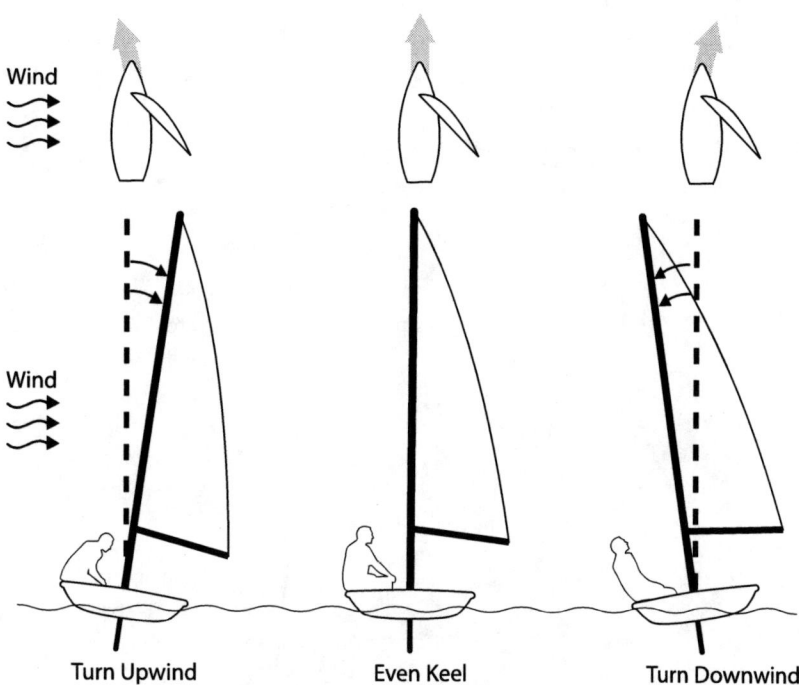

Fig. 7-5 Using Body Weight to Steer Boat

3. *Roll Tack*

The roll tack can be used in light to moderate winds to come about without slowing the boat. Therefore, it is a skill that is often used in racing. The technique creates increased lift during the turn resulting in a smooth fast tack. Begin from a close reach and lean in to heel the boat slightly to leeward while gently pushing the tiller in the same direction. As the boat turns into the wind, slide body weight about a foot aft (to help lift the bow), and hike the boat forcefully to windward "popping" the sail from one tack to the other. Immediately, duck, turn forward and cross the cockpit while changing hands on the tiller behind your back. Upon reaching the opposite side of the boat, place the feet under the hiking strap and quickly hike out to bring the boat flat on the new tack.

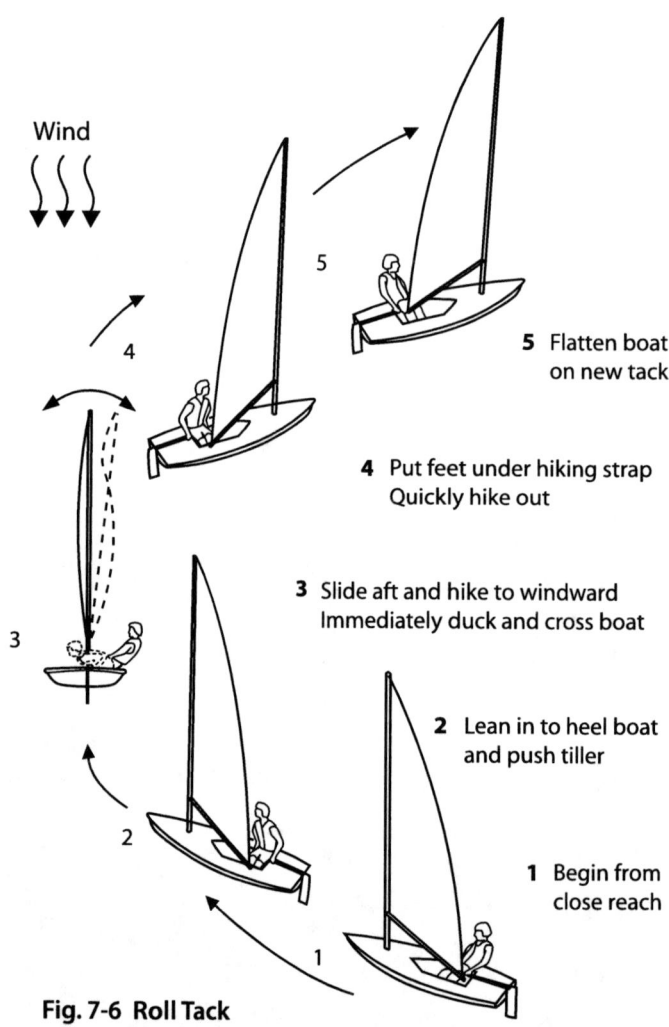

Fig. 7-6 Roll Tack

4. Capsize Step-Over Technique

If ready and agile, a skilled sailor can right a capsized boat without getting wet! As the boat goes on its side, the sailor leans back and puts weight on the windward gunwale with the

Intermediate Sailing Skills

hands, then steps over the gunwale onto the daggerboard. Maintaining balance with hands on the boat, the sailor steps backward on the centerboard to increase leverage. As the boat starts to come up, the sailor climbs back onboard.

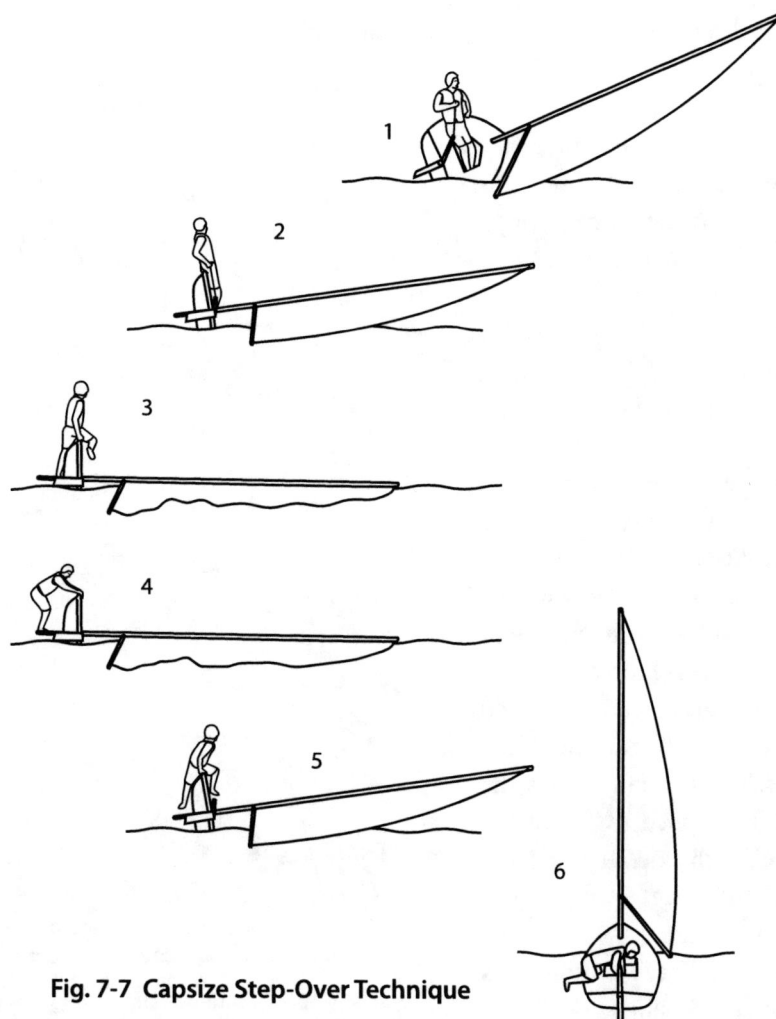

Fig. 7-7 Capsize Step-Over Technique

D. Sail and Daggerboard Adjustments

1. Sail Shape

The modern sail is not flat, it is constructed so that it will have shape or curve when attached to its spars. The depth of this curve is termed draft and is controlled by the lines that hold the sail in place.

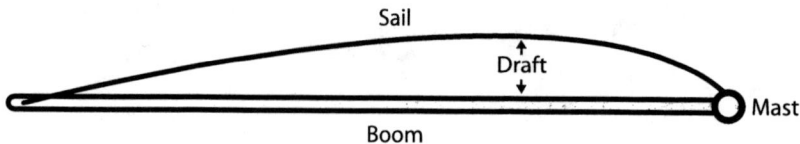

Fig. 7-8 Sail Shape

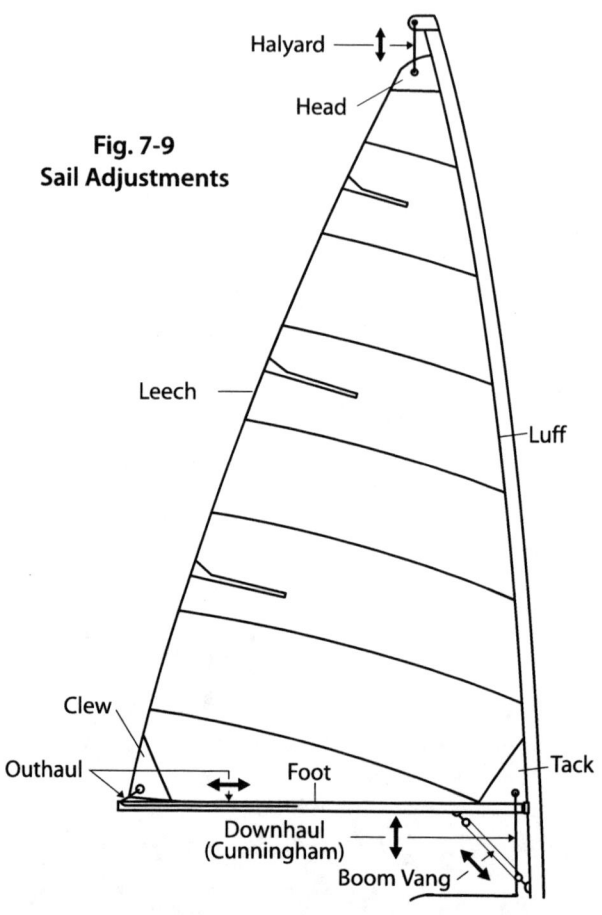

Fig. 7-9 Sail Adjustments

Depending on the sailboat rig, there may be one, two, or three sail adjustment lines for the three corners of a triangular sail. There may also be a device for adjusting the mast bend. The Laser sail attaches to the mast by means of a sailsock and does not have a sail adjustment line at the head of the sail. It does have a downhaul (Cunningham) attached to the tack of the sail to control luff tension and an outhaul attached to the clew of the sail to control foot tension. The Sunfish does not have a sail adjustment line at the tack of the sail but does have outhaul lines at both the clew and head corners of the sail. In addition, the **halyard**, which raises and lowers the upper spar, can be used to adjust the tension in the leech and luff and the shape of the sail. The term halyard originated from the order "Haul up the yards" given when large cotton sails had to be raised on ships. On some boats, all three corners of the sail can be adjusted.

The boom vang (line system which controls tension on the boom) can be used to adjust mast bend and therefore the shape the sail. Increasing tension in the boom vang will pull the boom down. Since the foot of the sail is attached to the boom, this action will result in a decrease in sail draft. The boom vang holds the boom down and resists the wind force tending to twist the sail and lift the boom when sailing downwind.

In general, the lines controlling the shape of the sail should be tightened as wind speed increases. Tightening these lines will decrease the draft (flatten the sail) resulting in less power ("de-powering" the sail) but more boat control. Conversely, if wind speed decreases, easing one or more of these lines will result in a fuller sail for increased power and speed ("powering-up" the sail).

In heavy wind it may be very difficult or dangerous to sail with the sail in its normal position. A technique for decreasing sail area and therefore de-powering the boat is **reefing**. Some boats permit the sail to be lowered and a bottom section of the sail is tied off to the boom. On the Laser, and some other catboats, the sail can be wrapped 1-3 times around the mast when rigging the boat. After stepping the mast and attaching the downhaul, the sail is turned around the mast the desired number of times. If three turns are to be used on the Laser, the upper batten will need to be removed before the sail is attached to the mast. Reefing will significantly decrease sail area.

2. Daggerboard Adjustments

The purpose of the daggerboard is to provide lateral resistance and enable the boat to sail upwind as well as across the wind. When sailing close-hauled, the daggerboard should be all the way down to minimize side slipping. This down position will also enable the boat to sail as high into the wind as possible. When sailing across or downwind, the required lateral resistance for sailing a track is reduced. Therefore, the daggerboard can be raised somewhat to reduce surface friction on the board and make it easier for the boat to pass through waves. It is recommended that the intermediate sailor use a 1/2 up daggerboard position for a beam reach, a 2/3 up position for a broad reach, and a 3/4 up position for a run. This is easy to remember if you match a half-out sail position (45°) on a beam reach with a half-up daggerboard and a two-thirds out sail position (about 60°) on a broad reach with a two-thirds up daggerboard. Check the boat's wake when sailing and lower the daggerboard a few inches if it appears the boat is slipping sideways. The ideal daggerboard position for each point of sail will depend on boat design and wind conditions, however, the above guideline will help the sailor get accustomed to adjusting daggerboard position as point of sail changes. Some authors recommend removing the daggerboard when on a run because it is not needed to steer the boat. However, the loss of stability in a catboat outweighs the reduced friction of leaving the board partially in, therefore, this author recommends leaving the board in at all times. Just be sure the top of the board is kept below the boom!

E. Stopping Alongside Another Boat

There will be times when you will want to come alongside another boat when out on the water. The intermediate level sailor should have the skills to safely perform this maneuver without a collision. Just like landing at a specific point on shore or at a dock, boat control is of the utmost importance.

First, the boat to be approached should be dead in the water and pointed into the wind. The approach to the target boat should be from a downwind position. It can be from a close reach or beam reach. Perform the maneuver slowly and *do not* get your hands or fingers caught between the boats. Use a padded bumper or some other object to prevent the boats from banging together. *Do not* attempt the approach from a broad reach or run (upwind position) because it is much more difficult to stop the boat from these points of sail.

The preferred approach is a close reach from downwind. The objective is to put your boat in irons right next to the target boat. If approaching on a port tack, it is best to stop on the starboard side of the target boat. If approaching on a starboard tack, it is best to stop on the port side of the target boat. This is done in order to minimize the possibility of colliding with the target boat. For example, if approaching on a port tack and attempting to stop on the port side of the target boat, the momentum of the boat will tend to take it into the target boat.

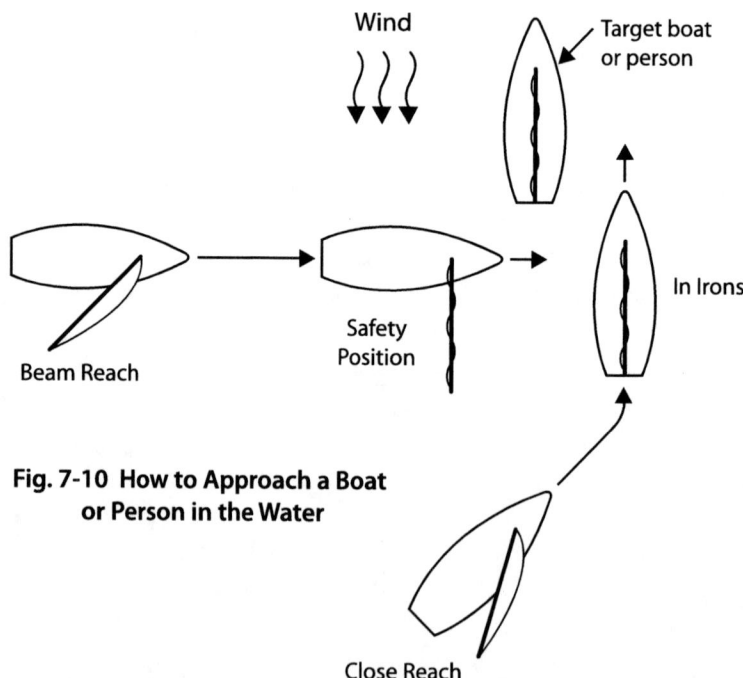

Fig. 7-10 How to Approach a Boat or Person in the Water

Intermediate Sailing Skills

The beam reach approach is from across the wind. As approaching, simply ease the mainsheet to de-power the sail and place the boat in the safety position just behind the target boat. Approach slowly, under complete control, and then allow the sail to luff. Stopping downwind (at the stern) of the target boat will minimize the possibility of a collision.

F. "Man Overboard" Recovery

If a person falls overboard, the first task is to call out "man overboard" and turn the boat around (come about or jibe). Keep an eye on the person in the water and approach him/her sailing on a close or beam reach from downwind. Stop the boat just downwind of the person to be recovered. The procedure is the same as stopping alongside another boat. Be sure to balance your boat when helping the person on board.

Practice the approach for stopping alongside another boat and the man overboard recovery using a mooring or buoy. Once the approach is learned and the boat can be stopped in the desired location, practice stopping alongside another boat. Then practice the man overboard recovery procedure under varying wind conditions.

G. Picking Up a Mooring

The approach to pick up a mooring is the same as stopping alongside another boat. However, since the objective is to make contact with the mooring, it is best to stop the boat on its windward side. In this way, the momentum of turning into irons, or the wind when in the safety position, will tend to move the boat into the mooring and make it easy to pick up.

H. Exercises and Review Questions

Complete Exercises and Review Questions for Chapter 7 in Appendix C *before* proceeding to Chapter 8.

Chapter 8
Right of Way and Racing

A. RIGHT OF WAY

There are marine traffic laws for boats just as there are rules of the road for cars. The Coast Guard sets the marine traffic laws (navigation rules) in the United States. Generally, the higher category in the following list has the "right of way":

- Unable to steer
- Limited in turning ability
- Restricted to channel water depth
- Commercial fishing
- Sailing
- Power driven

Note, even though a sailboat has the right of way over a powered craft, it *does not* have right of way over a commercial vessel (e.g. ship, barge, fishing boat, etc.). Also, there are certain instances when a sailboat does not have right of way over a power craft. For example, a narrow channel may be the only route the powered vessel can take due to water depth. Also, large/heavy vessels have limited maneuverability and can take a long time (and distance) to turn and/or stop. Another example of an exception is when a sailboat is overtaking a powered craft—the powered vessel has the right of way. Put another way, in this example, the slower boat has the right of way.

When two sailboats approach one another, one will have the right of way. The boat that has the right of way is called the **stand-on** boat and the other boat is called the **give-way** boat. The stand-on boat maintains course and speed while the give-way boat turns to avoid a collision. There are five basic rules of right of way for sailboats in relation to each other. The sailor needs to be aware of the tack (starboard or port) and direction (windward or leeward) of both boats in order to know which one has the right of way.

1. **STARBOARD TACK RULE. A boat on a starboard tack has right of way over a boat on a port tack**. See Fig. 8-1 (next page).

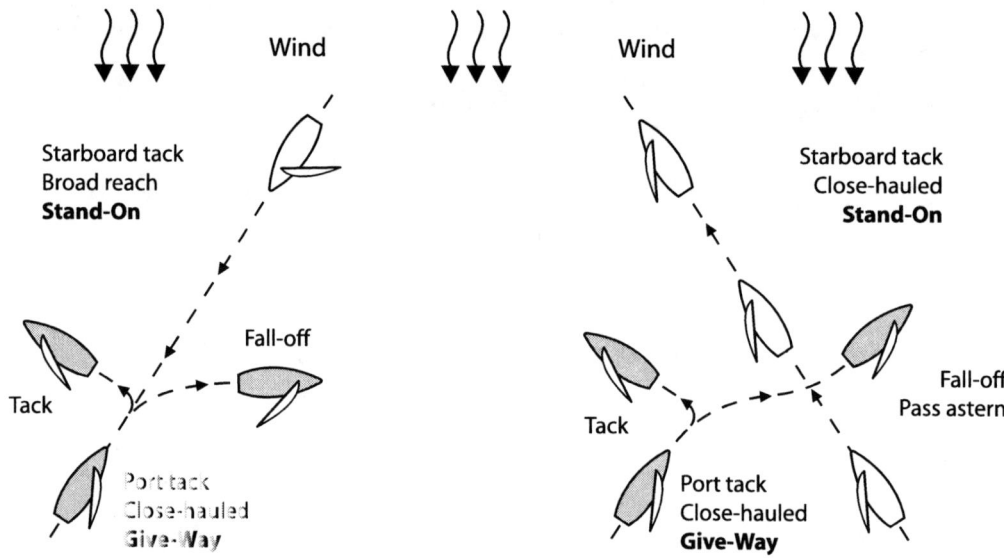

Fig. 8-1 Starboard Tack Rule

2. **SAME TACK RULE. If two boats are on the same tack, the leeward (downwind) boat has right of way over the windward (upwind) boat.**

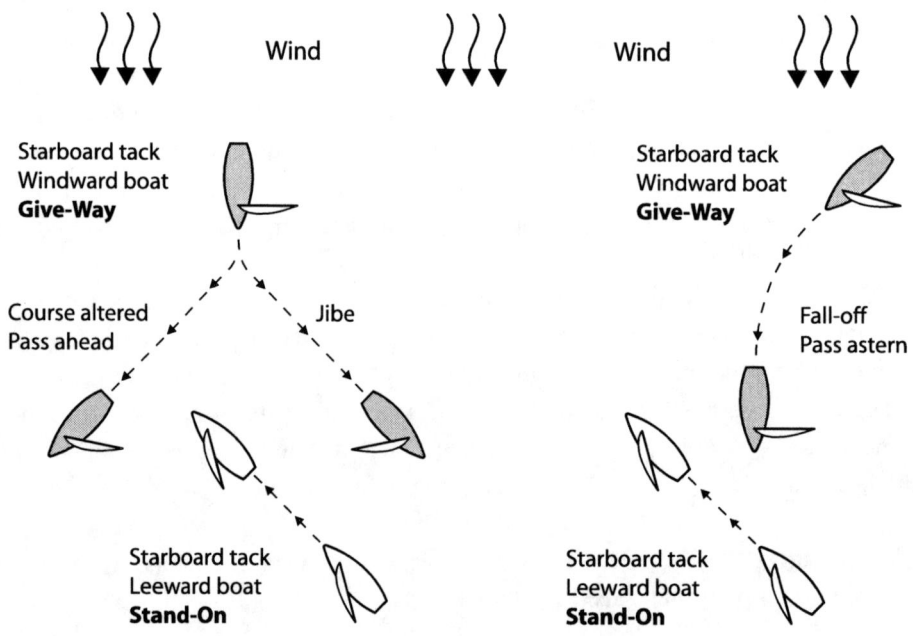

Fig. 8-2 Same Tack Rule

One reason for this rule is that the windward boat has more maneuverability than the leeward boat because the leeward boat cannot sail into the wind.

3. **OVERTAKING RULE. An overtaking boat must give-way when passing another boat.**

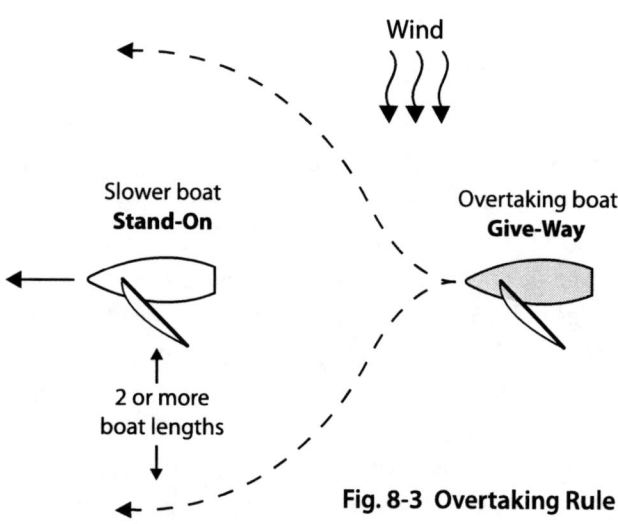

Fig. 8-3 Overtaking Rule

Further, it should stay clear (at least two boat lengths) when passing. This rule applies when passing another sailboat or a slower moving or stopped powerboat. A variation of this rule for racing states that the overtaking boat must keep clear of the boat ahead. However, if the boat passing to leeward on the same tack has overlapped the windward boat (i.e. bow of leeward boat has past stern of windward boat), it then has right of way to continue its course. At the same time, it may not sail above this course until clear of the boat that has been past.

4. **TURNING RULE. A boat sailing on any tack has the right of way over a boat that is coming about or jibing.**

When changing tack, be sure you are clear of other boats in your area before beginning the maneuver.

5. **PRUDENTIAL RULE. Do everything possible to prevent a collision!**

The sailor should constantly check the location and tack of all boats in the vicinity. This includes regularly looking below the boom on the downwind or leeward side of the boat. The captain of the other boat may not know who has right of way or may have a problem that prevents him/her from staying clear. Make the decision to change course to avoid a collision early. This will let the other boat know your intentions. Knowing you had the right of way will provide little consolation if staying the course results in boat damage or injury!

There are many other rules related to right of way, especially for sailing competition. However, knowing and abiding by the above rules should serve the recreational sailor well.

B. Racing

This section provides a very brief introduction to sailboat racing. Racing is a wonderful way to use and enjoy a sailboat. Friendly competition can provide many mental, physical, and social benefits. Typically the same kind of boats will race against each other. Boats that are built alike are called one-design class boats. The Laser, Sunfish, Optimist, Force 5, and Finn are examples of one-design boats. Racing regulations require that there be no modifications in one-design boats so that when they race against each other it is the skill of the sailors that determine the outcome of the race. A series of races over one or several days is called a **regatta**.

The racing committee (officials for the race) establishes the racing course with specified starting and finishing lines. Racecourses can have many shapes but the two most popular are; (1) a Windward-Leeward Course, and (2) a Windward-Leeward Triangle Course. Buoys (e.g. flag, nun, can), platforms, or anchored boats may be used as markers at the ends, corners, and/or at the start and finish lines.

Fig. 8-4 Examples of Race Course Markers

The starting line is typically set at right angles to the first leg of the course and is often set at a right angle to the wind. Therefore, the first leg will require tacking upwind. The course may be set up to require the sailor to sail clockwise or counter clockwise. In either

Right of Way and Racing

case the sailor will always be rounding the markers on the same side of the boat. If sailing clockwise, the markers will always be to starboard. If sailing counter clockwise, the markers will always be to port. It is permissible to sail on the inside of the triangle; however, the boat must sail around the outside of all markers. There are many rules related to racing. For example, if a boat strikes any part of a marker (including a flag) that is above the water, it must make one complete 360° turn, including one tack and one jibe, before continuing the course. If a boat illegally contacts another boat, it must sail around in a circle twice (720°) before continuing—or retire from the race. *The Racing Rules of Sailing* can be accessed on the internet at www.ussailing.org/rules

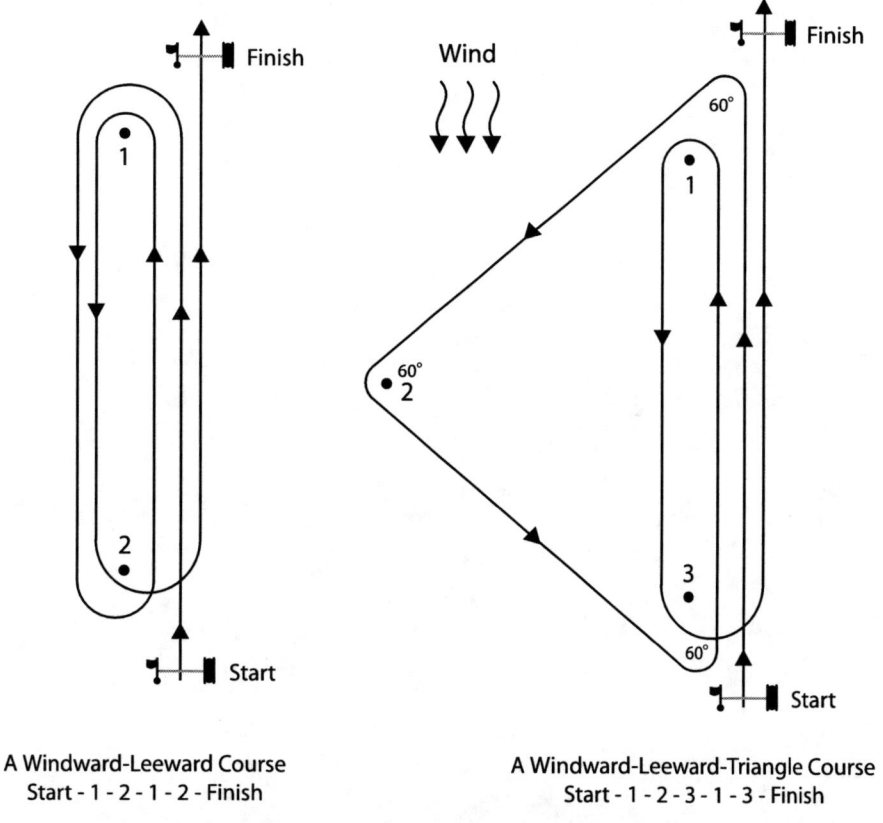

Fig. 8-5 Examples of Sailing Race Courses

Possible options for these racing courses include:
- Increasing or decreasing the number of laps
- Deleting the final windward leg
- Using a gate instead of a leeward mark for downwind legs (but not reaches)

- Using an offset mark at the windward mark (but not reaches)
- Using the leeward and windward marks as starting and finishing marks
- Varying the interior angles of the Triangle Course (e.g. 45°-90°-45°)

An example of points of sail for sailing a Windward-Leeward and Triangle Course counter clockwise is presented in Chapter 6, Section P—Practice.

C. EXERCISES AND REVIEW QUESTIONS

Complete Exercises and Review Questions for Chapter 8 in Appendix C *before* **proceeding to Chapter 9.**

Chapter 9
Useful Information

A. AIDS TO NAVIGATION

Aids to navigation serve much the same purpose as highway signs. Aids such as buoys, signs, lights, and beacons are designed to assist boaters by marking hazards and safe channels, helping determine location, controlling traffic, and protecting resources. A variety of colors, shapes, lights, numbers, and symbols give each navigation aid distinct characteristics. On charted waters these characteristics enable a boater to locate the aid on a nautical chart (roadmap of the waterway) and then determine their position.

1. Buoys

Buoys are floating signs placed to help make boating safer.

- **Informational Buoy**—a square is used on buoys giving directions to facilities or other information about the area.
- **Control Buoy**—a circle symbol is used to indicate a controlled area such as a no wake zone, open zone, ski zone, or speed zone.
- **Danger Buoy**—a diamond shape means danger; for example, rocks, stump, shallow area, reef, or shoal.
- **No Boats Buoy**—a diamond shape with cross in the middle means boats must keep out. The buoy may show only the symbol or may also indicate swim area, beach, keep out, no boats, closed area, dam, etc.

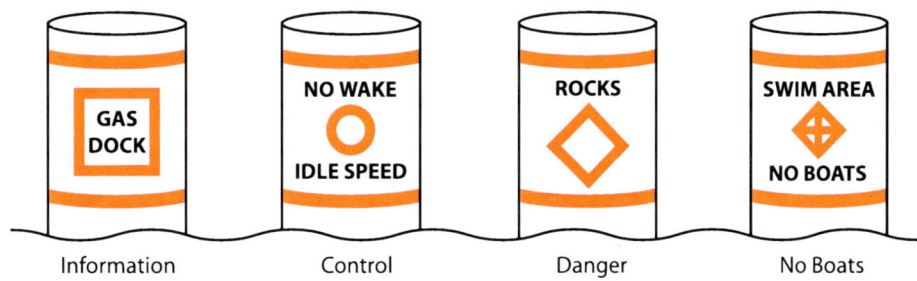

Fig. 9-1 Buoys are Floating Signs to Help Make Boating Safer

- **Channel Buoys**—indicate the deeper/safer channel for a harbor or marina entrance. They are also used for a dredged or natural channel.

Lighted, Can, or Square Sign Green Buoys—These buoys mark one side of a channel or river. Green (old color was black) buoys are kept on the right (starboard) side when proceeding out the channel or waterway and on the left (port) side when returning. These buoys have odd numbers with number 1 being the buoy found the farthest out in the waterway.

Lighted, Nun, or Triangle Sign Red Buoys—These buoys mark the other side of a channel or river. The red buoys are kept on the left (port) side when proceeding out the channel or waterway and on the right (starboard) side when returning. These buoys are even numbered with number 2 being the buoy found the farthest out in the waterway. A way to remember the side the buoys should be on is **Red Right Returning or RRR**.

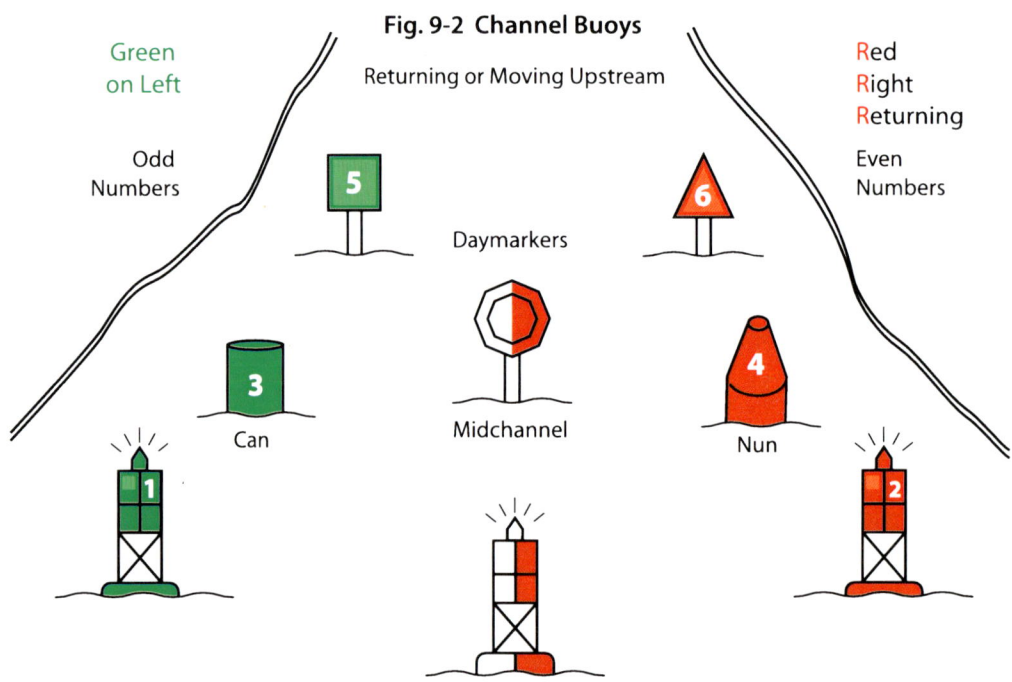

- **Mooring Buoy**—A white buoy with a blue horizontal band indicates a mooring buoy. This is the only type of buoy to which a boat may be legally tied. Be aware that most mooring buoys are private or rentals and permission is needed to use them.

Fig. 9-3 Mooring Buoy

Useful Information

- **Diver Buoy**—A red flag with a white diagonal stripe indicates SCUBA divers. Also, boats servicing diving operations will display a blue and white **alpha flag**. Avoid these areas.

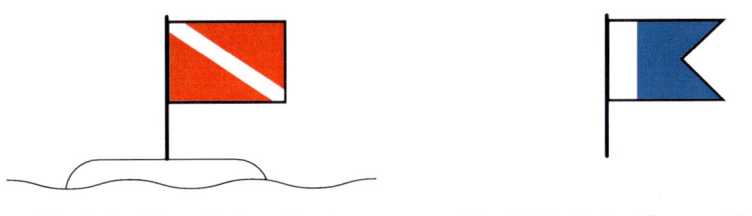

Fig. 9-4a Diver Below Flag   Fig. 9-4b Alpha Flag on Dive Boat

2 Lights

All non-motorized watercraft whether underway or at anchor at night must carry a white lantern or flashlight. This light should be strong enough so that other boats can see it from around the horizon at a distance of two miles or more. The light must be displayed in sufficient time to avoid a collision with another watercraft when sailing and must always be displayed while at anchor. Motorized sailboats must follow the light rules for power driven vessels.

3. Flags

There are many flag signals for boating. The most important one for small sailboats is the small craft warning signal. It is a single red triangular flag (pennant) displayed on shore to indicate wind conditions that are unsafe for small boats. Flag signals can be found on poles at Coast Guard stations and at marinas.

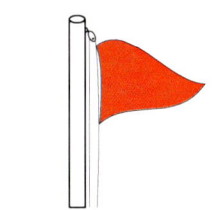

Fig. 9-5 Small Craft Warning Flag

B. Transporting Equipment

You, and only you, are responsible for any load being hauled on or behind the vehicle you are driving. Use a well-designed and firmly attached roof rack or trailer and be sure all equipment is securely tied down (using proper line and knots).

1. Car-Topping

There are a few key elements in car-topping a small boat. First, be sure you have enough help in lifting and removing the boat from the vehicle. Do not risk personal injury or damage to the boat or vehicle. Balance individuals around the boat and move it under control. Remember to lift with your legs; these are the strongest muscles in your body. Second, be careful of cleats, fairleads and other hardware that project up from the deck of the boat—lift these projections over the cross members of the roof rack so they are not damaged. Third, center the boat on the roof rack and provide padding across as large an area as possible. Fourth, securely fasten the boat to the roof rack using line, straps, and/or clamps. Next tie the bow to the front of the car and the stern to the rear to prevent movement forward or back. Ideally, there should be two bow and two stern lines, one to each corner of the vehicle. Finally, if the boat or spars project past the rear bumper, attach a red warning flag.

Fig. 9-6 Car Topping

2. *Trailering*

As with car-topping, make sure the boat and all related equipment is securely fastened to the trailer. Make sure there is adequate support for the hull and the boat is protected from road dirt, tar, and stones. Know and obey laws pertaining to trailers. Trailering safety instruction is recommended. The following figure illustrates how turning the steering wheel to the right causes the trailer to turn to the left (and vice versa) when backing up. Practice trailering techniques in an open area before attempting to maneuver in a congested one (e.g. backing a trailer down a boat ramp). Lightweight trailers and dollies can be purchased for small boats which will allow the sailor to single-handedly move the boat and launch it from a ramp or beach.

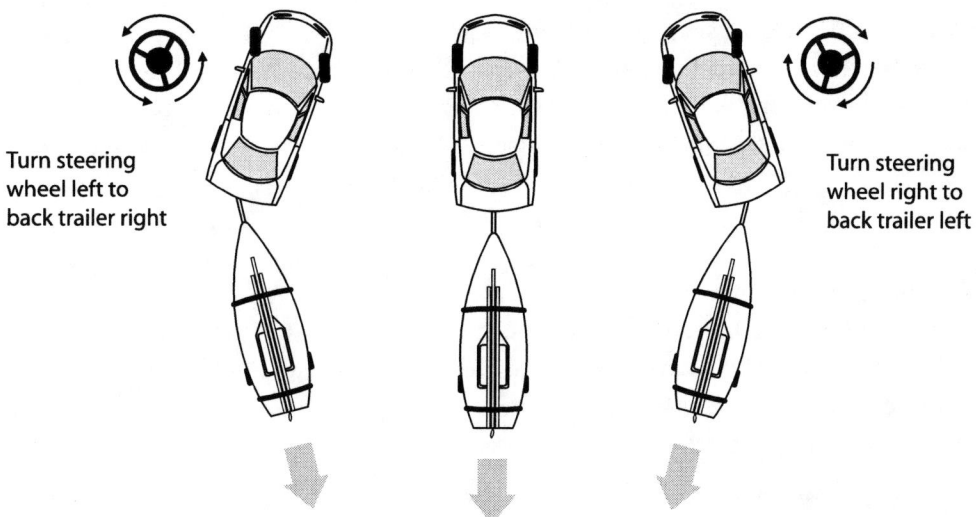

Fig. 9-7 Backing a Trailer

C. CARE AND STORAGE

1. Regular Care and Maintenance

Good care of equipment will insure that it functions properly, lasts a long time, and looks good. All sailing equipment should be inspected as the boat is being derigged. Any adjustments, repairs, or replacements should be taken care of right away. That way the boat will be ready the next time you want to go for a sail. There is nothing worse than having a beautiful day and "discovering" that there is a problem that either delays or prevents a sail.

Equipment should be clean and dry before being put away. If sailing in salt water, rinse, and then dry equipment. In the event this is not possible, clean and dry the equipment at the first available opportunity. If equipment is not going to be used for some time (e.g. weeks or stored through the winter) it is critical that it be stored properly to prevent deterioration and damage.

Line: The Do's and Don'ts of line care are covered in Chapter 2—Lines and Knots. If a line is worn or frayed it should be replaced. Choose good synthetic line for strength and durability. Though more expensive, it is well worth the cost. Know the best length and diameter for each line (check boat manual). When buying new line, consider different colors for different lines to make them more recognizable.

Sail: Inspect batten pockets, seams, and corners. It is usually best to remove battens to prevent wear and allow for easier folding of the sail. Fold the sail on a clean, dry, preferably soft surface (e.g. grass). Store the sail and battens in a sail bag.

Standing Rigging: Check the spars (e.g. mast and boom) and fittings to make sure they are sound. Look for dents, cracks, missing or loose rivets, straps, or caps.

Rudder Assembly/Daggerboard: Make sure parts are secure and functional—rudder head, pintles, tiller, hiking stick, daggerboard stop, etc.

Hull: Examine the hull, cockpit, daggerboard trunk, mast step hole, and gunwales for hairline cracks and signs of water leakage. Check all fittings (e.g. cleats and fairleads) attached to the hull for security and proper function. If there is water in the hull—there is a leak somewhere!

Gear/Parts: The boom vang, blocks, hiking strap, plugs, and other parts should be checked. Look for wear, cracks, corrosion, or malfunction. Make sure the sheaves (turning parts) of blocks turn freely.

Spare Parts: A damaged or missing small part could affect or prevent sailing a boat. Therefore, it is advisable to have a bag of spare parts and a few simple tools (e.g. regular and Philips screwdrivers, pliers, knife, and lighter) available at all times. For example, relatively inexpensive parts to have available for a Laser could include:

- line (which could be cut to desired length)
- clevis pins and securing ring dings (which are easily lost when dropped)
- vang key for attaching vang to boom
- large and small traveler blocks
- cockpit drain plug and line
- rudder retaining pin and line
- battens

2. Short and Long Term Storage

Whether storing equipment for a day or a season—store parts together. There are a variety of sailbags that have been designed for this purpose. It is very convenient and helpful to be able to put your daggerboard, rudder, and all other small parts and line in one bag. Parts will be less likely to get lost and will be easily accessible the next time you are ready to rig the boat.

Boats and spars can be stored on racks or on trailers. First be sure they are supported properly. There should be sufficient support to prevent bending or denting. This is especially important if the boat is stored right side up. The boat may also be stored on its deck (upside down), on its transom (standing on end), or on a gunwale (leaning on its side). In all cases there should be sufficient padding in several places to spread the load.

Prevent water collection in the cockpit and mast step hole. This can be accomplished by covering the boat if in the right side up position.

For long-term storage, the boat should be cleaned and then put indoors or covered and secured outdoors. Remove all drain plugs and drain the boat (if necessary) before storing. If there are inspection ports, open them to allow for ventilation through the hull. Cover the boat to prevent both water/dirt collection and deterioration from the damaging rays of the sun. Tie the cover and boat down to prevent wind damage. In colder climates, freezing water can and will damage a boat if it is not protected.

Useful Information

The end of the sailing season or off-season is an ideal time to repair, refinish, and replace equipment. The use of fiberglass, plastics, and alloy metals in boat construction has significantly reduced the amount of work necessary in caring for a boat. Still, there are basic tasks that need to be done to keep the boat and equipment in optimum condition. The handy sailor can easily perform most of these tasks. Boat yards and sail makers are available for repairs (e.g. hull damage, torn sail, etc.) that are beyond the expertise of the sailor.

D. Hull Identification Number (HIN)

The Hull Identification Number (HID) is displayed in 1/4 inch high characters on the upper right of the transom or on the starboard side within two feet of the stern. It may be engraved in the fiberglass or be on a metal plate. The HIN is a 12 character code that designates the boat manufacturer and serial number as well as the month and year of production. This number is used for warranty problems, to register the boat, and also for identification should the boat be stolen. Therefore, it is important to keep the HIN on file in a safe place. Look for the HIN when purchasing a boat (be sure it has not been altered), it will tell you the age of the boat.

HIN Example: BMA 45336 H4 96

BMA—Boat manufacturer's identification code
45336—Boat serial number
H4—Date of manufacture
96—Model year

E. Purchasing a Used Boat

Used boats can often be purchased at a fraction of new boat cost. Shop around; check newspapers, trader publications, postings at marinas, boat dealers, and the internet. "Know" the boat you are considering (check the boat manual). Information on specific boats and costs of new and used boats can be found on the internet. See Appendix A, Resources and References, for selected web sites.

Be familiar with the boats rigging and parts. Inspect the boat carefully looking for potential problems. Get an inventory of everything that comes with the boat and make sure it is complete. Factor in the cost of repair/replacement in determining the purchase price. The following check list may be helpful:

Hull: Bubbled Gel Coat
Loose Screws
Leaky Centerboard Trunk
Leaky Gunwales (hairline cracks?)
Damaged/Loose Cleats and Fairleads
Damaged Bottom

Spars:	Enlarged Screw/Rivet Holes
	Dented Mast
	Very Flexible Mast
	Bent Boom
Rudder Assembly:	Warped Rudder
	Loose Tiller Fit
	Worn Pintles
Sail:	Worn/Limp Fabric
	Frayed Seams
	Torn Batten Pockets
Parts:	Damaged Centerboard
	Broken/Missing Boom Vang or Blocks
	Missing/Frayed Sheets and Lines
	Damaged/Missing Drain Plugs

The boat does not have to be perfect to be functional. The key is to be sure that it can be sailed safely. If in doubt, have a knowledgeable person inspect the boat with/for you. Obtain a maintenance history and take the boat for a sail if possible. Beginning sailors may prefer a used boat as they practice their launching, sailing, and landing techniques. This could reduce the worry of boat damage (e.g. scrapes, dings, etc.) as skills are practiced.

F. Certification

Both the American Sailing Association (ASA) and the United States Sailing Association (US Sailing) administer sailing certification programs. These certifications range from basic or small boat sailing to various levels of keelboat and cruising certification. Both organizations require the demonstration of specific knowledge and skills to a certified sailing instructor of their association. To receive the certification, the student must then forward the application provided by the instructor and become a member of that sailing association.

Successful acquisition of the knowledge and demonstration of the skills contained in this book will enable the student to become certified by either association.

1. *American Sailing Association—ASA Basic Sailing Certification*

Small Boat Sailing Standard (110)
American Sailing Association 13922 Marquesas Way, Marina del Rey, CA 90292, 310-822-7171. http://www.american-sailing.com

Go to the above web site and link as follows: Learn to Sail—ASA Standards Summary—Basic Small Boat Sailing (110).

Useful Information

2. *US Sailing Association—Small Boat Sailor Certification*

Certification at any or all three wind speed ranges: **Light Air (5-9 mph)**
Medium Air (10-15 mph)
Heavy Air (16+ mph)

United States Sailing Association, P.O. Box 1260, 15 Maritime Dr., Portsmouth, RI 02871, 401-683-0800. http://www.ussailing.org 1-800-877-2451.

Go to the above web site and link as follows: Getting Started—Online Education—Small Boat Course.

G. EXERCISES AND REVIEW QUESTIONS

Complete Exercises and Review Questions for Chapter 9 in Appendix C.

Appendix A
Resources and References

A. BOATING ORGANIZATIONS

Boat Owner's Association of the United States (BoatU.S.), 880 S. Pickett St., Alexandria, VA 22304, 703-823-9550. http://www.boatus.com Courseline: 1-800-336-2628.

National Safe Boating Council Inc., P.O. Box 1058, Delaware, OH 43015, 740-666-3009. http://www.safeboatingcouncil.org

U.S. Coast Guard Headquarters Boating Safety, 2100 Second St. S.W., Washington DC 20593, 202-267-1077. Infoline: 1-800-368-5647. Boating links: http://www.uscg boating.org

B. SAILING ORGANIZATIONS AND SELECTED WEB SITES

American Sail Training Association, P.O. Box 1459, Newport, RI 22042, 703-206-7180. http://www.tallships.sailtraining.org

American Sailing Association, 13922 Marquesas Way, Marina del Rey, CA 90292, 310-822-7171. http://www.american-sailing.com

International Sailing Federation, Ariadne House, Town Quay, Southampton, Hampshire SO14 2AQ, United Kingdom, +44 1703 635111. http://www.sailing.org

National Sailing Industry Association, 200 E. Randolph Dr. Suite 5100, Chicago, IL 60601-6528, 312-946-6200. Sailing Hotline: 1-800-535-7245. http://www.discoversailing.com

SailNet, 3000 Gandy Blvd., St. Petersburg, FL 33702. 1-800-234-3220. http://www.sailnet.com

Starboard Tack, 1011 James Madison Ct., McDonough, GA 30253. New & Used Boats. http://www.starboardtack.com

United States Sailing Association, P.O. Box 1260, 15 Maritime Dr., Portsmouth, RI 02871, 401-683-0800. http://www.ussailing.org 1-800-877-2451.

C. ONE-DESIGN SAILING ASSOCIATIONS

DeWitt Dinghy Association, P.O. Box 70310, Pt. Richmond, CA 94807, 800-398-2440. http://www.dewittsailboats.com

El Toro International YRA, 1014 Hopper Ave., #419, Santa Rosa, CA 95403, 707-526-6621. http://www.eltoroyra.org

Force 5 Class Association, 10274 Wanda Circle, Hartville, OH 44632, 330-877-6281. http://www.sailingsource.com/force5

International Optimist Dinghy Association, Thormanby Road, Howth, Dublin, Ireland, 353-1-839-5587. http://www.optiworld.org

Laser Class North American Region, 5205 Beacon Drive, Austin, TX 78734, 512-266-8254. http://www.laser.org

National Butterfly Association, 515 Green Bay Road, Wilmette, IL 60091, 847-251-7884. http://www.butterflyer.org

U.S./International Sunfish Class Association, P.O. Box 300128, Waterford, MI 48330, 248-673-2750. http://www.sunfishclass.org

U.S./International Finn Class Association, Pentalpha Capital, 660 Steamboat Rd, Greenwich, CT 06850, 203-629-8900. http://www.finnclass.org

United States Optimist Dinghy Association (USODA), 301 Norwood Ave., PO Box 1301, Beach Haven, NJ 08008, 609-492-1612. http://www.usoda.org

D. SAILING VIDEOS

"At One with the Wind," executive producer, David Hill; director, Phil Hewitt; Richmond Hill, Ont.; a production of Sepia Arts; licensed and distributed by BFS Video, 1987. The Royal Yachting Association (Great Britain) beginner's sailboat training video.

"Learn to Sail," Bennett Marine Video, Selluloid Video presents a Sailing production in association with Offshore Sailing School Ltd.; Marine del Rey, CA, 1983. A comprehensive, easy to follow sailing course for beginning and intermediate students, taught by Steve Colgate.

"Michelob Sailing," a complete introduction to sailing with Gary Jobson, St. Louis, MO, Busch Creative Services Corporation, 1986.

"Sailing Fundamentals: The Official Learning to Sail Video of the American Sailing Association with Peter Isler," One hour video in four parts to compliment the text *Sailing Fundamentals* by Gary Jobson, 1985; American Sailing Association, 13922 Marquesas Way, Marina del Rey, CA 90292.

"Start Sailing Right Videos," 3 videos (approximately 44, 28, and 29 minutes each) to accompany the book *Start Sailing Right* by U.S. Sailing & the American Red Cross; copyright Emmett McNamara, 1991; United States Sailing Association P.O. Box 1260, 15 Maritime Dr., Portsmouth, RI 02871.

E. BOOK REFERENCES

Bond, B. (1992). *The handbook of sailing.* New York: Knopf.

Brown, A. (1971). *Invitation to sailing.* New York: Fireside, Simon and Schuster.

Cahill, A. E. (Ed.). (1995). *Small-boat sailing.* Irving, TX: Boy Scouts of America.

Colgate, S. (1996). *Fundamentals of sailing, cruising, and racing.* New York: W.W. Norton.

Conner, D. and M. Levitt. (1994). *Learn to sail.* New York: St Martin's Press.

Fries, D. (Rev. Ed.). (1997). *Start sailing right!* Portsmouth, RI: United States Sailing Association.

George, M. B. (1984). *Basic sailing.* New York: Hearst Marine Books.

Goodman D. and I. Brodie. (1994). *Learning to sail: the Annapolis sailing school guide for all ages.* Camden, ME: International Marine/McGraw-Hill.

Isler, J.J. and P. Isler. (1997). *Sailing for dummies.* Foster City, CA: IDG Books.

Isler, P. (1993). *Let's go sailing.* Marina del Rey, CA: American Sailing Association and Hearst Marine Books.

Jobson, G. (2004). *The winner's guide to Optimist sailing.* Camden, ME: International Marine/Ragged Mountain Press.

Lewis, L. (1996). *The Sunfish Bible.* Sarasota, FL: Omega Cubed Press.

Reekie, S. H. M. (1986). *Sailing made simple.* Champaign, IL: Leisure Press.

Royce, P. M. (1993). *Royce's sailing illustrated: the best of all sailing worlds.* Newport Beach, CA: Royce Publications.

Sargeant, F. (1998). *The complete idiot's guide to boating and sailing.* New York: Alpha Books.

Seidman, D. (1995). *The complete sailor: learning the art of sailing.* Camden, ME: International Marine/McGraw-Hill.

Terry, J. (1992). *The fundamentals of sailing.* New York: St. Martin's Press.

Tillman, D. (2000). *The complete book of Laser sailing.* Blacklick, OH: McGraw-Hill.

Tillman, R.L. (2005). *The complete book of Laser sailing.* Camden, ME: International Marine/Ragged Mountain Press.

United States Coast Guard Auxiliary. (1985). *Sailing and seamanship.* Washington, D.C.: U.S. Coast Guard Auxiliary.

White, W. (1983). *The Sunfish book.* Boston: SAIL Books.

F. BOOKLET

Ohio Boat Operator's Guide 2005/06. Ohio Department of Natural Resources, Division of Watercraft, 2045 Morse Road, Building A, Columbus, OH 43229.

Appendix B
Sailing Class Information

A. INTRODUCTION

The sailing class information in this section is based on a course offered in a school academic setting. The major class objectives are:
- To assist the student in the acquisition of knowledge/understanding related to sailing
- To assist the student with the acquisition and development of sailing skills
- To develop an appreciation for and compliance with boating safety rules
- To assist in the development of a lifelong leisure activity that will provide mental, physical, and social benefits

As an academic course, the Sailing class must follow department and school guidelines and requirements. This course consists of 30-40 hours of instruction/practice/testing in conjunction with the completion of required exercises and review questions (from this book), the viewing of instructional sailing videos, and the review of relevant sailing information and video clips on the Internet.

The best way to learn to sail is by sailing with a certified instructor. Sailing with a knowledgeable and skilled sailor can also provide a good learning experience. In a beginning sailing class, the opportunity to sail with an experienced person is limited. Therefore, "land" instruction is very important. The beginning sailor needs to understand the basics of the skills to be practiced *before* going out on the water. Studying, listening alertly to descriptions, and watching demonstrations of techniques and videos should prepare the individual for the skills to be practiced. There is an attempt to pair each beginner with an experienced sailor. However, in the event that sufficient experienced sailors are not available, beginners are paired with each other to practice skills. The instructor(s) will be present on land and/or out on the water to provide direction, instruction, and control.

B. SAILING CLASS RULES

1. **Students must pass a swim test in order to take the class.** The swim test used by this instructor has two parts. First, a non-stop (no time limit but must keep moving and not touch bottom) fifty-yard swim while fully clothed (i.e. wearing long pants, long sleeve shirt, and shoes). Many individuals will not have previously experienced

swimming while fully clothed. This is an opportunity to discuss the importance and reasons for staying with a capsized boat rather than attempting to swim to shore.

The second part of the swim test consists of spending five minutes (fully clothed) in deep water (e.g. in eight or more feet of water). For example, students are first fitted with Personal Flotation Devices (PFDs—life jackets) and then asked to line up around the deep end of a pool. PFDs are then removed and placed on the edge of the pool. On a signal, the students jump into the deep end and begin to swim, tread, and/or float. After five minutes, life jackets are pushed into the pool and each student must retrieve, put on, and properly secure his/her life jacket while in the water. This is an opportunity to discuss the importance and reasons for wearing a PFD whenever on or near the water.

2. Students must complete a Student Information form and an Affirmation and Liability Release form in order to participate in class. Students must inform the instructor of any limitation, disability, or medical condition that could affect their performance or safety in the class. Students must inform the instructor of all allergies, including those to dust, insect bites or stings, medicine, etc. Students must also inform the instructor of any medication(s) they are taking while participating in the class. Finally, students must report all injuries to the instructor, regardless of how minor.

3. **All students will assist with unloading, loading, and caring for equipment.** It is expected that students will care for, clean, and properly store equipment according to the directions provided by the instructor.

4. **Footwear is required, e.g. sandals with ankle straps, water shoes, deck shoes, old sneakers, etc.**

5. **Students without sufficient protective clothing will not be permitted to participate in class.** Protective clothing must be available for each class. Weather can change rapidly; it could be warm and sunny with a light breeze at the beginning of class and then turn cold, wet, and windy during the class period. At a minimum, each student should have an insulation layer and a wind protection layer. See the Clothing/Gear Checklist in the next section.

6. **Students must wear their properly secured life jackets (PFDs) whenever on or near the water.** It is the students' responsibility to remember to put his/her PFD back on after spending time on shore for instruction or a rest break.

7. **Each student is responsible for inspecting his/her boat before sailing. It is also the students' responsibility to be sure that the instructor has inspected the boat, for proper and complete assembly, before it is used.**

8. **Students must stay within the boundaries stipulated by the instructor.** Sailing or drifting outside these boundaries could subject you to hazards your instructor intended for you to avoid. These boundaries have been carefully selected for your

safety. If you reach these boundaries, you will be expected to turn around or Self-Rescue back into the designated area. The boundaries are also intended to keep students in an area that will facilitate instruction and supervision. Finally, going too far could prevent you from reaching safety in the event of a sudden storm.

9. **Only use techniques that are taught in class or approved by the instructor.** Horseplay will not be tolerated and students will be held liable for any injuries or equipment breakage that results. Students will also be responsible for repair or replacement of equipment that is misused or lost. Sailboat parts are *expensive!*

10. **Obey whistle signals.** A whistle or horn may be used to communicate with students when verbal communication is impractical:
    - 1 whistle blast—message for everyone OR instruction for student being pointed at
    - 2 whistle blasts—everyone return to launch site immediately; class session is over or foul weather approaches.
    - 5 whistle blasts—everyone seek nearest shore and/or shelter. Example of use would be a sudden storm with lightning.

11. **Smoking, alcohol and illegal substances are not permitted in class and will not be tolerated. Individuals suspected of being "under the influence" will not be permitted to participate in class.**

C. SAILING CLASS EVALUATION

There is a required attendance policy in order to fulfill school and department academic requirements. More than one (1) absence will result in failure of the course and an NC (no-credit) on the transcript. The student may drop or withdraw (W) from the course by the designated deadline without penalty. This is a pass/fail class with the student receiving an S (Satisfactory) or NC (no-credit) as a final grade. The student must fulfill the following requirements to pass the course:

- Pass a comprehensive written final examination on safety rules, sailing terminology, and sailing technique at the 80th percentile or higher
- Completely and correctly rig a sailboat using proper knots
- Successfully launch, sail a designated triangle course, and land a sailboat within a time limit based on size of the triangle course and wind conditions

D. CLOTHING/GEAR CHECKLIST

Each day bring a bag to class containing all of the items that you might need. That bag should contain clothing for *all* possible conditions. Your clothing should allow you to "layer" what you wear making it possible to add or remove clothing at any time. Use this check list to be sure you have everything you need.

_____ U.S. Coast Guard approved Personal Flotation Device (PFD)
_____ Carrying bag or pack (ideally, waterproof)
_____ Swimsuit
_____ Shoes: sandals with ankle straps, water shoes, deck shoes, old sneakers, etc.; be sure they have non-skid soles; they *will* get wet
_____ Towel and set of dry clothes for after sailing
_____ T-shirt: white for warm days
_____ Hat, sunscreen, drinking water: for hot days
_____ Rain/Wind Suit: Gore-Tex or other breathable fabric is great but other synthetic will do
_____ Underwear: polypropylene (poly-pro) or synthetic fibers, long sleeve shirt and long pants
_____ Socks: poly-pro, wool, synthetic
_____ Shirt: poly-pro, wool, synthetic
_____ Hat/Hood: poly-pro, wool, synthetic—warm
_____ Gloves: leather, poly-pro, wool, synthetic—which will insulate and not deteriorate when wet. Gloves can help with grip and prevent irritation to hand and fingers.

Optional: Pants: heavy polypropylene, wool, fleece, synthetic
Wool sweater, fleece or synthetic jacket
Coat
Wet suit, dry suit
Sunglasses (with strap)

- **No rain ponchos are permitted**—they are a risk to wear in the water.
- Cotton *is not* a good cold weather fabric—it has little insulation value when wet. **Do not wear** cotton jeans, sweat pants, T-shirts, sweat shirts, socks, etc. on cold days.
- If you wear glasses, be sure you have a strap to hold them on.
- If you wear a watch, make sure it is waterproof.
- It is recommended that you not wear jewelry. It can be lost, broken, or get caught on equipment resulting in injury.

If you are cold/wet and out-of-doors—you will be miserable, not to mention a likely candidate for hypothermia. Also, you will not feel comfortable sailing or learning sailing skills. Therefore, be prepared for all weather conditions.

E. First Assignment

Complete the following Student Information form and the Affirmation and Liability Release form and submit them to your instructor. Read Appendix B, Chapter 1 and Chapter 2. After reading, complete the Exercises and Review Questions for Chapter 1 and Chapter 2 in Appendix C.

Student Information*

Name: _____ (print) Age: _____

Indicate your swimming ability: _____ novice _____ good _____ excellent

Indicate your sailing ability: _____ none _____ novice _____ good _____ excellent

Do you have any fears about being out on the water in a boat by yourself?
_____
_____

What *size* and *types* of sailboats have you sailed on? Were you a passenger or did you crew?
_____
_____

Do you or your family own a boat? What kind? What body of water do you usually boat on?
_____
_____

Have you ever participated in a regatta or other sailing event?
_____
_____

Do you now or have you ever held any type of sailing certification? Describe:
_____
_____

Do you have any health problems that will affect your participation in this class? List your health problems and any medications that you are currently taking:
_____
_____

I certify that I am in good health and that I am able to participate in this activity without adversely affecting any health problems. I have notified the Instructor of any condition that may affect my participation and any medicine that I am currently taking.

Signature: _____ Date: _____

*Do not participate in any skill practice until you have fully completed and turned in this form and the Affirmation and Liability Release form to your instructor. If you have any questions or concerns, consult your instructor before participating.

AFFIRMATION AND LIABILITY RELEASE

(Print information, read carefully before signing)

I, _____, hereby affirm that I have thoroughly read Chapter 1 and Appendix B of *Sailing is a Breeze: Learning to Sail a Laser, Sunfish, or Other Small Boat* and certify that I have been well advised and thoroughly informed of the inherent dangers of Sailing. I understand and appreciate the hazards, risks, and rules contained in these sections. By signing this Release, I acknowledge that I am cognizant of the basic risk and danger of sailing and that it is my intention to voluntarily assume such risk and danger.

In consideration of being permitted to enroll in this course of instruction and to participate in this activity, I hereby release the _____, and its agents and employees, and the author and publisher of this book, from any liability arising from any occurrence in connection with this class and activity which results in injury, death or other damage to me or my family, heirs or assigns. I also hereby personally assume all risks in connection with this course and this activity, for any harm, injury, or damage, which may befall me while I am enrolled as a student in the course and participating in this activity, including all risks, connected therewith, whether foreseen or unforeseen. Further, I agree to save and hold harmless _____, and its agents and employees, and the author and publisher of this book, from any claim by me or by my family, estate, heirs or assigns, which arises out of my enrollment and participation in this course and activity.

I am eighteen years of age or older and legally competent to sign this Affirmation and Liability Release, or in the event that I have not attained the age of eighteen years, I have acquired the written consent of my parents or legal guardians. I understand that the terms stated in this Release are contractual and are not merely recitals. I have signed this document of my own free act.

I HAVE FULLY INFORMED MYSELF CONCERNING THE RISKS AND DANGERS INHERENT IN SAILING AND WITH THE CONTENTS OF THIS AFFIRMATION AND RELEASE BEFORE SIGNING IT.

Course Name: _____ Course Number: _____

Student's Name: _____ Age: _____

School Address: _____

E-mail Address: _____

School Phone: (_____) _____

Signature _____ Date _____

Emergency Contact
Name and Relationship: _____

Address: _____

Phone Daytime: (_____) _____ Evening/Weekend: (_____) _____

Signature of Parent: _____ Date _____
Or Guardian (students under age 18)

Name _____ Date _____

Appendix C
Exercise and Review Questions

Chapter 1

Risk Analysis Exercise—read the following paragraph, which is a compilation of circumstances taken from actual fatal accident reports:

One beautiful morning in April, Steve arrives at Ann's house with his brand-new sailboat. Ann is surprised, and since she has never been in a sailboat, she suggests they go sailing. Dressed in a T-shirt and jeans, she jumps into Steve's car and they drive to the lake. Steve has never sailed at this lake before but it looks like a good day to sail. It is a sunny day, temperature of 62 degrees, and a strong breeze is blowing. There are no other boats out on the lake and they are pleased there is no wait at the launch ramp. Some dark clouds are on the horizon, but they are a long way off. It seems to take forever to get the boat rigged. Finally they are ready and Steve remembers to throw the new life jackets and his car keys into the boat before they head out. There is an off-shore wind and they catch a sudden gust as they sail out into the center of the lake.

List eight risks related to Steve and Ann's sailing adventure. **ALSO,** *explain* how each of these risks could have been eliminated or minimized.

Risk 1: _____
_____
_____

Risk 2: _____
_____
_____

Risk 3: _____
_____
_____

Name _____ Date _____

Risk 4: _____
_____
_____

Risk 5: _____
_____
_____

Risk 6: _____
_____
_____

Risk 7: _____
_____
_____

Risk 8: _____
_____
_____

Circle or Fill-In the correct answer:

1. Cold water cools the body _____ times faster than cold air of the same temperature:

    a. 10-15
    b. 15-20
    c. 20-25
    d. 25-30

2. What is the first sign of hypothermia? _____

3. Which of the following is not an approved US Coast Guard PFD?

    a. Type I—Off-Shore Life Preserver
    b. Type II—Near-Shore Life Vest
    c. Type III—Special Purpose Flotation Aid
    d. Type IV—Throwable Flotation Device

4. High pressure (barometric) is associated with clear, dry weather. True or False

Name _____ Date _____

Chapter 2

1. Sailing commands are transmitted to the boat through _____, movement of the _____, and shifting of _____.

2. Before storing, line should be _____ and _____.

3. The _____ is the recommended stopper knot for lines on a sailboat.

4. The _____ is used whenever a loop is needed in a line.

Chapter 3

1. What is the purpose of a daggerboard? _____

2. How are a centerboard and keel similar? _____

3. How are a centerboard and keel different? _____

4. A sail is a flat two-dimensional surface used to catch the wind. True or False

5. Describe a catboat: _____

6. A dinghy is a small centerboard boat that is less than 17 feet long. True or False

7. How is a sloop rig different from a catboat rig? _____

Chapter 4

Labeling

The following labeling (learning) exercises are divided into three parts: (1) Hull Terms; (2) Spar, Steering Assembly, and Depth Terms; and (3) Sail and Running Rigging Terms.

LABEL EACH OF THE FOLLOWING PARTS ON THE DIAGRAM OF YOUR BOAT

Only label the diagram for the boat you are sailing (e.g. Laser or Sunfish). Complete this exercise by writing the name of the part on the diagram next to the correct number and then crossing it off the list. Continue until all parts have been labeled. Note that some parts are labeled two (2) or three (3) times. Resist the temptation to check your answers until you have placed **ALL** of the terms on the diagram—this is a learning exercise. Some terms have

Name _____ Date _____

already been defined and some are defined here; all can be found in the Nautical Dictionary in Appendix E.

LASER—Label Fig. C-1 Laser Parts p. 150

Hull Terms—Laser

Stern	**Hiking strap**
Transom (2)	**Mainsheet swivel block**
Gudgeon (2)	**Daggerboard trunk**
Traveler line	**Mast step hole (Tabernacle)**
Cockpit	**Deck**
Gunwale (2)	**Bow (2)**

Cockpit drain plug—hole where water can drain out of cockpit. Some Lasers have an automatic bailer which will bail water from the cockpit while moving.

Traveler clam cleat—clam cleat used to hold and adjust the traveler line

Small block with brummel (2) (traveler block)—pulley to attach traveler to large block with brummel

Traveler fairlead—fairlead used to change direction of traveler line

Mainsheet cam cleat—optional cam cleat used to hold the mainsheet

Downhaul clam cleat—clam cleat used to hold and adjust the downhaul line

Bow eye—used to attach a painter. A **painter** is a piece of line attached to a boat for towing, directing, or tying off.

Downhaul fairlead—fairlead used to change direction of downhaul

Rudder lift stop—snaps snugly on top of the bottom rudder strap to prevent the pintle pin from lifting and coming out of the gudgeon; it keeps the rudder attached to the transom of the boat (e.g. when the boat capsizes).

Transom bung (drain plug)—hole where water can drain out of hull

HIN—hull identification number

Spar, Steering Assembly, and Depth Terms—Laser

Mast	**Draft**
Boom	**Daggerboard**
Boom vang	**Daggerboard stop**
Gooseneck	**Rudder blade**
Forward boom block	**Pintle pin**
Waterline	**Tiller**
Freeboard	**Tiller extension/Hiking stick**

Name _____ Date _____

Outhaul clam cleat—clam cleat used to hold and adjust the outhaul line
Aft (Becket) boom block—aft pulley on boom through which mainsheet runs and is used to secure mainsheet
Large block with brummel—pulley to attach mainsheet to small block with brummel
Tiller retaining pin—pin that prevents the tiller detaching from the rudder head
Rudder head—top part of the rudder; it is hinged to the stern
Eye strap—a metal strap (loop) that allows free passage of the mainsheet while keeping it close to the boom

Sail and Running Rigging—Laser

Mainsail	**Tack**
Luff	**Head**
Foot	**Batten**
Leech	**Batten pocket**
Clew	**Mainsheet**

Luff sleeve (sailsock)—pocket in luff of mainsail that fits over the mast securing the luff edge of the sail to the mast
Downhaul grommet—grommet (metal ring) in the tack of the sail for attachment of the downhaul line
Downhaul line (Cunningham)—line used to adjust tension in the luff edge of a sail. The downhaul is attached to the downhaul grommet (tack of the sail), runs down through the downhaul fairlead (changes direction), and inserts in and is attached to the downhaul clam cleat.
Outhaul grommet—grommet (metal ring) in the clew of the sail for attachment of the outhaul line
Outhaul line and outhaul fairlead—The outhaul line is used to adjust foot edge tension on the sail. It is attached to the outhaul grommet in the clew (lower back corner) of the sail, runs down through the outhaul fairlead (changes direction), runs forward along the boom, and then inserts in and is attached to the outhaul clam cleat.

Name ______________________________ Date ______________

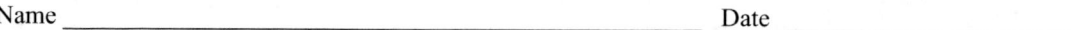

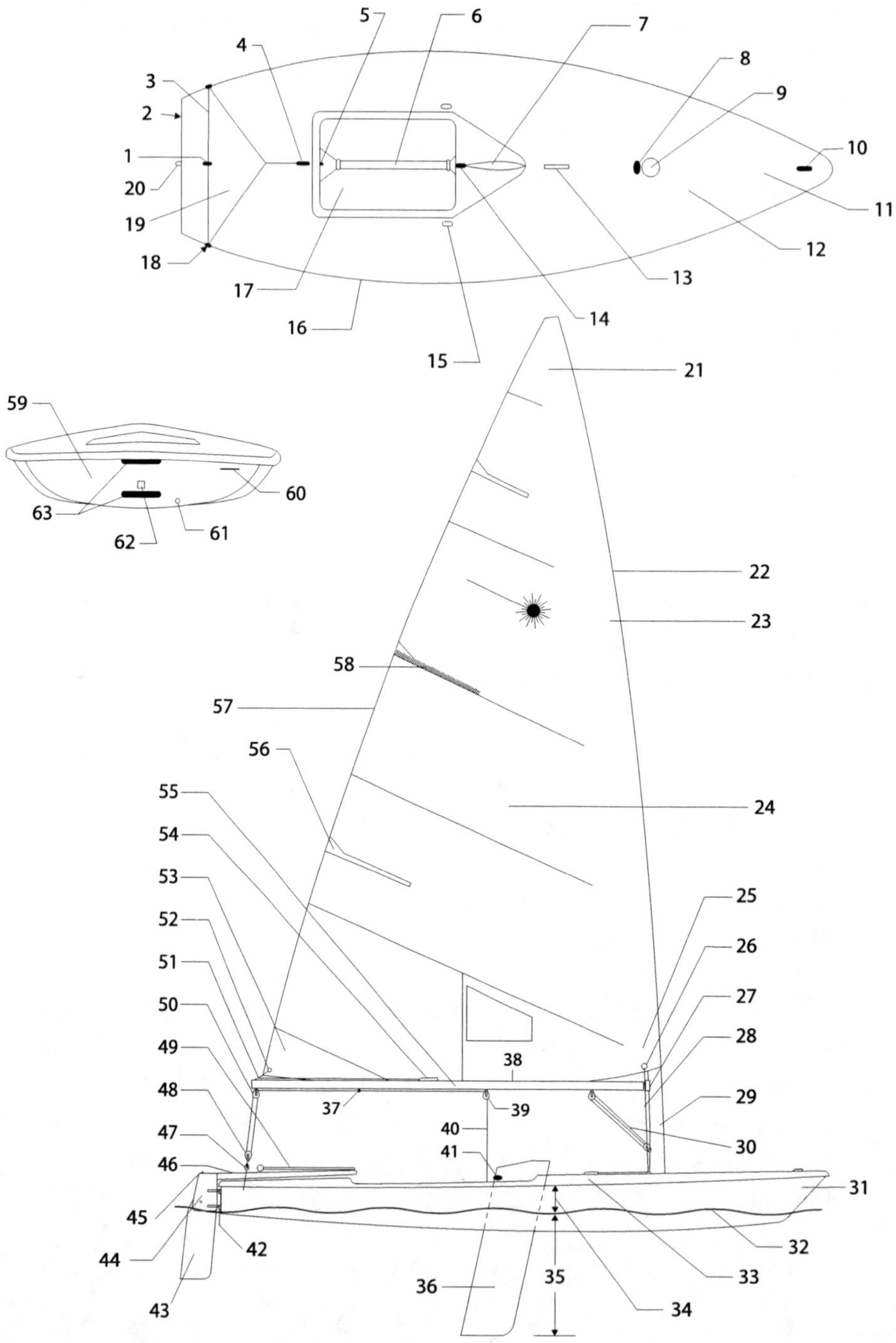

Laser

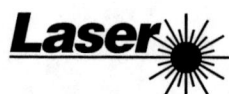

Fig. C-1 Laser Parts

Name _____ Date _____

SUNFISH—Label Fig. C-2 Sunfish Parts p. 153

Hull Terms—Sunfish

Stern	**Hiking strap**
Transom	**Mainsheet swivel block (2)**
Gudgeon bracket (2)	**Daggerboard trunk (slot)**
Traveler line (2)	**Mast step hole**
Cockpit	**Deck**
Gunwale (2)	**Bow (2)**

Traveler eye strap—a metal strap for securing the traveler line to the stern

Drain plug—hole where water can drain out of hull

Bailer (Cockpit drain plug)—hole where water can drain out of cockpit. The automatic bailer will bail water from the cockpit while moving.

Bow handle—used for attaching a painter and controlling the bow. A **painter** is a piece of line attached to a boat for towing, directing, or tying off.

Coaming—raised framework or railing around cockpit and deck openings to prevent water from the deck running below

Small bullet block (2) (traveler block)—pulley to attach traveler to mainsheet

Bullseye fairlead for halyard—fairlead used to change direction of the halyard

Halyard cleat—cleat used to hold and adjust the halyard line

Spar, Steering Assembly, and Depth Terms—Sunfish

Mast (3)	**Draft**
Gooseneck (2)	**Daggerboard**
Forward boom block	**Rudder blade**
Aft boom block	**Pintle pin**
Waterline	**Tiller**
Freeboard	**Tiller extension/Hiking stick**

Pintle spring—permits rudder to be attached to gudgeon and then holds it in place

Lower boom (3)—spar used to support the foot of the sail

Upper boom (3)—spar used to support the luff of the sail

Boom cap with eye—end cap with hole for passage of outhaul line

Daggerboard retaining line—line used to prevent daggerboard from sliding all the way out of the daggerboard trunk (slot). For example, should the boat "turtle" (i.e. turn upside down) when capsized.

Mast base cap—cap used to protect the bottom end of the mast and the mast step hole

Name _____ Date _____

Sail and Running Rigging—Sunfish

Mainsail	**Clew**
Luff	**Tack**
Foot	**Head**
Leech	**Mainsheet**

Halyard (3)—line used to hoist the upper boom and sail up the mast. It is also used to adjust tension on the upper boom and therefore the sail

Outhaul line (2)—line used to attach a corner of the mainsail to an end of a boom. It is laced through a grommet in the corner of the sail and then both ends are passed through the eye in the boom cap. The ends are secured with figure 8 knots. The outhaul is used to adjust tension on the corner of the sail. The Sunfish has two booms, therefore, it has two outhaul lines.

Sail ring (2)—rings used to attach the sail to the booms

Grommet—eyelet in sail

Name _____ Date _____

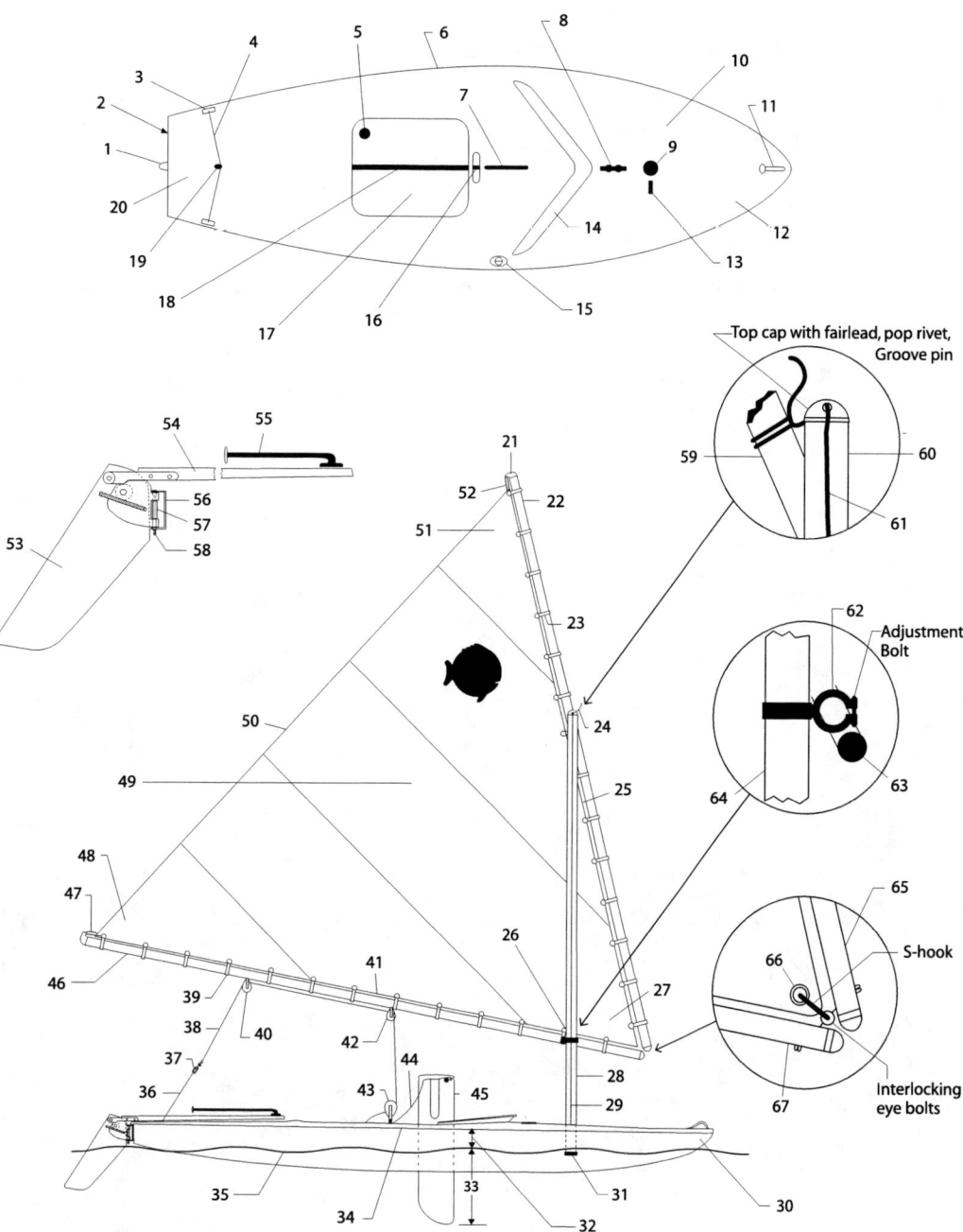

Fig. C-2 Sunfish Parts

Name _____ Date _____

Chapter 5

1. Center of Gravity (CG) is defined as _____

2. Movement around a longitudinal axis through the center of gravity of a boat is called: _____

3. Movement around a bilateral axis through the center of gravity of a boat is called: _____

4. Movement around a vertical axis through the center of gravity of a boat is called: _____

5. Hiking is a sailing technique used to counteract heeling of the boat. True or False

6. What side of the boat do you sit on? _____

7. What does it mean to sail on an even keel? _____

8. The higher the center of gravity of a boat, the more stable it is. True or False.

9. Label the tack of each sailboat—port tack or starboard tack:

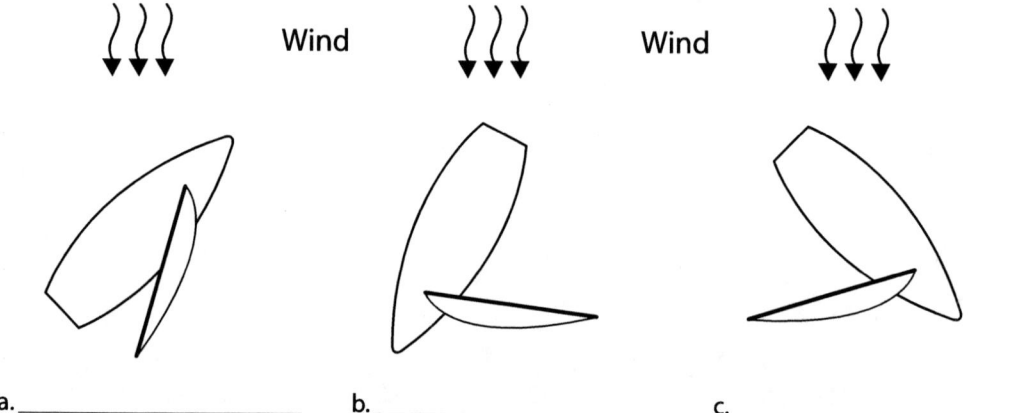

a. _____ b. _____ c. _____

Fig. C-3 Tack of Boat

Name _____ Date _____

10. Given wind direction toward the bottom of this page, draw and label a boat in irons and sailing on each of the four main points of sail. Be sure that you include (draw) the correct position of the boom/sail for each point of sail. (5 x 3 = 15 points)

⇣⇣⇣ Wind   ⇣⇣⇣ Wind   ⇣⇣⇣

Fig. C-4 Points of Sail

11. How can you tell what point of sail you are on? _____
_____

12. The side of the boat that the boom is on is the name of the tack the boat is sailing. True or False

13. When a boat sails into the wind at less than a 45° angle, the sail will _____ and the boat is said to be _____

155

Name _____ Date _____

14. After tacking upwind, the new course will be at least 90° from the old one. True or False

15. A boat's heading is always the same as the course made good. True or False

16. "Fall-Off" means to point the bow farther away from the wind. True or False

17. To turn the boat to port, you would turn the tiller to _____

18. To turn the boat to starboard, you would turn the tiller to _____

19. Label the high and low pressure areas, on the top view of the sail diagram.

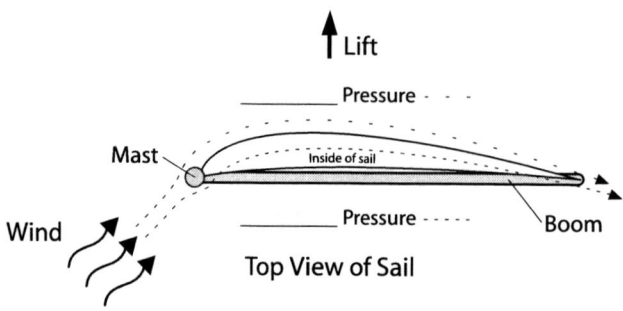

Fig. C-5 Top View of Sail

20. The fastest point of sail is usually a _____

21. Boat resistance to sideways movement in the water is called _____ resistance. In small boats this is provided mainly by the _____, but also by the _____ and the _____

22. The point on a sail where the wind can be said to be concentrated is termed the center of effort (CE). True or False

23. If the center of effort (CE) of a boat is behind its center of lateral resistance (CLR), the boat will have a weather helm and tend to turn upwind. True or False

Name _____ Date _____

Chapter 6

1. A boat moving at 10 knots is moving faster than a boat moving at 10 mph. True or False

2. The direction the wind is blowing from is called the direction of the _____ wind.

3. When a sailboat is moving, the wind felt on a sailor's face is called the _____ wind.

4. Draw arrows to indicate the direction of the true wind:

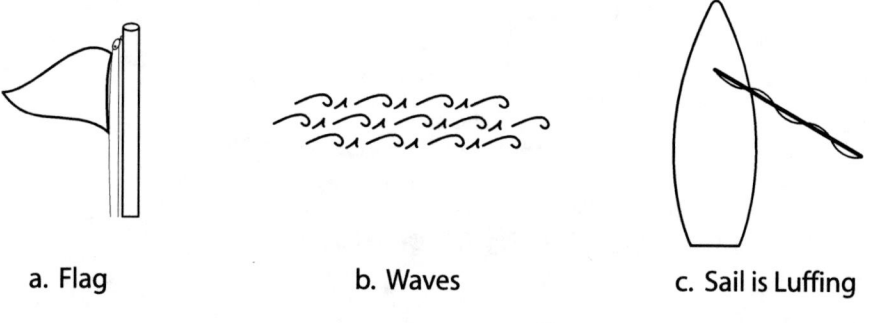

a. Flag   b. Waves   c. Sail is Luffing

Fig. C-6 Direction of True Wind

5. Why does the apparent wind feel stronger when sailing on a close reach compared to sailing on a broad reach? _____

_____

6. When there is an area on the surface of the water that appears darker, what does it indicate? A puff or a lull? _____

7. In rough weather, would you sail your boat to the windward or leeward side of an island for protection? a. _____

   Why? b. _____

Name _____ Date _____

8. Draw, label, and briefly explain the Go and No-Go zones when launching from a beach in an on-shore breeze (3 points):

Beach/Land

Fig. C-7 On-Shore Wind

9. Ideally, from which side of a dock should a boat be launched? _____

10. Name the three things that determine how (and if) a sailboat moves:

   (1) _____ (2) _____ (3) _____

11. What are the commands given by the captain to the crew when coming about?

   (1) _____

   (2) _____

12. List three common errors in coming about—that can result in a boat being caught in irons:

   _____

   _____

   _____

Name _____ Date _____

13. In light wind, come about slowly. True or False

14. You are sailing on a port tack. Pushing the tiller will cause the boat to turn to (circle)—Port or Starboard

15. When a boat is in the Safety Position, the sail will be pointed into the wind and it will be luffing. True or False

16. Before attempting to right a capsized boat, the bow should be pointed _____

17. Your boat is caught in irons; what is the name of the technique used to get it out?
    _____

18. Your boat is caught in irons. IN ORDER, describe the steps you would take to get it out of irons and start sailing:

    (1) _____

    (2) _____

    (3) _____

19. What are the two main ways of slowing or stopping a boat?

    (1) _____

    (2) _____

Name _____ Date _____

20. Draw the path (courses) you would sail to dock your boat at the point indicated. Draw your boat in *at least* three positions with proper sail trim (boom/sail angle to boat) along the drawn path you would sail to stop your boat at the X. Label the point of sail and tack (starboard or port) of each boat position. Also, label any tacking maneuver (i.e. coming about or jibing) that you would perform. Start with the boat that is labeled Close reach, Port tack. (3 × 4 + 1 = 13 points)

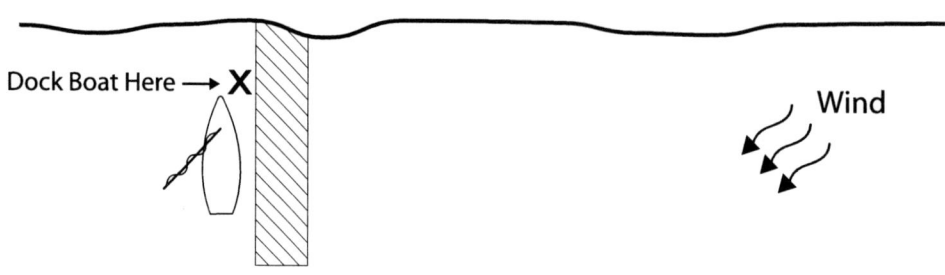

Fig. C-8 Dock Boat Here

Close reach
Port tack

21. If the sail is not luffing, then it is properly trimmed. True or False

22. Sailing close-hauled on alternating tacks in order to make progress upwind is called _____

23. While sailing on a close reach your sail starts to luff. Which way has the wind shifted, further ahead of the boat or further to beam? _____

24. An example of sailing by the lee is when a boat on a port tack broad reach has the wind blowing on the starboard side of the sail. True or False

25. Sailing by the lee is a good strategy and will help the boat sail faster. True or False

Name _____ Date _____

26. What are the commands given by the captain to the crew when jibing?

   (1) _____

   (2) _____

27. _____ (coming about or jibing) is changing direction (tacking) by turning the stern of the boat across the wind. _____ (Push or Pull) the tiller _____ (toward or away) from the sail.

28. _____ (coming about or jibing) is changing direction (tacking) by turning the bow of the boat across the wind. _____ (Push or Pull) the tiller _____ (toward or away) from the sail.

29. List two causes of capsizing a boat: (1) _____

    (2) _____

30. Match the corresponding number to the correct description:

_____ Jibe

_____ Falling-off

_____ Safety Position

_____ Come About

_____ Heading-up

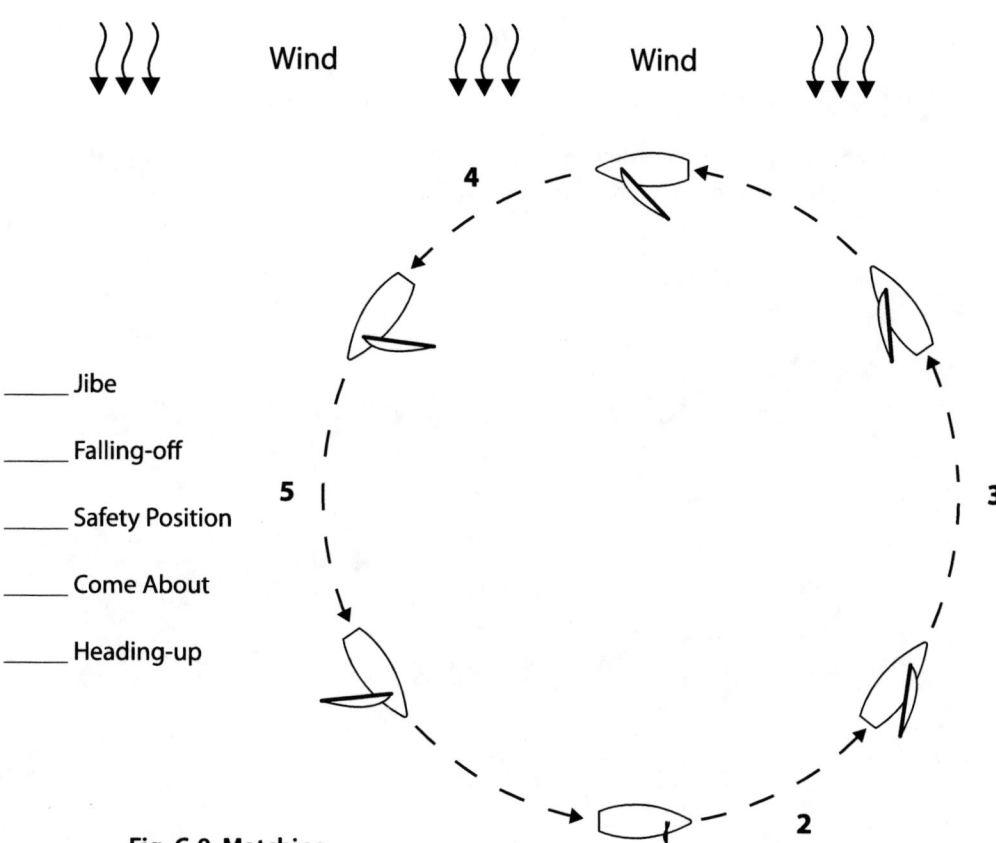

Fig. C-9 Matching

Name _____ Date _____

Chapter 7

1. "Sailing on the Wind" refers to sailing _____

2. When pinching (i.e. sailing on the windward side of the "groove") it is correct to have a slight flutter (luff) in the front of the sail. True or False

3. In light wind, boat speed can be increased by moving body weight forward and to leeward thereby heeling the boat 5-10 degrees to leeward. True or False

4. When sailing on an even keel, moving body weight to leeward will cause the boat to turn downwind. True or False

5. Name each corner of a triangular sail and name the line that could be used to adjust (tension or loosen) it.

    (1) corner _____ line _____

    (2) corner _____ line _____

    (3) corner _____ line _____

6. When sailing on a beam reach, the daggerboard should be about _____ up.

7. In attempting to come alongside another boat or pick up a person in the water, it is best to approach from windward. True or False

Name _____ Date _____

Chapter 8

1. Four right of way questions. All boats are moving. Circle the letter (A or B) of the stand-on boat, the other boat is the give-way boat.

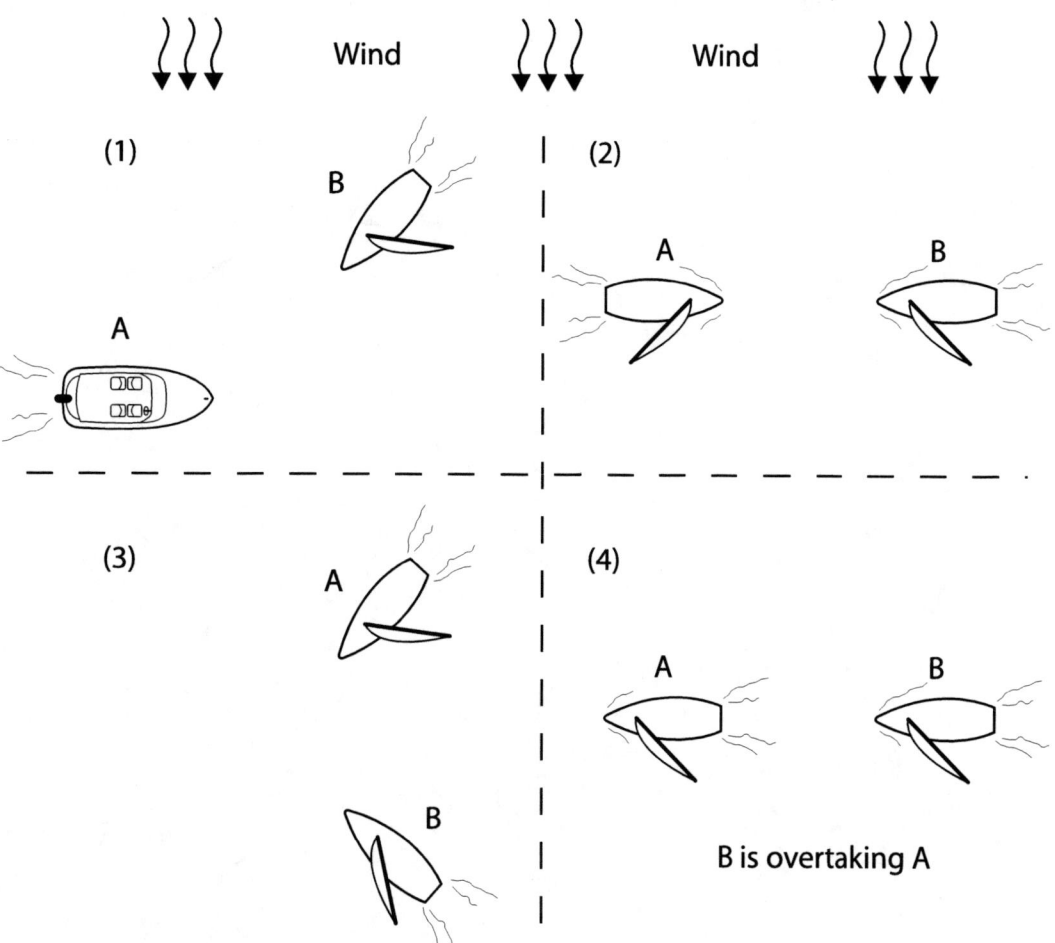

Fig. C-10 Right of Way

2. A series of sailboat races over one or several days is called a _____

3. In sailing a triangle course in competition, it is permissible to sail on the inside of the triangle. True or False

Name _____   Date _____

Chapter 9

Fig. C-11: Examine the buoys lining the Channel—(1) number the nun buoy that is furthest out in the lake, (2) number the next nun buoy, (3) number the can buoy that is furthest out in the lake, (4) number the next can buoy. Place the correct symbol on the buoys representing the other five sets of buoys; (5) swimming area, (6) Dam, (7) rocks, (8) shallow area, and (9) launch ramp. (10) What should be the color of the nun buoys lining the channel? The color of the nun buoys should be _____

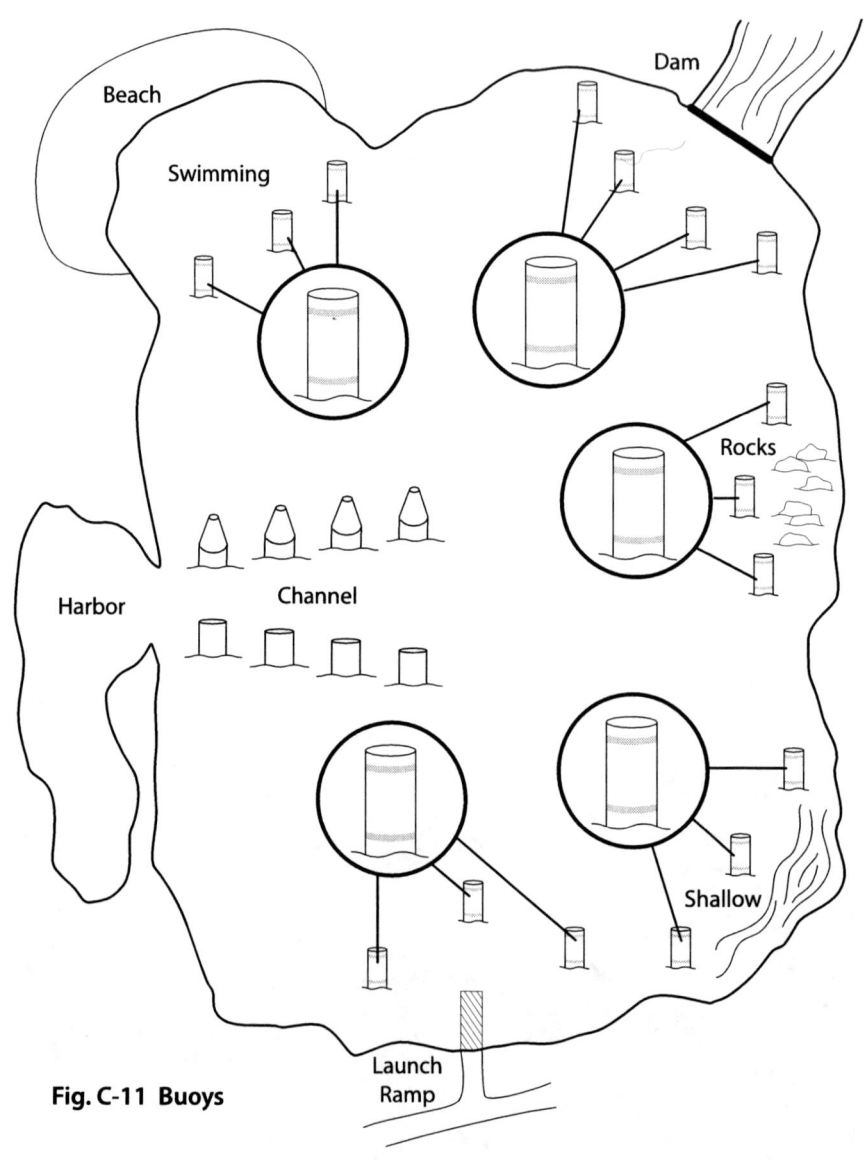

Fig. C-11 Buoys

Appendix D
Answers

A. Answers for Labeled Figures in Chapter 3

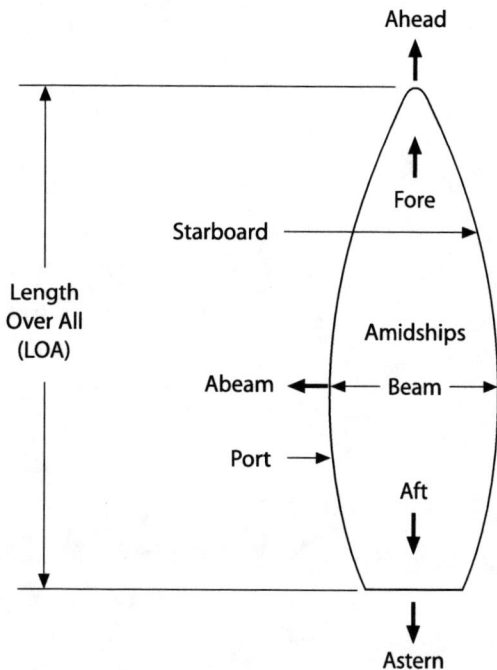

Fig. D3-2 Basic Boat Terms

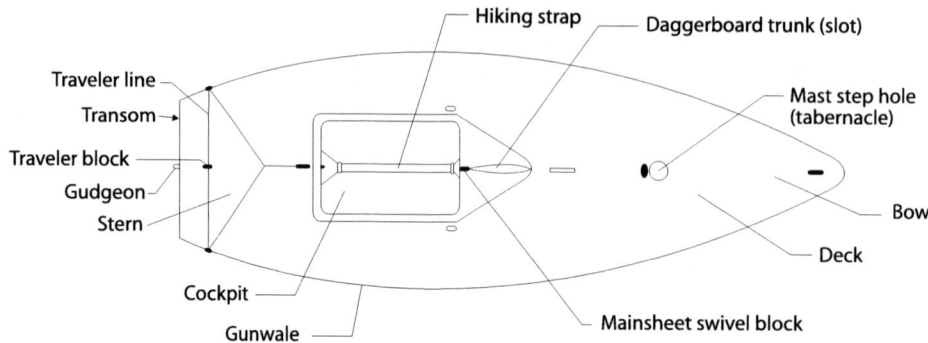

Fig. D3-3 Hull Terms

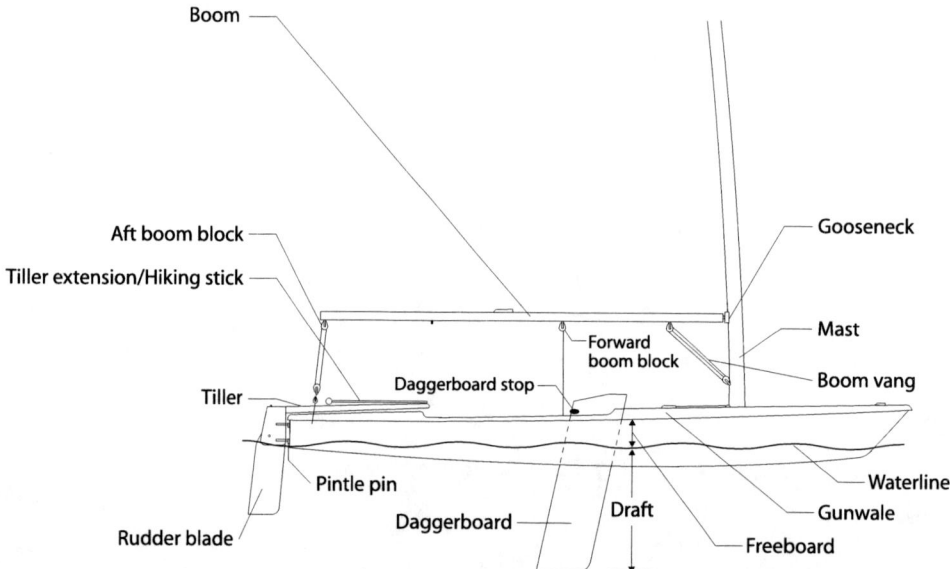

Fig. D3-4 Spars and Steering

Answers

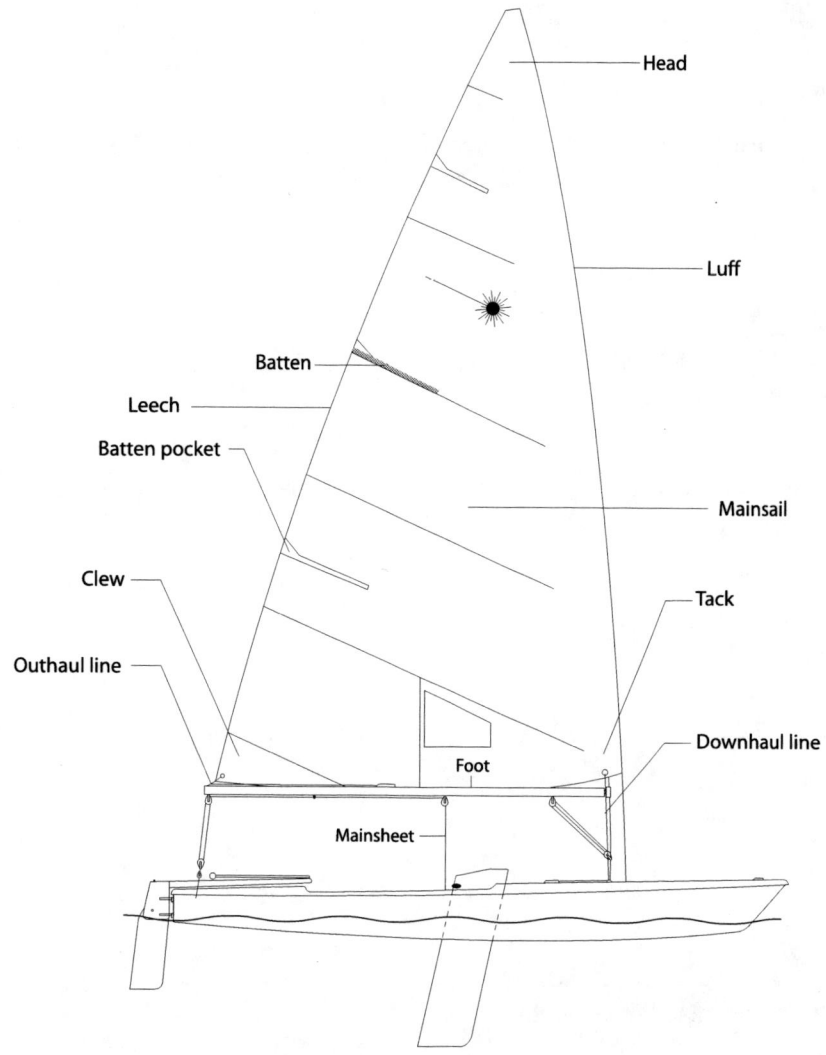

Fig. D3-5 Sail and Running Rigging

B. Answers to Exercises and Review Questions in Appendix C

CHAPTER 1

Risks—at least 8, also explain how each could have been eliminated or minimized:
1. inexperience
2. unfamiliarity with equipment
3. immersion or drowning
4. hypothermia
5. cold water immersion
6. off-shore wind
7. severe weather
8. sailing in area where there is no means of communication with other boats or people
9. never sailed at this lake
10. equipment failure or misuse
11. loss of property
12. natural hazards

9. d
10. shivering
11. d
12. True

CHAPTER 2

1. lines, rudder, and body weight
2. clean and dry
3. figure 8
4. bowline

CHAPTER 3

1. to provide lateral stability (resistance)
2. both provide lateral stability
3. keel has ballast
4. False
5. has one mast stepped well forward and a single sail

Answers

6. True
7. sloop has a jib sail

CHAPTER 4—LABELING

Laser—see Fig. 4-1 Laser Parts in Chapter 4
Sunfish—see Fig. 4-3 Sunfish Parts in Chapter 4

CHAPTER 5

1. the weight or mass center of an object; the point around which all parts or molecules of an object balance
2. roll
3. pitch
4. yaw
5. True
6. windward
7. sailing with the boat flat (balanced)
8. False
9. a. port, b. starboard, c. port
10. (1) in irons, sail luffing down center of boat; (2) close reach, boom/sail at 30° to long axis of boat; (3) beam reach, sail at 45° to long axis of boat; (4) broad reach, sail at 60° to long axis of boat; (5) run, sail at 90° to long axis of boat. See Fig. 5-8 Points of Sail in Chapter 5.
11. direction of boat in relation to wind
12. False
13. luff; in irons
14. True
15. False
16. True
17. starboard
18. port
19. low pressure on leeward, high pressure on windward (inside)
20. beam reach
21. lateral resistance, daggerboard (centerboard), rudder, hull
22. True
23. True

CHAPTER 6

1. True
2. true
3. apparent
4. (a) horizontal left, (b) horizontal right, (c) directly at luff edge and in line with sail
5. because one feels the sum of the true wind and motion wind
6. puff
7. (a) leeward, (b) leeward side has calm water, is protected, is safer
8. correctly drawn and labeled: (1) Go zone is from 45°-90° each side of the wind, (2) in irons is No-Go zone, and (3) shallow is No-Go zone See Fig. 6-5 in Chapter 6
9. leeward side
10. (1) direction of the wind, (2) point of sail (heading) of the boat, (3) trim of the sail
11. (1) Ready About, (2) Hard-A-Lee
12. (1) trying to come about from a broad or beam reach and not having enough momentum, (2) not having enough speed (i.e. momentum), (3) releasing the mainsheet before the tiller is pushed hard to leeward, (4) not pushing the tiller out far enough, (5) straightening the tiller before the bow has crossed the wind and the sail starts to fill on the new tack
13. True
14. port
15. True
16. into the wind
17. backwind
18. (1) push boom out to produce sternway, (2) push tiller to produce turn, (3) backwind more than 45° off-wind, and (4) pull in mainsheet to start sailing
19. (1) let out the mainsheet, (2) turn into the wind

Answers

20.

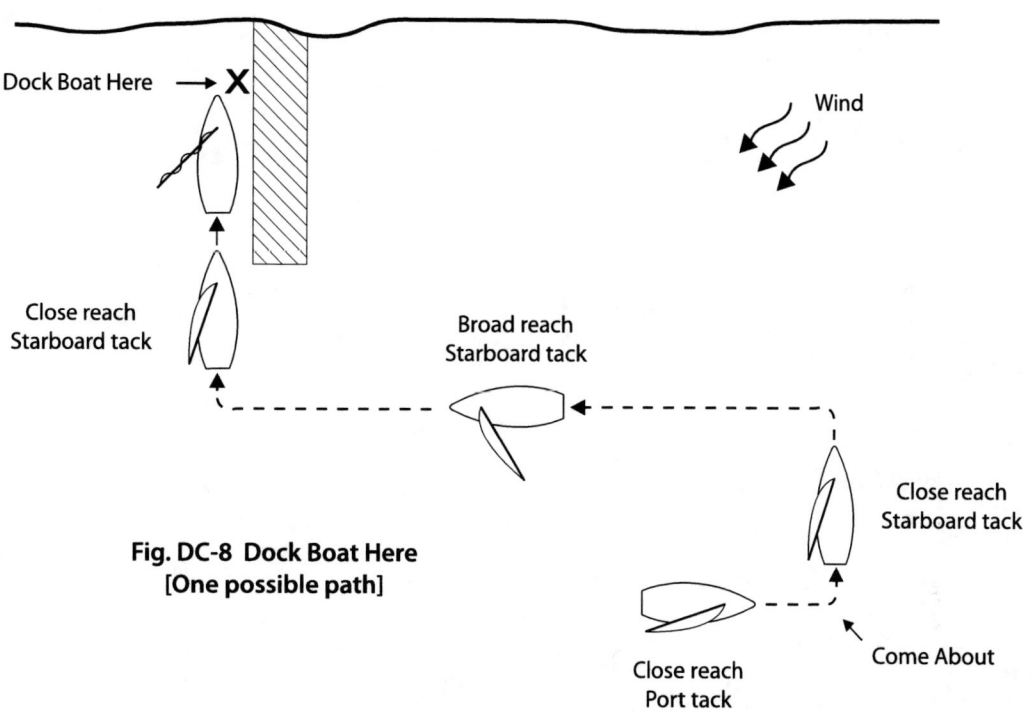

**Fig. DC-8 Dock Boat Here
[One possible path]**

21. False
22. beating
23. further ahead
24. True
25. False
26. (1) Ready to Jibe, (2) Jibe Ho
27. (1) jibing, (2) pull, (3) away
28. (1) coming about, (2) push, (3) toward
29. (1) accidental jibe, (2) improper position of body weight when tacking or jibing, (3) not adjusting to gust of wind
30. (5) Jibe, (4) Falling-off, (1) Safety Position, (3) Come About, (2) Heading-up

CHAPTER 7

1. to windward or upwind
2. True
3. True
4. False
5. (1) head, halyard; (2) tack, downhaul or Cunningham; (3) clew, outhaul
6. half way
7. False

CHAPTER 8

1. (1) B, (2) B, (3) B, (4) A
2. regatta
3. True

CHAPTER 9

1. 2
2. 4
3. 1
4. 3
5. Swimming area—no boats symbol (diamond with cross in middle)
6. Dam—no boats symbol (diamond with cross in middle)
7. Rocks—danger symbol (diamond)
8. Shallow—danger symbol (diamond)
9. Launch ramp—control symbol (circle)
10. red

Appendix E
Nautical Dictionary

Abeam—the bearing 90° from ahead; perpendicular to the centerline of the boat

Aft—at, near, or toward the stern

Aft Boom Block—aft pulley on boom through which the mainsheet runs

Ahead—in front of the boat

Amidships—between fore and aft; the middle of the boat

Apparent Wind—wind "felt" by the sailor when the boat is moving; a combination of the true wind and the effect of the boat's movement (motion wind)

Astern—behind the boat

Backstay—a wire support from the mast to the stern of the boat

Backwind—a technique where wind on the back of the sail is used to get out of "Irons"

Bail—remove water from a boat

Ballast—weight concentrated at the lowest point in a boat to aid in stabilization by lowering the center of gravity. Weight (lead or iron) in keels is called "outside ballast," while movable weights inside the boat are called "inside ballast."

Batten—thin wooden or plastic strip inserted in pocket along the leech of a sail to help hold its form

Batten Pocket—pocket for holding a batten

Beam—widest point of the boat

Beam Reach—sailing with the wind coming directly over the beam of the boat, wind is perpendicular to the long axis of the boat

Bearing—the direction of an object measured in compass or relative degrees

Beat—to sail close-hauled to windward

Beating—sailing close-hauled on one tack (e.g. starboard) and then the other (e.g. port) in order to make progress upwind

Becket Block—an aft boom block on a Laser that is use to secure the mainsheet

Bight—any part of a line except the end; usually refers to a bend in a line

Bilge—bottom part of boat where water may collect

Block—a nautical pulley; it is used to change the direction of a line and/or exert force on a line

Boltrope—rope sewn into the luff and foot of the sail giving the edge more strength; in some rigs, fed along a groove in the mast and/or boom

Boom—horizontal spar that attaches to the mast and supports the foot of the sail. Be careful, it got its name by hitting people in the head!

Boom Vang—line system secured to the boom; it controls tension on the boom, holds it in place and prevents it from lifting

Bow—the front of the boat

Broad Reach—sailing between a beam reach and a run

Buoy—a floating marker which provides information (e.g. danger, depth, and direction)

Cam Cleat—cleat that holds a line between two rotating sets of cam teeth, released by jerking line perpendicular to the load

Can Buoy—black or green cylindrical buoy found on the port side on entering a channel, odd numbered with the lowest number being farthest out in the body of water.

Capsize—to overturn

Cast Off—to let go

Catboat—sailboat with one mast stepped well forward and a single sail (mainsail)

Catamaran—a twin hulled craft

Catspaw—isolated ruffling of water surface by wind

Centerboard—moveable board (fin) that is lowered to reduce sideways drift

Centerboard Trunk—slot or housing for centerboard

Center of Buoyancy (CB)—is the center of gravity of the volume of water displaced

Center of Effort (CE)— the point on a sail where the wind can be said to be concentrated

Center of Gravity (CG)—the weight or mass center of an object. It is an imaginary point around which all parts or molecules of an object balance.

Center of Lateral Resistance (CLR)—is the point where the lateral resistance balances. In other words, there is the same amount of lateral resistance fore and aft of this point. As a result, the boat turns (to port or starboard) around a vertical axis through the CLR.

Chain Plate—metal plate bolted to the side of the boat to which a stay is attached

Chine—line where sides and bottom of boat meet

Clam Cleat—cleat with grooved inner faces to grip line

Cleat—fitting to which lines are attached

Nautical Dictionary

Clew—lower back corner of a sail

Close-hauled—sailing as close as possible to the wind without the sail luffing; sail is hauled in close to hull. Boat would be on a beat.

Close Reach—sailing between close hauled and beam reach

Coaming—raised framework or railing around cockpit and deck openings to prevent water from the deck running below

Cockpit—open area behind the mast where you sit or place your feet

Cockpit Drain Plug—used to plug the hole where water can drain out of cockpit

Coil—to lay a rope in a circle

Come About—change boat's course so the bow crosses the wind and the sail fills on the opposite side

Course—the direction that a boat is steered to reach a destination

Cunningham—downhaul attached to the tack of the mainsail

Cutter—one-masted sailboat with mainsail and two headsails

Daggerboard—centerboard which is inserted by hand; it provides lateral resistance

Day Sailer—small sailboat used for brief sails

Deck—the horizontal flat surface enclosing the hull

Dinghy—a small retractable centerboard boat; also a small boat used as a tender

Downhaul—line used to adjust the luff edge tension of the sail; it pulls down on the tack of the sail

Draft—distance from waterline to the deepest part of the boat; also the depth or fullness of a sail

Ease—to let out

Ebb—the outgoing or falling tide; the opposite is the incoming or flood tide

Eye Strap—metal strap that keeps line in place while providing free passage

Fairlead ("fairleed")—device used to guide or change the directional of a line or wire

Fall-Off (head-off or bear-off)—means to point the bow farther away from the wind. Do not fall off your boat!

Fathom—a nautical measurement for the depth of water; one fathom is equal to 6 feet

Fluke—protruding arm of anchor that lodges in sea floor

Foot—the bottom edge of a sail

Fore—forward ("for-rad"), toward the front

Foresail—any sail set in front of the leading mast

Forestay—stay supporting the mast in a forward direction

Forward Boom Block—forward pulley on boom through which the mainsheet runs

Freeboard—distance from the waterline to the deck or gunwale

Furl—to gather up and secure a sail

Gaff—spar to which the head of a fore-and-aft sail is secured

Genoa—an overlapping jibsail.

Gooseneck—hinged or swivel fitting that attaches the boom to the mast

Grommet—eyelet in a sail

Gudgeon (Gudgeon bracket)—fitting (bracket) on the transom into which a pintle pin from the rudder head is inserted to hold the rudder onto the boat

Gunwale ("gunnel")—edge of the boat at deck level; term from the past when ships carried guns along a wall

Gybe (Jibe)—changing tacks when sailing to leeward (downwind); changing a boat's course so that the stern crosses the wind and the sail fills on the opposite side

Gybe Ho—command sounded just before pulling the tiller to windward. This is preceded by the command "Prepare to Gybe."

Halyard—line used to hoist a sail up a mast. It is also used to adjust tension on the top of the sail. The name originated from the order "Haul up the yards" given when large cotton sails had to be raised on ships.

Hard-a-Lee—command sounded just before pushing the tiller to leeward. This is preceded by the command "Ready-About."

Head—top corner of a sail. Also, a marine toilet.

Heading—the direction the bow points

Headway—describes a boat moving forward

Head-Up—means to point the bow more into the wind

Heeling—the tilting action of the boat caused by wind; rolling in the direction the wind is blowing

Helm—steering mechanism; a tiller or wheel used to move the rudder; the place where the boat is controlled

Helmsman—person who steers the boat

Hike—lean out to counter act the heeling force of the wind and keep the boat balanced

Hiking Stick—tiller extension used to steer the boat when hiking (leaning) out

Hiking Strap—line or webbing across cockpit; feet are placed under it in order to hike (lean) out to balance the boat

Hoist—to raise

Hull—main body of boat (without mast or gear)

In Irons—caught headed directly into the wind

Jib—a triangular sail used in front of the mast

Jibsnap—fitting used to attach the leading edge of the jib to the forestay

Jibe (Gybe)—changing tacks when sailing to leeward (downwind); changing a boat's course so that the stern crosses the wind and the sail fills on the opposite side

Jibe Ho—command sounded just before pulling the tiller to windward and when pulling the boom across the centerline of the boat. This is preceded by the command "Prepare to Jibe."

Jury Rig—any emergency rig using what remains after breakage

Keel—longitudinal "ridge" on the bottom of the hull which reduces leeway; in some sailboats, a heavily weighted lower projection of the hull for stability

Ketch—two-masted sailboat with the shorter mast aft of the mainmast but forward of the tiller

Knot—one knot is one nautical mile per hour. In comparison to land speed, one knot is 1.15 mph. Also, the result of tying a line.

Lateen Rig—rigging where the sail extends forward of the mast

Lateral Resistance—the resistance to lateral or sideways movement of the boat in the water; it depends on the lateral surface area of the hull, the lateral surface area of the centerboard, and the lateral surface area of the rudder

Leeboard—a board used as a centerboard but secured over the side of a flat-bottomed boat

Leech—the back edge of a sail

Lee Helm—a boat where the center of effort (CE) is forward of its center of lateral resistance (CLR); it will tend to turn away from the wind; the boat will turn downwind when not sailing

Leeward ("loo-ard")—away from the wind

Leeway—the drift to leeward caused by the wind or current

Length Overall (LOA)— is the distance measured along the centerline of the boat from the tip of the bow to the stern

Line—nautical term for rope

Loose-Footed—sail is attached to the boom only at the tack and clew

Luff—the front or leading edge of a sail. When the sail flutters along the luff edge (e.g. when the boat heads into the wind) it is said to be "luffing."

Mainsail ("mainsul")—the principle sail attached to the main mast

Mainsheet—line which controls the boom and therefore the position of the mainsail

Mainsheet Block—pulley through which mainsheet runs

Mast—the vertical pole that supports the sail

Mast Step Hole (Tabernacle)—place to mount the mast in the deck of the boat

Masthead Fly—telltale at the top of the mast

Mizzenmast—the shorter mast aft on a ketch or yawl

Moor—to secure a boat to a post, dock, or buoy

Motion Wind—wind resulting from movement of boat

Nautical Mile—6080.27 feet

Nun Buoy—red buoy with a conical top found on the starboard side when entering a channel. Nun Buoys are even numbered with the lowest number being farthest out in the body of water.

One-Design—class of identical racing boats

Outhaul—line used to adjust tension on a corner of a sail

Painter—a piece of line attached to a boat for towing, directing, or tying off

Pennant—a three sided flag

PFD—Personal Flotation Device; life jacket

Pinching—from a close-hauled position, steering slightly closer to the wind

Pintle Pin—pin that attaches rudder head to gudgeon on the transom of the hull

Pitch—motion around a bilateral (side to side) axis through the center of the boat; up and down motion of the bow

Planing—to travel on top of the water rather than through it

Point of Sail—boat heading in relation to the direction of the wind

Port—left side of the boat when looking toward the front; note, left and port each have four letters

Port Tack—boat sailing with the wind coming over the port side

Pounding—a flat hull surface rising, falling, and hitting the water's surface

Pram—a small sailboat known for its square flat bow

Prepare to Jibe (Gybe)—warning order before jibing

Privileged Vessel—boat which has the right of way

Rake—angle a mast is tilted forward or back

Reaching—sailing on a course between close hauled and running; sailing across the wind

Nautical Dictionary

Ready-About—warning order before coming about

Reef—to reduce sail area in heavy weather so the boat may be more easily kept upright

Regatta—series of boat races over one or several days

Rig—refers to the number and arrangement of spars and sails on a boat. To set up spars, standing, and running rigging on a sailboat.

Rigging—lines securing masts and sails

Right of Way—marine traffic laws for boats specify which boat has precedence over others on conflicting courses. That is, the boat that can continue without altering its course is said to have right of way. It is also referred to as the stand-on boat.

Roll—motion around a longitudinal axis through the center of the boat; sides of the boat move up and down

Rudder Blade—flat blade attached to the stern; used to steer the boat

Rudder Head—top part of the rudder; it is hinged to the stern

Rudder Lift Stop—prevents pintle pin from coming out of gudgeon; it keeps rudder attached to transom of boat (Laser)

Running—sailing directly before the wind, wind coming directly over the stern

Running Rigging—consists of the sheets, halyards, and other lines used to hoist, trim, and control the sails

Sailing by the Lee—is when a boat is sailing with the sail on the wrong side of the boat; it is dangerous and should be avoided

Sailsock—the sleeve along the luff edge of the sail that slips over the mast (e.g. on Laser)

Schooner—sailboat with two or more masts, the mainmast being as tall or taller than the foremast

Sculling—moving rudder side to side to propel boat

Shackle—a U-shaped metal fitting with a pin or screw across the open end, used to join sheets and/or halyards to sails

Sheet—any line used to control a sail, e.g. mainsheet, jib sheet, etc.

Sheeting—refers to pulling in (trimming) or letting out (easing) the line that controls the sail

Shrouds—mast side stays of rope or wire

Shove Off—push off or depart from dock

Skeg—the continuation of the keel aft, protecting the propeller and sometimes taking the heel of the rudder.

Sloop—sailboat with one mast, mainsail, and jib

Spar—a mast, boom, gaff, or pole used to support a sail

Spill—to spill wind is to allow wind to escape from the sail so that force is reduced

Spinnaker—a large, lightweight, balloon-like sail, used when boat is broad reaching or running.

Sprit—small spar used for extension of sail away from boat

Squall—sudden strong wind, usually of short duration

Standing Part—the end of a line that is secured

Standing Rigging—is the rigging used to attach and hold the mast to the boat

Starboard—right side of the boat when looking toward the front

Starboard Tack—boat sailing with the wind coming over the starboard side

Stays—are ropes or wires used to support the mast (e.g. headstay, jibstay, backstay)

Step—socket into which butt of mast fits; to raise and secure the mast

Stern—the back of the boat

Sternway—describes a boat moving backward

Stow—to put in place

Swamp—fill with water

Tack—lower front corner of a sail. Also, direction of a boat in relation to the wind (e.g. a starboard or port tack).

Tacking—changing from a starboard to a port tack (or vice versa)

Telltales—small lengths of wool, nylon, or other lightweight material attached to standing rigging to determine the direction of the wind; telltales attached to a sail indicate the flow of air across the sail and are used as a reference to correct sail trim

Thwart—seat or support across a boat

Tiller—bar or handle used to turn the rudder and steer the boat

Tiller Extension/Hiking Stick— extension of the tiller, used to steer the boat when leaning out (hiking)

Tiller Retaining Pin—pin that prevents the tiller detaching from the rudder head

Transom—the stern surface of the boat

Transom Drain Plug—used to plug the hole where water can drain out of hull; transom bung

Trapeze—wire from mast, to which crew is attached, so he/she can hike out when standing on gunwale

Traveler—line and blocks at the stern of the boat to which the mainsheet is attached

Traveler Block—pulley on traveler to which mainsheet is attached

Nautical Dictionary

Trim—to take in on a sheet, tightening a sail; difference in draft between bow and stern

Trough—hollow between two waves

True Wind—actual speed and direction of the wind, wind felt when standing still

Turnbuckle—a metal thread and screw device used for adjusting stays

Turtle—overturn 180°, mast points straight down

Waterline—the water level at which the boat floats

Weather Helm—a boat where the center of effort (CE) is aft of the center of lateral resistance (CLR); the boat will tend to turn into the wind; the boat will turn into the wind when not sailing

Weather Mark—upwind buoy on race course reached by beating to it

Weigh—to lift the anchor off the bottom

Whipped—line end bound to prevent fraying

Winch—drum with mechanical advantage used for winding in line

Windward—towards the wind, upwind

Wing and Wing—sailing before the wind with jib on one side and mainsail on the other

Yaw—motion around a vertical axis through the center of the boat; the bow of the boat moves left and right

Yawl—two-masted sailboat with the shorter mast aft of the rudder